# BUYING AND MAINTAINING A
# 126 S-CLASS
# MERCEDES

# BUYING AND MAINTAINING A 126 S-CLASS MERCEDES

## NIK GREENE

THE CROWOOD PRESS

First published in 2017 by
The Crowood Press Ltd
Ramsbury, Marlborough
Wiltshire SN8 2HR

**www.crowood.com**

This impression 2018

**British Library Cataloguing-in-Publication Data**
A catalogue record for this book is available from the British Library.

ISBN 978 1 78500 244 1

**Disclaimer**
Safety is of the utmost importance in every aspect of an automotive
workshop. The practical procedures and the tools and equipment
used in automotive workshops are potentially dangerous. Tools should
used in strict accordance with the manufacturer's recommended
procedures and current health and safety regulations. The author
and publisher cannot accept responsibility for any accident or injury
caused by following the advice given in this book.

Designed and typeset by Guy Croton Publishing Services,
Tonbridge, Kent
Printed and bound in Malaysia by Times Offset (M) Sdn Bhd

# CONTENTS

# ACKNOWLEDGEMENTS

One of the most exciting things about classic-car ownership is being able to share the passion with others, so first and foremost I would like to thank The Crowood Press for having faith in my enthusiasm for a car that is not quite yet a full-blown 'classic'.

In the preparation of this book I have badgered many people for information and photographs. It would be impossible to name everyone in the space provided but I do thank you all wholeheartedly for your support.

I also wish to thank the following for going the extra mile, as well as those who allowed me to use the images of their own 126s for technical clarity: Ian Luscombe, Ian Hunter, Charlie Deycon, Josh Mayo, Michael Pillay, Norman von Kraus, Bert van de Bovenkamp, Michael Clare, John Prins, Ken Davis, Sam Ng, Steven de Coninck and Roland Muller.

I would also like to thank the various people I have spoken to at the 'classic' department of Daimler Germany.

Lastly I would like to thank my dear wife Trudy, who has had to put up with me staring at a screen for hours on end and mumbling to myself. She has tolerated my 'eureka' moments in the middle of the night, which usually entailed me dashing off to the workshop to go and photograph something before I forgot, and has supplied me with copious amounts of tea.

# INTRODUCTIONS

As a youngster my fascination for beautiful cars was always a bit askew when compared to my peers. While they were generally more interested in 0 to 60 figures and top speeds, I always felt much more comfortable immersing myself in a car's design, history and function; this inevitably led to me dismantling things to see how they worked. Back in those days, car parts were not as readily available as they are today, so we used to have to trawl greasy scrapyards, where vehicles were often stacked four high, to find, clean and rebuild parts that were better than the ones we already had.

As the years rolled by, even though I had no kind of formal engineering qualifications I built up the courage to tackle anything, dismantling, restoring and recommissioning all sorts of cars, from V12 Jaguars to Citroen 2CVs.

This has nothing directly to do with the Mercedes 126, except that it might help to explain my approach in writing this book. Apart from a brief affair with a buy-to-sell 280TE, my first real Mercedes was in the guise of the G-Wagen, which I have owned now for fifteen years. My first 126 came along by complete accident, when I was not even looking for one. A dear friend lost her father and did not have the heart to sell his big Mercedes, which remained untouched on the driveway for eight years. I hate to see a majestic car going to rack and ruin for no reason and I did ask my friend more than once to sell it to me. One day out of the blue, she called me to say that they needed the driveway again. The scrap man had offered them £300 and if I could match the price, the car was mine – as long as I could move it in four days. I did not need to be told twice.

*Meet Brunhilde, my 1990 560SE.*

That Mercedes was an Astral Silver 420SE and, even though it had only 90,000 miles on the clock, it needed completely recommissioning just to get it back on the road. The project turned into a six-year running restoration to get it perfect and that was the beginning of my love affair with the 126 S-Class Mercedes. Having bought, restored and recommissioned four examples to date, I now own the rarest model of all; the short-wheelbase 560SE, of which only 1252 were made, on special order.

For many years, I have wittered on about there being too few books or TV programmes for the real classic-car enthusiast. There is always a place for a glossy coffee-table car book – I have shelves full of them – but ownership of a classic car is about more than just a line of immaculate examples at a show. The real value comes from what it takes to get cars into that condition. The true passion lies with the person standing in front of the shiny car on display, who has most likely given blood, sweat and tears to get it there.

Some people buy a car because they love the look and style of it, but they may have no interest in maintaining it themselves. However, I am assuming that the reader of this book has some inclination towards a deeper understanding of one of the finest Mercedes ever built. I have nothing at all against using mechanics or garages; I have a 'go-to guy' who is not only marque-trained but also an old-school engineer, and he is invaluable. The main problem for me is that commercial enterprises are often limited by time constraints and profit margins, which will dictate what they do and when they need to move on to the next job. This may be fine for a daily runner and for general mechanical repair, but a classic car needs something different.

I have endeavoured not to sound pretentious in this book and wish only to share my own enthusiasm as well as the benefit of my forty years' experience of classic-car ownership, ten years of which have been around the 126 S-Class. Hopefully, the reader will gain some insight as to what to expect, but he or she must be aware that this is not an official workshop manual; it is an informal manual based on nothing more than my own meandering experience. It cannot cover everything, as space is limited, but it should give you plenty of information about the little things (and some of the big things) that you will need to know when buying, owning and maintaining one of the world's greatest-ever vehicles.

# SAFETY FIRST

*For want of a bolt the bracket was lost;*
*For want of a bracket the pipe was lost;*
*For want of the pipe the brakes were lost;*
*For the failure of the brakes a life was lost…*
*All for the want of a bolt in a bracket.*

The original quote referred to nails and horseshoes, but the principles are the same: there is more to safety than just being safe. Safety is about having the right frame of mind, attitude, and awareness and, even more importantly, self-awareness. Accidents do happen but they are usually the result of a subtle accumulation of circumstances that, with a bit of thought and care, could have been avoided.

## GENERAL POINTS

There are a number of points to consider before you start working on your vehicle:

- Never drop your guard: it is very easy to get lazy and slapdash when you get used to your surroundings and tools; remaining alert and sharp will limit any potential for accidents.
- A 'that-will-do' attitude has no place in a garage: there is only one way to do a job and that is the right way.
- Take your time and never rush a job to finish it: working on a car will nearly always take you longer than you estimate, so do not try to squeeze the work in between other deadlines. Remember the old adage, 'More haste less speed'. Rushing a job is probably the number-one cause of accidents.
- Be self-aware: trips, falls and spills happen when you bumble about without thought, so remain observant and methodical at all times.

- Be methodical and be prepared: think about the tools you need and have a couple of pots handy for nuts, bolts and parts.
- Be tidy and orderly: find a clean spot and prepare a convenient work area. Set out your equipment, laying out the tools you need so that they are easily reachable.
- A workshop is no place for alcohol: leave it at home or in the man cave.
- Use eye protection: have a clean pair of eye protectors readily available. If they are packed away in a box or a drawer somewhere, you might not bother to pick them up when you need them. Hang them from the bench grinder so that you cannot use it without moving them.
- Wear gloves and/or barrier creams: mechanics' gloves are popular now due to advancements in fine strong mesh materials. Have a box of Nitrile and rubber gloves for the wet jobs; they not only keep oil from ingraining but also protect from chemical toxins.
- Keep loose clothing and long hair tucked away: running engines, power tools or machines such as grinders and wire wheels will easily trap anything loose, with dangerous outcomes.
- Remove all jewellery: not only loose necklaces or bracelets, but also rings.
- Always use the correct tool for the job: never force a tool to fit or use a loose-fitting tool. Slipping with an ill-fitting screwdriver in your hand carries a surprising amount of force.
- Get someone to check on you at regular intervals: let people know what you are up to if you plan to do something that you recognize as potentially hazardous.

## GENERAL HAZARDS

- Scalding/burning: coolant, engine oil, exhaust manifolds, engines, brakes, metal burs, nut and bolts can all burn you badly.
- Crushing: always have something to support heavy objects you are removing – a starter motor can knock you out, a gearbox can break bones. Never get under a car that is being supported only by a jack. Never support a vehicle on blocks or bricks, which can crumble or roll over.
- Fire: fuel leaks and spills are bad, but it is the volatile vapour that is the most dangerous; it can be easily ignited by a spark from something as simple as a heater igniter or a spark from a battery terminal. Electrical overloads may creep along wires and ignite something flammable. The propellant used in aerosols can ignite in a flash with the smallest of sparks in a confined space. Always keep a fire extinguisher near by.
- Electric shocks: an ignition high-tension circuit can be dangerous for someone with heart problems or a pacemaker. All electrically powered tools should have a breaker (RCD). Dropping a heavy object on to a cable could cut it or at the very least expose wiring.
- Fumes: battery fumes can be explosive and breathing in fumes from paint thinner can be very quickly disorienting. Carbon monoxide is a silent killer; never run a vehicle in an enclosed garage. Petrol fumes are heavier than air and will sink to the floor or down a pit.
- Poisonous and irritant substances: battery acid will burn as bad, if not worse than fire, vehicle fluids can be an irritant with prolonged use, Strong cleaners and paint thinners can cause skin problems.
- Air bags: take care when removing items with air bags attached, as they can cause injury if they go off inadvertently.

## WORKING SAFELY UNDER A CAR

Follow these tips and stay safe when working under a vehicle:
- Park the vehicle on a hard level surface such as a concrete driveway.
- Before you raise the vehicle, chock the unlifted wheels and engage the handbrake/parking brake.
- Refer to the car's workshop manual to locate the lifting point to position the jack under the vehicle. If the incorrect lifting point is used, the jack could slip or tip.
- Watch carefully while raising the vehicle. Check that the lift plate of the trolley jack is sitting squarely on the point you are lifting.
- A trolley jack does not lift vertically, but in an arc. Make sure the jack is able to roll slightly to allow for the change of angle as the vehicle is raised, otherwise you will be trying to drag the car sideways.
- If you are planning on working under a vehicle, always use support stands or ramps. When using support stands, ensure you locate the correct position for them before slowly lowering the jack so the vehicle is resting on the stands. Ensure the vehicle is secure on the stands before getting under it.
- Never work under a car on the street or in a car park.
- Never allow a person or pet to remain in the vehicle while it is being jacked.
- Never exceed the weight capacity of the jack.

**TIP:** If you are removing a road wheel to work on a car, slide it under the chassis rail. It keeps it out of the way but could also save you if the car becomes unstable on its jack or stands.

# PART I

# INTRODUCING THE 126 S-CLASS

Although there have been 'S' classifications for Mercedes cars since the early 1950s, the first official flagship Sonderklasse – the German term for 'special class' – was officially introduced as late as 1972, with the 116.

The 126 premiered at the Internationale Automobil-Ausstellung (International Motor Show, or IAA) in Frankfurt in September 1979 with an initial line-up of eight models: the 280S, 280SE, 280SEL, 380SE, 380SEL, 500SE and the 500SEL, and a diesel version 300SD for the US/Canada only.

Generally, the term '126' has been used throughout the book, even though the car has become widely known as the W126. For the sake of accuracy, though, it is necessary to distinguish between the models. The standard-wheelbase or 'SE' model was so named by abbreviating the German words *Sonderklasse Einspritzmotor* for petrol-injected engines; 'SD' indicated the diesel version. The factory codename of these cars was W126. The long-wheelbase models – the 'SEL' (for *Sonderklasse Einspritzmotor-Lang*) and 'SDL' (diesel) – were codenamed V126. In 1981, a two-door sports coupé version C126 (*Sport Einspritzmotor-Coupé*, or SEC) was premiered at the IAA.

Four years after the introduction of the first generation of 126 models the range was further reworked and presented at the IAA in Frankfurt. There had been visual changes to the bumpers, side covers and alloys, but more significant were the engine variants that were now offered. Two newly constructed six-cylinder engines and two reworked V8s were added, and other engines were further upgraded. The 260

had the new Mercedes M103 2.6-litre straight-six engine and a new 3.0-litre petrol engine was also introduced. The 420 (4.2-litre) replaced the 380 3.8-litre V8 engine. The 500 remained and an upgraded 560 with a sportier 5.6-litre V8 engine joined the family.

The 126 S-Class was replaced by the 140 in 1991, although a satellite factory in South Africa is known to have continued production until late 1992.

## PRODUCTION NUMBERS

It is easy to imagine a small-volume manufacturer creating a car that turns into an instant classic but it is more complicated for a mass producer. Thankfully Mercedes Daimler have, for the most part, built models that are considered 'special' and, as such, do become sought after, even if they take their time to achieve that reputation. One way to keep ahead of the game is to know the numbers.

Overall, the 126 S-Class achieved a sales total of 892,126 units, made up of 818,066 saloons and 74,060 coupés. The following tables provide a breakdown of total production numbers by the year and model, separating Generation 1 and 2, remembering, of course, that the 500SE, SEL and SEC were the only 126s produced for both generations.

Mercedes Daimler wanted to end production of the 126 in 1988 and introduce the 140 model S-Class at around the same time, but a number of issues – officially described as 'budget and patent delays' – led to a two-year extension for the car. It was not until 27 August 1991, after twelve years of production,

## Mercedes 126 Generation I

| Model | Type | 1979 | 1980 | 1981 | 1982 | 1983 | 1984 | 1985 | Total |
|---|---|---|---|---|---|---|---|---|---|
| 280S | 126021 | 408 | 6,348 | 7,212 | 8,761 | 8,568 | 6,203 | 5,496 | 42,996 |
| 280SE | 126022 | 812 | 22,482 | 26,654 | 23,287 | 25,229 | 22,656 | 12,835 | 133,955 |
| 280SEL | 126023 | 1 | 887 | 2,423 | 3,843 | 4,302 | 4,598 | 4,601 | 20,655 |
| 380SE | 126032 | 217 | 7,935 | 8,603 | 7,429 | 8,147 | 14,618 | 11,290 | 58,239 |
| 380SEL | 126033 | 1 | 1,648 | 6,726 | 8,496 | 6,270 | 2,016 | 1,857 | 27,014 |
| 500SE | 126036 | 149 | 5,312 | 3,308 | 3,349 | 3,646 | 2,790 | 3,194 | 21,748 |
| 500SEL | 126037 | 2 | 2,206 | 5,942 | 8,966 | 12,095 | 14,808 | 17,251 | 61,270 |
| 380SEC | 126043 | | 3 | 945 | 4,393 | 3,829 | 1,310 | 787 | 11,267 |
| 500SEC | 126044 | | 1 | 726 | 4,059 | 6,058 | 6,664 | 5,865 | 23,373 |
| 300SD | 126120 | 3 | 4,857 | 16,595 | 18,122 | 20,291 | 12,546 | 6,311 | 78,725 |
| **Total by year** | | **1,593** | **51,679** | **79,134** | **90,705** | **98,435** | **88,209** | **69,487** | **479,242** |

that the last 126 rolled off the Sindelfingen production line; it was a coupé version with VIN 610819.

The last saloon version, an SEL with VIN 605721, had already rolled off the line four months previously, in the first week of April. It was immediately put aside as a museum piece and remains at the factory museum, occasionally being used as a promotional vehicle.

## MERCEDES 126 SALES POSITIONS

The following table gives the overall sales position and the percentage relating to all 126s sold. It is interesting to note the following:

• The W126 took 55 per cent of the total 126 market, with 490,905 vehicles.

• The V126 took 36.6 per cent of the total 126 market with 327,161 vehicles.

• The C126 took 8.3 per cent of the total 126 market with 74,060 vehicles.

## Mercedes 126 Sales Positions

| Position Number | Model | Percentage of Sales |
|---|---|---|
| 1 | 280SE | 15.02 |
| 2 | 300SE | 12.03 |
| 3 | 300SD | 9.32 |
| 4 | 560SEL | 8.41 |
| 5 | 420SEL | 8.30 |
| 6 | 500SEL | 8.15 |
| 7 | 380SE | 6.53 |
| 8 | 280S | 4.82 |
| 9 | 300SEL | 4.59 |
| 10 | 500SE | 3.75 |
| 11 | 500SEC | 3.38 |
| 12 | 560SEC | 3.24 |
| 13 | 380SEL | 3.03 |
| 14 | 260SE | 2.34 |
| 15 | 280SEL | 2.32 |
| 16 | 420SE | 1.57 |
| 17 | 300SDL | 1.55 |
| 18 | 380SEC | 1.26 |
| 19 | 420SEC | 0.41 |
| 20 | 350SDL | 0.33 |
| 21 | 350SD | 0.23 |
| 22 | 560SE | 0.14 |

**Mercedes 126 Generation 2**

| Model | Type | 1985 | 1986 | 1987 | 1988 | 1989 | 1990 | 1991 | 1992 | Total |
|---|---|---|---|---|---|---|---|---|---|---|
| 260SE | 126020 | 2,222 | 6,198 | 4,657 | 3,120 | 2,455 | 2,100 | 84 | | 20,836 |
| 300SE | 126024 | 5,432 | 18,134 | 15,104 | 20,431 | 20,289 | 21,058 | 4,974 | | 105,422 |
| 300SEL | 126025 | 1,379 | 4,815 | 6,886 | 8,686 | 10,985 | 6,428 | 1,777 | | 40,956 |
| 420SE | 126034 | 1,689 | 4,181 | 2,704 | 2,368 | 1,528 | 1,345 | 181 | | 13,996 |
| 420SEL | 126035 | 6,102 | 19,238 | 18,623 | 9,467 | 9,181 | 8,324 | 3,082 | | 74,017 |
| 500SE | 126036 | | 2,351 | 1,722 | 1,895 | 2,676 | 2,308 | 718 | | 11,670 |
| 500SEL | 126037 | | 4,032 | 2,163 | 2,087 | 1,560 | 1,331 | 244 | 6 | 11,423 |
| 560SE | 126038 | | | | 486 | 428 | 337 | 1 | | 1,252 |
| 560SEL | 126039 | 2,097 | 16,559 | 13,494 | 12,832 | 12,990 | 13,728 | 3,339 | 32 | 75,071 |
| 420SEC | 126043 | 273 | 896 | 714 | 593 | 534 | 451 | 219 | | 3,680 |
| 500SEC | 126044 | | 2,020 | 1,107 | 1,056 | 1,062 | 1,067 | 499 | | 6,811 |
| 560SEC | 126045 | 989 | 4,745 | 5,476 | 5,012 | 5,299 | 5,270 | 2,138 | | 28,929 |
| 300SDL | 126120 | 47 | 8,274 | 5,509 | | | | | | 13,830 |
| 350SD | 126134 | | | | | | 1,181 | 885 | | 2,066 |
| 350SDL | 126135 | | | | | 18 | 2,032 | 875 | | 2,925 |
| **Total by year** | | 20,230 | 91,443 | 78,159 | 68,033 | 69,005 | 66,960 | 19,016 | 38 | 412,884 |

*There were a few minor differences to the full production numbers. One noticeable difference was a lack of rounded rub strips on the front and rear bumpers.*

## Production Identification

- 280S – 408 units
- 280SE – 812 units
- 280SEL – 1 unit
- 380SE – 217 units
- 380SEL – 1 unit
- 500SE – 149 units
- 500SEL – 2 units
- 300SD – 1 unit

**Total – 1,590 units**

Production started with what was known as a 'pre-production series' set of vehicles. These were generally test, show, press and showroom models to 'pre-empt' full production. They are much sought-after cars among the die-hard 126 fans and quite rare now.

There were a total of 1,590 'pre-production' vehicles built, across the models, as shown in the table above. It is always nice to know where a particular vehicle fits in the model line and with most limited-number manufacturers it is possible to follow model numbers via vehicle identification numbers (VIN). Although this initially applied to the 126, the system changed around the end of 1982/beginning of 1983, making it impossible to know now exactly where each vehicle fits.

The first two years of production saw a model-relevant consecutive VIN system, which equated to the first 281,192 cars. It was relatively simple: all VINs started with WDB126 and model number, then the last six numbers started at 000001 for each model. Once they reached the number listed as the 'Last VIN', the numbering system changed so that the numbers increased with all 126 vehicles built, and were not model-related. Following the 'Last VIN before change' list, all subsequent 126 vehicles produced followed a total production number thereafter. For example, a 500SEC Coupé might be numbered WDB126 044 1A 555555 and if the next vehicle on the build line was a 280SE it would be WDB126 022

1A 555556. Unfortunately, this only gives a total 126 build between numbers.

This is evident with the 'Last of the line' in the previous section. The SEL was 605721 and the SEC was 610819. This means that the factory produced 5,098 126 units of all models between this time.

## PRODUCTION CHANGES

Like any manufacturer, Mercedes constantly developed and evolved its models, and this applied to the 126. Many of the important changes are listed below, by date and, where possible, in relation to the vehicle identification number. Note: the non-model-related VIN did not start until late 1983 so it is impossible to give a more accurate breakdown before this date.

When attempting to find the nearest build date for a particular 126, it is important to remember that, even though revisions were implemented across the vehicle range from the date or VIN shown, that vehicle may have had the revised part added at some point in its past. For the sake of accuracy, it is important to use accumulated data, not just one item change.

(**Note:** SA = Special Equipment order only)

09/1979 – World premiere of the W126 series at the 48th IAA in Frankfurt.

01/1980 – Start of the main series (after pre-series) at the Sindelfingen plant.

*[Only 42 vehicles a day were being produced at this early stage.]*

02/1980 – The vacuum pump was moved from the engine compartment to the spare-wheel well to avoid it being affected by the heat from the engine.

03/1980 – The bumpers were amended by adding front and rear rub strips.

04/1980 – Start of main production of the SEL models.

12/1980 – SA Airbag for driver and front passenger and seatbelt tensioners were made available as a special equipment order.

07/1981 – SA Air conditioning was now activated via a switch and electronically controlled (previously manual dial); a recirculation switch was added.

07/1981 – Interior temperature sensor moved to the instrument panel in the roof frame trim installed to improve control and performance.

08/1981 – Steering gearbox upgraded for automatic play compensation.

09/1981 – Introduction of the so-called 'Mercedes energy concept' for all models, a programme aimed at reducing fuel consumption and harmful emissions. In addition to an increase in compression, the list of improvements included camshafts with modified valve timing, air-bathed injection valves and electronic idle-speed control. Camshafts with modified valve timing enabled maximum torque to be achieved at a lower engine speed and, in the case of the 3.8-litre engine, torque was increased.

09/1981 – Ceiling light, now with delay on exit control.

10/1981 – Coupé models in 380 and 500 form were released.

11/1981 – Surface heat exchanger added below the windscreen in the storage area to prevent snow and ice build-up.

09/1982 – Fuel-level warning light illuminates immediately when the ignition is switched on.

07/1983 – SA Seat heating upgraded to feature automatic shut-off.

08/1983 – New Hirschman Auto EL 6000 Automatic Antenna, which was lighter in weight, and better gearing for less wear and tear on electronic motor.

09/1983 – SA Burl Walnut available as option.

01/1984 – Assignment of road springs and rubber seating pad bearing is calculated and constructed on a points system.

04/1984 – SA Trip computer available for the V8 models all other models from 08/1984 – SA Trip computer available for all other models.

08/1984 – SA Coupé front seats and coupé-style rear sculptured singles available for the SEL.

08/1984 – SA Introduction of electric seat adjustment with two memory seat positions, now also includes electric headrest adjustment from VIN A 094293.

09/1984 – Seatbelt tensioners for both front seats as standard (indicated by the 'RS' on the buckle tongue) from VIN A 094293.

09/1984 – SA New orthopaedic backrest adjustment by means of electrically driven vacuum pump and adjusting the seat from VIN A 094293.

09/1984 – SA Headlight wiper and washer with larger wipers and integral spray nozzle (as Gen 2) from VIN A 096820.

09/1984 – SA Heated outside door mirror glass available.

02/1985 – Bonnet latches and grille slightly amended to accommodate safety bonnet tongue latch similar to that of the 123 and 124 models from VIN A 134098.

09/1985 Introduction of the 2nd series, from A 186069.

09/1985 – New electrically adjustable steering column available for all models.

11/1985 – New, lighter airbag unit in steering wheel, more visually integrated to the wheel shape.

12/1985 – 58D controller terminal upgraded, to improve switch illumination.

04/1986 – SA New seat switches now in more modern design similar to that of the 124 model, and new storage tray below the ashtray from VIN A 243517.

04/1986 – Fanfare horn switch no longer positioned at the top of the centre console, but below ashtray similar to that of the 124 model from VIN A 243517.

06/1986 – Central locking, electronic supply pump improved to respond more quickly and more quietly from VIN A 252372.

07/1986 – Spare tyre mounted the other way around, now with a removable tray (as W124) from VIN A 268602.

08/1986 – Introduction SA HPF II (Hydropneumatische Federung) self-levelling system with automatic lowering of the body by 24mm above about 120km/h and operating controls for adjusting the shock absorber hardness from VIN A 281436.

08/1986 – SA EDW (factory-fitted alarm system) with improved tow-away protection from VIN A 284611.

09/1986 – Introduction of ASR traction control for the V8 and ASD for the six-cylinder models from VIN A 288303.

09/1986 – New surge protection relay from VIN A 288303.

11/1986 – Amended stereo system with more space for larger speakers (better surround sound) from VIN A 296642.

12/1986 – ABS standard on all models (previously only V8 models) from A 309743.

01/1987 – New cruise-control unit with coding for each vehicle type (unification) from VIN A 311370.

03/1987 – SA EDW (factory-fitted alarm system) and elimination of towing protection.

03/1987 – Fault diagnosis by duty cycle now in the KE control unit.

03/1987 – Revised fuel tank swirl pot with integrated separation chamber and fumes separation, thereby eliminating splashing noises from fuel tank from VIN A 327880.

05/1987 – Elimination of vacuum tank for the headlight levelling, new setting switch with incorporated shut-off valve from VIN A 338234.

05/1987 – Additional security for the terminal 58D (not for trip computer) in the left instrument cluster.

06/1987 – Fuel injectors made of brass with Viton seals (M103 engine).

07/1987 – Electric rear shade available as SA.

08/1987 – More compact pre-tensioners with about 80mm shorter tube.

09/1987 – Introduction of the up-rated V8 engine with anti-knock control.

09/1987 – New instrument cluster with modified control of the tank reserve indicator to stop light flicker when cornering from VIN A 350465.

09/1987 – Central vent, climate control flap receives new bar clamps from VIN A 354453

09/1987 – Icon switches for sliding-lifting roof illuminated from VIN A 357231.

09/1987 – Completely new airbag system (SA) with improved electronics and triggering algorithm, recognizable by the SRS logo on the airbag; SA passenger airbag is now available from VIN A 363212.

09/1987 – Heated washer nozzles now standard (SA code 875; only for LHD) and new heated windscreen-washer nozzles (PTC-resistor is replaced by a fixed resistor), as well as additional panels for windscreen-washer jets on the inside of the bonnet from VIN A 363212.

09/1987 – SA Air conditioning revised, now with microprocessor control and electronic recirculation switch from VIN A 363799.

09/1987 – SA Heated seats, only one controller for both front seats from VIN A 368215.

09/1987 – SA New sound system available.

10/1987 – Chrome rings for the door lock pins changed into black plastic rings from VIN A 388633.

02/1988 – Comfort control relay for electric windows and seat adjustment: performance of the diode is increased from 1 to 3 amperes.

03/1988 – Amending the toolbar to the right in the instrument cluster for SA airbag, instead of RS now SRS (Safety Restraint System) from VIN h07304.

03/1988 – HT lead set improved with soldered terminals improving resistance to moisture.

07/1988 – Improved sound insulation, including special foam pieces around the rear speakers in the rear shelf glued into place as well as the shelf base being covered in sound-proofing material. Extra panels added to seal cable insertion slots in the rear wall and C post. Water drain hoses from the sunroof now sealed in the C post with foam. Fire-proof sound-dampening fleece (20mm) lain loose over the fuel tank and into the C post areas also between the rear seat wall and tank partition

09/1988 – New model type 560SE is introduced as SA only.

09/1988 – Softer damping adjustment of the shock absorbers on front and rear with revised adjustment of base score in the spring selection from VIN A 428209.

09/1988 – Ruffled solid pockets replace cargo-style nets on the seat backs as standard from VIN A 428659.

09/1988 – Installation of a heated exterior mirror passenger side (both mirrors now connected with a single cable set) from VIN A 430736.

09/1988 – Boot lights can be deactivated via switch from VIN A 434459.

09/1988 – Wiring for anti-theft alarm system (ATA) now integrated from VIN A 434548.

09/1988 – Revised wiring loom set for the exit (puddle) lights changed from VIN A 434549.

09/1988 – New seat-heater control unit to control power increase due to introduction of soft leather from A 439287.

09/1988 – Amended resistance arrangement for the front passenger seat airbag (R32) from A 439844.

09/1988 – Improved standard equipment: four electric windows, steering wheel and gearshift lever in leather, folding armrest, Head restraints in the rear and outside temperature display from VIN A 440401.

09/1988 – Soft leather available.

09/1988 – Introduction of twelve colours (instead of four) for the bumpers and side planking.

10/1988 – New supply pump of the central locking system for increased performance and faster unlocking of the vehicle (distinguishable by white base to the motor unit) from VIN A 443217.

11/1988 – Amended headlight control device.

12/1988 – SA HPF II (self-levelling system) given revised connecting piece to avoid oil-flow noise during acceleration or cornering.

01/1989 – SA New relay (green) to headlight cleaning system, controlling shutting off the wipers from VIN A 451890.

03/1989 – SA Revised electric sliding-lifting roof mechanism, eliminating the closing noise.

03/1989 – New comfort control relay for electric windows and seat adjustment from VIN A 461998.

04/1989 – Revised door contacts to improve glovebox and exit lighting from VIN A 474336.

06/1989 – Guide funnel in fuel-tank filler pipe as standard (previously only KAT-vehicles and USA) from VIN A 484390.

06/1989 – Brand-new design of the front bumper, with hydraulic impact absorbers as standard from VIN A 485222.

07/1989 – VIN plate change: reference to Daimler-Benz AG changed to Mercedes-Benz AG from VIN A 491298.

07/1989 – Electronic dimmer rheostat replaces ceramic type for terminal 58D, also new warning symbol in the speedometer in SA ASD/ASR (day/night) from VIN A 491585.

09/1989 – Broader transmission support with extra frame for automatic transmission from VIN A 495960.

09/1989 – New ignition from A 496760.

09/1989 – Steering wheel size changed to 400mm diameter (previously 410mm) from VIN A 496760.

09/1989 – New wheel covers, in addition to the already existing chrome star now with chrome ring on the edge; on special request now painted in one of the twelve side cover colours since VIN A 496760.

09/1989 – Introduction of ASR II SA (now also available for 260/300SE) from VIN A 496760.

09/1989 – Capacitor of the SA air conditioning increased using double-fan for W and V126 only from VIN A 496760.

09/1989 – Use of new soft boot lining material only for V and C126 from VIN A 496760.

09/1989 – Gear shift point increase between 2 and 3, as well as faster heating of the $CO_2$ sensor and catalytic converter (V8 models only).

09/1989 – New bracket for fire extinguisher SA, taken from R129. With interior matching velour from VIN A 502270.

10/1989 – Revised brake discs from VIN A 506204.

10/1989 – Revised wrinkled hose to the left-hand bonnet air filter intake (only M116/117) from VIN A 513364.

12/1989 – Parking lock latch (shift lock) with automatic transmission from VIN A 524864.

01/1990 – Revised steering lock from VIN A 525779.

01/1990 – Fuel injectors made of brass with Viton seals, in M116/117.

07/1990 – Improved check valve (noise optimization) vacuum line from the brake booster (distinguishable by black line colour).

07/1990 – Introduction of Becker radios from the 2000 series SA.

## THE EXPORT MARKET

Mercedes had an excellent export sales regime and managed to export around 40 per cent of its total units built, which contributed to making the 126 the most successful 'S'-classified Mercedes ever produced, even to the present day.

Approximately 55,000 units went to the Middle East, 45,000 units to Japan and 30,000 to the Far East. In addition, early sales results in South Africa were so

Generation One

Generation Two

Larger Bumpers

*Due to complicated anti-dazzle and beam-direction regulations in the US DOT system, the Euro H4 headlamp units were replaced by gas-filled sealed units to come into line with the FMVSS 108 regulations.*

good that Mercedes decided it was prudent to build a factory in the territory. The South Africa plant continued building the 126 for another 6 months after Sindelfingen ceased production.

Almost a third of the entire production numbers, approximately 283,000 units, were sold to the USA and Canadian markets through dedicated main dealers. The official US-/Canada-specification 126s were easily identified by the larger bumpers; DOT regulations meant that they had to incorporate the shock-absorbing mounting struts as well as the large steel beams in the inner bumper structure. This also resulted in narrower chrome bumper embellishments.

Not all the DOT regulations led to changes that were immediately visible. The engines were considerably restricted in horsepower due to the stricter emission rules and incorporated a belt-driven air pump under the alternator. However, as respect and admiration for the 126 grew in the US market, the demand for something a little less restricted also increased, resulting in many 5-litre models (500s) and later 560 models finding their way on to the 'grey market' system. These cars still had to get through the same DOT federalized testing system and changes were made to bring them into line with the 'officially imported' models; many 126s managed to pass through the system by the greasing of palms. Even though the vehicles were adapted to come into line with the regulations, many of the original 'euro parts' removed by the private importer, such as lights and bumpers, were sold with the 'federalized vehicle' to refit later.

US/ Canada Version

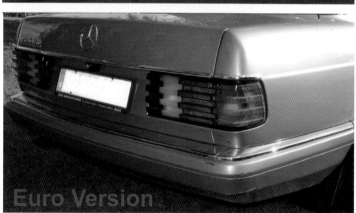

Euro Version

*The tail-lights were also slightly different, incorporating an extra red sidelight in comparison to a Euro model.*

## PRICES

It is very difficult to give an accurate indication of the original price of a 126 due to the concessions and taxes involved in each country. These are the basic factory prices, given in Deutschmarks. The end price of a particular vehicle may have varied according to the supplying dealership.

The average US Dollar to DEM over the twelve-year period was 1.00 to 1.90 although during 1985 the average was 1.00 Dollar to 2.90DEM, which would have made the 126 a good deal cheaper in the US around that time.

The average GBP to DEM over the twelve-year period was 1.00 to 3.30 although during 1981 the year averaged 1.00GBP to 4.20 DEM.

In some of the Asian markets the price of a 126 trebled and even quadrupled with the addition of local taxes due for imported models.

## Generation-One Prices

| | Production Start Price | Production End Price |
|---|---|---|
| 280S | April 1979 | April 1985 |
| Price in Deutschmark | 35.877,50 | 47.743,20 |
| | | |
| 280SE | September 1979 | April 1985 |
| Price in Deutschmark | 38.815,50 | 52.041,00 |
| | | |
| 280SEL | September 1979 | April 1985 |
| Price in Deutschmark | 41.188,50 | 55.176,00 |
| | | |
| 380SE | September 1979 | April 1985 |
| Price in Deutschmark | 46.669,00 | 65.949,00 |
| | | |
| 380SEL | September 1979 | April 1985 |
| Price in Deutschmark | 49.042,00 | 69.084,00 |
| | | |
| 500SE | September 1979 | April 1985 |
| Price in Deutschmark | 50.680,50 | 72.162,00 |
| | | |
| 500SEL | April 1979 | April 1985 |
| Price in Deutschmark | 56.161,00 | 78.831,00 |
| | | |
| 300SD | September 1979 | August 1985 |
| Price in Deutschmark | NA in Europe | NA in Europe |
| | | |
| 380SEC | September 1981 | April 1985 |
| Price in Deutschmark | 69.495,00 | 89.034,00 |
| | | |
| 500SEC | July 1980 | April 1985 |
| Price in Deutschmark | 73.902,00 | 94.620,00 |

# PART II

# BUYING A 126 S-CLASS

With prices having reached rock bottom in recent years and online auction sites making it easy to buy any type of vehicle, unseen, on a whim, never before has the old adage 'Purchase in haste, repent at leisure' been so apt. The fact that the 126 was a well-built Mercedes will stand the prospective purchaser in good stead – to a degree – but the chances of finding a good one are still probably only about 50–50.

When it was new and in its flagship form, the 126 cost about the same as a semi-detached house in the UK. In the worst-case scenario, the very persistent (or reckless) buyer could end up needing a re-mortgage in order to return a particular example to its original form. For the less persistent purchaser who may become increasingly disheartened by a difficult refurbishment project, the result could be another 126 consigned to the SORN declaration or taking up room in a garage or on a driveway. Eventually, the disillusioned owner will probably need the space back and pass the car on to the scrap man.

Armed with enough knowledge, it should be possible to weed out the rubbish instead of buying it and thus have the real pleasure of owning one of the greatest, best-built vehicles ever produced.

# CHAPTER ONE

# OPTIONS

## BODIES

- The SE, or W126, was the short-wheelbase version. It took 55 per cent of the total sales market.
- The SEL, or V126, was the long-wheelbase version. The extra 140mm over the SWB version was placed aft of the B post to allow for extra legroom in the rear. It took 36.6 per cent of the total sales market
- The SEC, or C126, was the two-door sports coupé introduced in September 1981. It took 8.3 per cent of the total sales market.

### Generation One 1979-1985   Generation Two 1985-1991

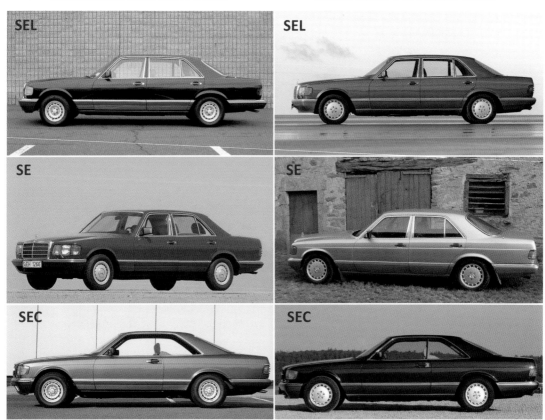

*The various body shapes available in the 126 range.*

## ENGINES

### PETROL V8S

#### *Eight-Cylinder M116 and M117*

The eight-cylinder engines were, by far, the best match for a heavy car such as the 126, offering great comfort and versatility and proving to be incredibly smooth in operation. Performance-wise, the V8 engines were better than their six-cylinder counterparts, but at the cost of higher fuel consumption.

The first versions available were the 3.8- and 5.0-litre engines but only until 1985. Although having very robust blocks and bottom ends, the early 3.8 versions did have a tendency to wear out their camshafts more quickly. The single-row timing chain on the very early versions had a tendency to stretch and, if not corrected in time, could break, causing catastrophic failure.

In the autumn of 1985 the V8s were revised and upgraded. The 3.8-litre was replaced by the 4.2-litre, the 5.0-litre was upgraded and improved and a 5.6-litre version was introduced, adding a little more oomph. All these engines have since proved themselves to be exceptionally reliable, with several hundreds of thousands of miles being easily obtainable without problems.

The 4.2 was the smallest of the second-generation V8 engines. The version before the 1987 upgrade had performed little better than the 300 but the 4.2 that was offered after 1987 had an extra 20bhp, which helped to widen the gap.

After August 1987, all the V8s were tweaked again, to compensate for the loss of power that came with the catalytic converter and the more popular use of unleaded fuels. It is worth looking out for the RUF and ECE versions, which offered increased performance, with or without a cat.

Throughout the entire life of the 126 the 5.0-litre was considered the most durable and well-balanced of all its V8s – the second-series 5.0-litre M117 engine is especially recommended. The rpm to power band ratio were lowered, while bhp was raised to 265 in the euro engine, providing an even quieter and more durable engine – if that were possible.

*The M116 and M117 V8 engine. The eight-cylinder engines were by far the best match for a heavy car like the 126.*

The 5.6-litre was a revelation. Although it was only marginally more powerful than the 5-litre on paper, the way in which the extra power was spread helped it run more smoothly and consequently more quietly when treated gently. With the application of a slightly heavier foot, however, it really came into its own; the higher revving capabilities gave it a feel of raw power, encouraging a sportier driving style and justifying its nickname of 'The Porsche Hunter'.

Fuel economy of the 5.6-litre is just marginally more than that of the 5.0-litre on a combined test. However, it is not too difficult to get it down to single figures with a bit of frisky driving. The 5.6 was also the engine of choice to tune and there have been many upgrades over the years; for example, AMG built a retuned 5.6 and a quad-cam 6.0-litre version.

### PETROL STRAIGHT-SIXES

#### *Six-Cylinder M110*

The M110 2.8 engines were introduced into the Mercedes line-up in 1972 and proved themselves to be among the most robust six-cylinder petrol engines ever produced by MBD – or any other car manufacturer for that matter. The tame overhead

*The M110 2.8 straight-six. The number-one bestselling 126 engine.*

*The M103 straight-six came in the two engine sizes of 2.6 and 3.0. It was sometimes referred to as the 'million-miler'.*

camshaft set-up went a long way to provide decent fuel efficiency for its size and a long life expectancy. The 280S 126021 cars were carburettor-fuelled.

Even though the 280SE was only made in the first series it was the number-one bestselling of all 126s and took over 22 per cent of the total market.

Of course, there are probably as many well-conditioned examples of the first series as there are abused 126s of the second series. However, when considering a 280 model it is important to take into consideration the fact that it may incur a slightly higher maintenance cost purely because of the age of this engine.

### Six-Cylinder M103

Replacing the 2.8-litre M110 in August 1985, the M103 engine came in two sizes – a 2.6-litre and a 3.0-litre. Although it was a new engine at the time, both versions proved themselves strong and reliable in a number of Mercedes models, besides the 126. The 126 powered by the 3.0-litre version became the second biggest-selling of its type; as a result, the 300SE 126024 remains by far the most plentiful example available on the second-hand market today. The 2.6 version was fitted to the 126

only to comply with the tax legislation in certain countries and it does teeter on the edge of being under-powered. It is perhaps better suited to the more relaxed driver...

Although 180bhp was not considered powerful enough for the 126 initially, the engine's high torque capabilities went a long way towards making it a smooth alternative to the V8s. Later in their life, the engines were often referred to as the 'million-milers' due to their robust nature. They were also the European taxi engine of choice in the pre-diesel boom, most often in W124 form.

### DIESEL FIVE-CYLINDERS (US AND CANADA MARKET ONLY)

The OM617 engine family is a straight-five diesel, initially entering the market in 1974 on the W115 model. It has been referred to as one of the most reliable engines ever produced by any manufacturer, capable of reaching over 1,000,000km without being rebuilt. It is one of the key reasons for the popularity of the Mercedes brand in North America in the early 1980s. Offered in its turbo form, it quickly became a popular option fitted in the 300SD from 1980 to 1985. Although it was produced only for

*The OM617 Turbo was the first diesel version offered for the 126 and, even though it was offered only to the US and Canadian market, it became the third-highest-selling 126.*

*The OM603 was not the manufacturer's finest hour, but most problems should have been ironed out by now, if you can find one.*

the US and Canadian market, it achieved close to 9 per cent of the overall market and was the power behind the third biggest-selling 126. It was never offered outside the US, but in recent years a small number of SD/Ls have come up for sale online in Europe.

The very same engine, minus the turbo, is the unit in my own G-Wagen. During fifteen years and 150,000 miles of ownership, it let me down only once, as a result of contaminated fuel drawn from a faulty station.

## THE DIESEL SIXES (US AND CANADA MARKET ONLY)

The OM603 was offered in two engine sizes for the 126. The 300SDL had the 3.0-litre version between 02/1986 and 09/1987 and then the 3.5-litre version was offered for the 1991 350SD and the 06/1990 to 08/1991 350SDL; all had a turbo.

All early OM603s suffered from cylinder-head problems, which were not eliminated even after extensive head revisions in the later W140.

The 300SDL sold 13,830 units but the 350s only managed 4,991 units between them.

## SPECIAL OPTIONS

For those who wanted something different, there were many tuners willing to add a little extra to the 126. The most popular by far was AMG, who offered everything from body kits to full-blown tuned DOHC 32-valve engines. Unable to compete with the popularity of AMG, Mercedes Daimler Benz signed a co-operation agreement with the company in 1990 to allow their tuned versions to be offered officially in Mercedes showrooms. Of course, anyone can stick a badge on a 126, call it an AMG and charge double, so it is vital to ensure that any potential purchase is indeed a genuinely 'AMG breathed-upon version'.

## SPECIAL PROTECTION VEHICLES

Daimler-Benz AG had recognized very quickly that the 116 S-Class lent itself effectively to a potentially lucrative market of specially prepared vehicles for VIPs and dignitaries. This carried on through to the 126, with the short-wheelbase W126 being mostly

# MERCEDES BENZ 126 S-CLASS ENGINE SPECIFICATIONS

| Engine | Cyl. | Power | Torque | 0–100 km/h | Maximum speed | Model Year |
|---|---|---|---|---|---|---|
| Gasoline | | | | | | |
| 2.6 | I6 | 166 PS (122 kW; 164 hp) | 228 Nm (168 lb-ft) | 10.2s | 205 km/h (127 mph) | From MY 1986 |
| 2.6* | I6 | 160 PS (118 kW; 158 hp) | 220 Nm (162 lb-ft) | 10.8s | 205 km/h (127 mph) | From MY 1986 |
| 2.8 Carb | I6 | 156 PS (115 kW; 154 hp) | 223 Nm (164 lb-ft) | 11.0s | 200 km/h (124 mph) | MY 1980–1985 |
| 2.8 Inj | I6 | 185 PS (136 kW; 182 hp) | 240 Nm (177 lb-ft) | 10.0s | 210 km/h (130 mph) | MY 1980–1985 |
| 3.0* | I6 | 180 PS (132 kW; 178 hp) | 255 Nm (188 lb-ft) | 9.6s | 210 km/h (130 mph) | From MY 1986 |
| 3.0 | I6 | 188 PS (138 kW; 185 hp) | 260 Nm (192 lb-ft) | 9.3s | 210 km/h (130 mph) | From MY 1986 |
| 3.8 | V8 | 218 PS (160 kW; 215 hp) | 299 Nm (221 lb-ft) | 9.7s | 215 km/h (134 mph) | MY 1980–1981 |
| 3.8 | V8 | 204 PS (150 kW; 201 hp) | 315 Nm (232 lb-ft) | 9.3s | 205 km/h (127 mph) | MY 1982–1985 |
| 4.2* | V8 | 204 PS (150 kW; 201 hp) | 310 Nm (229 lb-ft) | 9.8s | 210 km/h (130 mph) | MY 1986 |
| 4.2 | V8 | 218 PS (160 kW; 215 hp) | 330 Nm (243 lb-ft) | 9.0s | 218 km/h (135 mph) | MY 1986 |
| 4.2* | V8 | 224 PS (165 kW; 221 hp) | 325 Nm (240 lb-ft) | 8.3s | 218 km/h (135 mph) | From MY 1987 |
| 4.2 | V8 | 231 PS (170 kW; 228 hp) | 335 Nm (247 lb-ft) | 8.1s | 222 km/h (138 mph) | From MY 1987 |
| 5.0 | V8 | 223 PS (164 kW; 220 hp) | 365 Nm (269 lb-ft) | 8.0s | 220 km/h (137 mph) | From MY 1986 |
| 5.0 | V8 | 240 PS (177 kW; 237 hp) | 402 Nm (296 lb-ft) | 7.8s | 225 km/h (140 mph) | MY 1980–1981 |
| 5.0 | V8 | 231 PS (170 kW; 228 hp) | 405 Nm (299 lb-ft) | 8.1s | 220 km/h (137 mph) | MY 1982–1985 |
| 5.0 | V8 | 245 PS (180 kW; 242 hp) | 400 Nm (295 lb-ft) | 7.6s | 230 km/h (143 mph) | MY 1986 |
| 5.0* | V8 | 223 PS (164 kW; 220 hp) | 358 Nm (264 lb-ft) | 7.8s | 220 km/h (137 mph) | MY 1986 |
| 5.0* | V8 | 252 PS (185 kW; 249 hp) | 390 Nm (288 lb-ft) | 7.5s | 230 km/h (143 mph) | From MY 1987 |
| 5.0 | V8 | 265 PS (195 kW; 261 hp) | 405 Nm (299 lb-ft) | 7.3s | 235 km/h (146 mph) | From MY 1987 |
| 5.6* | V8 | 242 PS (178 kW; 239 hp) | 390 Nm (288 lb-ft) | 7.6s | 228 km/h (142 mph) | MY 1986 |
| 5.6* | V8 | 279 PS (205 kW; 275 hp) | 430 Nm (317 lb-ft) | 7.2s | 240 km/h (149 mph) | From MY 1987 |
| 5.6 | V8 | 272 PS (200 kW; 268 hp) | 421 Nm (311 lb-ft) | 7.0 | 250 km/h (155 mph) | MY 1986 |
| 5.6RÜF | V8 | 299 PS (220 kW; 295 hp) | 456 Nm (336 lb-ft) | 6.9s | 250 km/h (155 mph) | From MY 1987 |
| 5.6ECE | V8 | 299 PS (220 kW; 295 hp) | 455 Nm (336 lb-ft) | 6.9s | 250 km/h (155 mph) | MY 1986/87 |
| Diesel | | | | | | |
| 3.0 TD | I5 | 125 PS (92 kW; 123 hp) | 245 Nm (181 lb-ft) | 15.0s | 170 km/h (106 mph) | MY 1980–1985 |
| 3.0 TD | I6 | 150 PS (110 kW; 148 hp) | 273 Nm (201 lb-ft) | 13.0s | 195 km/h (121 mph) | MY 1986/87 |
| 3.5 TD | I6 | 136 PS (100 kW; 134 hp) | 310 Nm (229 lb-ft) | 11.8s | 175 km/h (109 mph) | MY 1990/91 |

*= Catalyst version*

*Basic engine specification (variations to the data may occur when applied to various models).*

## Mercedes 126 Special Protection Vehicle Production Numbers

| Model | Type | From | To | Units |
|---|---|---|---|---|
| 380SE | 126032 | 1981 | 1985 | 86 |
| 380SEL | 126033 | 1981 | 1985 | 88 |
| 500SE | 126036 | 1981 | 1985 | 3 |
| 500SEL | 126037 | 1981 | 1985 | 376 |
| 420SE | 126034 | 1985 | 1991 | 229 |
| 420SEL | 126035 | 1985 | 1991 | 63 |
| 500SE | 126036 | 1985 | 1991 | 7 |
| 500SEL | 126037 | 1985 | 1991 | 262 |
| 560SEL | 126039 | 1986 | 1992 | 349 |

**Total 1465**

*A fine example of a first-generation special protection vehicle, including blast-proof wheels with Continental run-flat tyres and triple-glazed bullet-proof glass.*

*The 32-valve quad-cam 6-litre AMG engine was the ultimate incarnation of the M117, officially called the M117/9 and producing around 370bhp.*

used by special police forces, and the V126 SEL proving to be ideal for the VIP market.

The vehicles were pretty much bespoke but among the general upgrades were bullet-proof glass, armoured body panels, strengthened chassis and special wheels and tyres made by Continental, called the CTS system. Such vehicles come up for sale more often than the numbers would imply. They are basically the same as a normal 126 but carrying an extra couple of tons in weight, so regular work on the steering and suspension will be necessary. Some items may be prohibitively expensive, too; for example, a new front screen is between £16,000 and £17,000 and Continental CTS tyres are about £500 each.

## STATUS AND VALUE OF THE 126

Is the 126 a 'true classic'? Well, what makes a 'true classic'? Is it memorable? Yes. Is it special? Yes. Is it desirable? Yes; of course it is; the 126 is everything a classic car could and should be, however there is always that tendency to link 'classic' with 'age and/or value'. Whether classic or otherwise, all vehicles go through a value cycle, during which they will reach a point of being almost worthless.

The 126 started life as a prestigious car so it automatically has a head start compared with a more 'run-of-the-mill' domestic vehicle. It has already gone through its decline years, bottoming out, in Europe at least, around the end of 2012, when the cost of its individual parts outweighed its total value. At this point, there is usually a process whereby a number of cars are 'parted out' or crushed. Although it may be upsetting to a fan of a particular model, this 'thinning out' is entirely necessary if that car is going to appreciate in value.

Value is a relative concept, depending on whether you are buying or selling. When you sell a car it is worth every penny of the asking price, but when you buy a car, there are a multitude of things to do to it and it is not worth anywhere near what they are

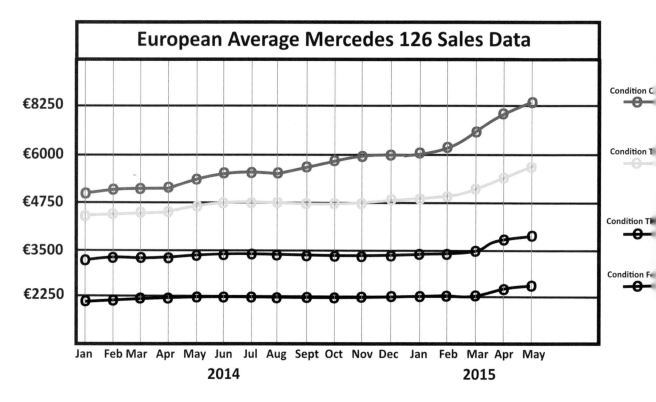

# European Average Mercedes 126 Sales Data

Condition C

Condition T

Condition Th

Condition Fo

Jan Feb Mar Apr May Jun Jul Aug Sept Oct Nov Dec Jan Feb Mar Apr May

**2014**          **2015**

*Even though there was a similar 20–30 per cent rise in value from January to May 2015 throughout the condition ranges the growth was exponential. For example, a Condition 4 126 increased by only around £250 whereas a Condition 1 car increased by over £1500 – a good reason to keep your 126 as near-perfect as possible.*

asking. The only sensible approach is to be realistic and do your homework.

The classic-car market has always been ever-changing and trying to keep up with what designates a classic – as opposed to a beaten-up jalopy – is difficult. One buzz word of the moment is 'young-timer', which applies to those middle-market vehicles that do not really fit into the full 'classic' status. It is a term often used in relation to the 126. It is irrelevant how often the enthusiast waxes lyrically about how special the 126 is, and how deserving it is of classic status; it does not necessarily make it so in the real world and this fact must be considered when it comes to spending money on it.

Once you take the beast home, the desire to 'get the car right' can very easily empty your wallet. If you

do it because you love it, you want to drive one of the finest motor vehicles in the world, and you do not really care how much it is worth, then the investment in time and money is down to you. At the moment, however, you are highly unlikely to recoup everything you spend on it. It is not all doom and gloom, though. The work you do on your car will always improve the amount it is worth; condition or perception of condition is everything.

The first vehicles in any marque to start appreciating in value will be the most sought-after, high-end and rare models and the same will apply to the 126 family – the pretty coupé sport GT 560SEC, the flag-ship 560SEL, and the rarest of them all, the 560SE. The other models will follow but in monetary value they will always lag behind those at the top of the range.

## Mercedes 126 Comparative Value Percentages

| Model | Type | From | To | Percentage |
|---|---|---|---|---|
| 260SE | 126020 | 1985 | 1991 | 35 |
| 280S | 126021 | 1979 | 1985 | 40 |
| 280SE | 126022 | 1979 | 1985 | 40 |
| 300SE | 126024 | 1985 | 1991 | 50 |
| 380SE | 126032 | 1979 | 1985 | 60 |
| 420SE | 126034 | 1985 | 1991 | 75 |
| 500SE | 126036 | 1979 | 1991 | 80 |
| 560SE | 126038 | 1988 | 1991 | 85 |
| 280SEL | 126023 | 1979 | 1985 | 45 |
| 300SEL | 126025 | 1985 | 1991 | 50 |
| 380SEL | 126033 | 1979 | 1985 | 75 |
| 420SEL | 126035 | 1985 | 1991 | 80 |
| 500SEL | 126037 | 1979 | 1992 | 85 |
| 560SEL | 126039 | 1986 | 1992 | 90 |
| 380SEC | 126043 | 1979 | 1985 | 75 |
| 500SEC | 126044 | 1979 | 1991 | 85 |
| 420SEC | 126043 | 1985 | 1991 | 80 |
| 560SEC | 126045 | 1985 | 1991 | 100 |
| 300SD | 126120 | 1979 | 1985 | 60 |
| 300SDL | 126125 | 1985 | 1987 | 50 |
| 350SD | 126134 | 1990 | 1991 | 55 |
| 350SDL | 126135 | 1989 | 1991 | 60 |

Values in different currencies are unhelpful, as they are soon out of date, but percentages in relation to each model will give an approximate idea of value, regardless of market or country. The following table works on the basis that the most sought-after and thus expensive model will be the 100 per cent value; the remainder will show the percentage of that value for a vehicle of equivalent condition. It does not include specials, rare barn finds with 600 miles on the clock or concours cars. It is based on Condition 1 cars that have been well cared for, regularly serviced and remain in original condition. Anything other than this is buyer/seller option.

At this early stage in status, neither age – Generation 1 (1979–1985) or Generation 2 (1986–1992) – nor the amount of options a particular car has will make any great difference to the general value. However, you need to be aware that this will change eventually as they become rarer and certain items become increasingly sought after. When making a decision about a purchase, you also need to remember that, although buyers in the UK rarely have a problem owning a left-hand-drive vehicle, the chances of selling on a right-hand-drive car in Europe are very slim.

# CHAPTER TWO

# GETTING STARTED: CHOOSING A CAR

## WHAT AND WHO IS IT FOR?

There are three very different body sizes to choose from, as well as three different engine options mixed in with nine different engine sizes. When choosing what to buy, you will save yourself time by narrowing down the options.

First, think about how you are going to use it and who you need to accommodate. Will it be a weekend car or a 'daily driver?' If you have a family, how big is it? Do you want a sporty coupé feel or a sedate Sunday stroll? Do you feel more at ease with a less complicated six-cylinder than a V8?

Hopefully some of the following information might help you with your decision.

## ACCOMMODATION AND CAPACITY

In terms of accommodation, all four doors open wide with a double-check door stop, which gives ample room to enter and exit safely and comfortably. The front seats of any 126 are ample enough for even the most corpulent driver or passenger; however, although the 126 is a big vehicle, made to look imposing, the SE and SEC models do lack legroom in the rear, especially by today's boxy standards. The SEL is no wider than an SE but it does have an extra 140mm of legroom, which makes all the difference to rear passengers.

*The rear seats of the SE will take two adults comfortably and even a third smaller person in the middle, but inevitably there will be a compromise between front seat positions and rear legroom.*

*Sculptured seats limit the rear passenger capacity to two small adults or children.*

*Even with its multiple adjustable seating and a laterally adjustable steering wheel, there is enough room in the 126 for all but giants.*

Being a sports coupé, the SEC has a slightly lower roof line at the back and the rear seats are sculptured for two individuals, which gives the impression of less space, even though it is not that different from the SE. The two front seats are more 'Recaro' in shape so, while offering more support, they can also restrict the occupant somewhat.

The boot capacity is a massive 510 litres (18 cubic feet) – more than enough to accommodate most luggage.

## DRIVING AND OWNING PRACTICALITIES

### AGILITY AND HANDLING

For such a heavy, imposing car the 126 is surprisingly agile and compliant, and easy to drive. A number of minor changes over the years resulted in a good option list, including SLS (self-levelling) hydraulic rear suspension, hydraulic all-round suspension, LSD (limited-slip differentials), which all went a long way towards assisting with the feel of the ride.

One of the only limitations is the compliant rear suspension of the non-SLS version. Too much and you will find it will bounce on to its bump stops and, as it already has an ample rear-end overhang, bottoming out on sleeping policemen and high kerbs is not unheard of.

When I drove Brunhilde through the Stelvio Pass (see picture, overleaf), we swung effortlessly back and forth on the hairpin road with ample power to pull up the curving steep inclines. More importantly, the car held the road beautifully poised, even on the way down with the weight behind.

When it comes to manoeuvring in a standard road, it will not be possible to do a U-turn in one action because of the extensive turning circle of the 126. The saloon versions have a minimum turning circle of 12.4m (488in or 40ft), while the coupé versions have a minimum turning circle of 11.6m (456in or 38ft).

### STORAGE AND PARKING

The SEL is 5285mm long by 1820mm wide (208in x 71.6in), the SE is 5145mm long by 1820mm wide (202.5in x 71.6in) and the SEC is 5060mm long by

*Stelvio Pass in Italy, which featured on the BBC's* **Top Gear** *programme as one of the best driving roads in the world.*

1828mm wide (199.2in x 71.9in). The 126 is a big car by any standards and parking is likely to be an issue, especially in supermarkets or shopping centres, where the tiny spaces rarely seem to comply with the 'recommended' dimensions of 4.8 x 2.4m. Even with bays of that size, the 126 would struggle to fit into just one space.

## RUNNING COSTS AND MAINTENANCE

Even if you have managed to avoid buying a 'pup', it is very difficult to calculate likely running costs. The 126 can fool you into thinking that you are driving a modern vehicle and it is very easy to forget you are actually driving a car that is, at the very least, twenty-five years old. Although terms such as 'over-engineered' and 'bullet-proof' are always bandied about whenever Mercedes cars are mentioned, the 126 is still 'old school' and needs looking after.

The 126 was a very expensive car to buy new and by today's standards it is not cheap to run. Some

thought needs to be given to fuel costs if you plan to run the car on a regular basis. All the engines, even the diesels, run in the mid- to low 20s for miles per gallon (14 litres per 100km), depending on the weight of your right foot of course.

With a 126 that has been well looked after, you may be able to just jump in and drive at your leisure, but the problems may come with 'deferred maintenance'. It is generally a robust and reliable vehicle that was well put together, and will benefit from being used regularly. However, any example will be at least twenty-five years old and catching up with all the issues that have been neglected by previous owners can get very costly. Mercedes parts can be ridiculously cheap or ridiculously expensive from a dealer but if you make friends with your local expert, you may be surprised at the parts discounts you get.

Parts can be purchased cheaply from the likes of eBay and other online sellers, but it is vital to choose wisely. The desire for cheap items has led to the creation of pattern parts of abysmal quality, which

*It is never good to see a car you adore in a state like this, but it is all a part of the process.*

are to be avoided at all costs. It is not impossible to find OEM (original equipment manufacturer) parts of reasonable quality, but there are also counterfeit items purporting to be OEM. If something is very cheap, there is probably a good reason for that.

It is advisable instead to budget for dealer prices and official Mercedes parts suppliers and if you manage to get OEM parts a bit cheaper it is a bonus. Around 99 per cent of serviceable parts are still available and getting used to what manufacturers use as original equipment will help enormously. Bosch, Lemforder, Mahle are all recognized suppliers, for example. When it comes to non-serviceable items, the situation is not so good; more and more parts are becoming NLA (no longer available) or BO (back order), which means they could become available in the future, although they are not at the moment.

Just a couple of years ago, the 126 was actually worth more as a sum of its parts than as a complete vehicle and this was reflected in the amount of second-hand parts offered for sale on auction sites.

However, this in itself caused problems. Cars were stripped of the items that would sell well and the remainder was crushed with the body shell, with the result that items such as interior parts and main body parts are now proving more difficult to find.

When all is said and done, this iconic car will put a smile on your face every time you drive it, especially in these days of bland soulless vehicles. However, you really need to ask yourself a number of questions about the condition of car that you can manage. Do you have the time and skills to do most of the work yourself, or are you going to pay a mechanic? Are you going to restore the car and are you planning to drive it and maintain it? A general and 'in-sequence' service will cost £150–250 in parts, while an extensive service could cost over £800 in parts. If these services are carried out at a garage, these costs could easily double.

It is important to be aware that many serviceable items can be worn by time as well as by mileage. One of the riskiest ways to go is to buy a below-average vehicle, with the intention of taking the 'rolling restoration' route. The 126 was an innovative and complicated vehicle in its time and the chances of removing and replacing one item at a time are pretty slim; what might appear to be a worn ball joint, for example, can very easily turn into a full suspension rebuild. While it is not an impossible task – my first 126 is proof of that – it is one that needs careful consideration, in terms of space, money, time and enthusiasm. If you lack any of these, it will quickly become either an immobile full restoration, awaiting completion of certain items, or a non-existent restoration that never gets done, ending up as a donor car or in the scrapyard. To avoid all this, buy the best car you can afford.

## LIVING WITH IT

This Mercedes is one of the old-school cars that need to be used. It can be all right sitting around, but a lack of activity can cause problems. The more you use the car, the better, smoother and more reliable it will become. As a daily driver it will eat up the miles. Whatever you chose to do with it, keep it pampered and serviced regularly and it will serve you well.

On the question of insurance, even the youngest (1991) 126 is approaching the age of twenty-five, so finding a reasonably priced insurance policy is fairly easy, especially with limited mileage. However, you do get what you pay for. If you want to protect your investment, it is worth considering an 'agreed value' insurance. This may require a vehicle assessment from a club official but it will offer better protection of the money and time you have invested.

This is predominantly a big, luxury car, with a feel and ride to match, but it is not necessarily easy to live with. It was innovative in its time but that was in the 1980s. It is certainly no mere 'runaround' and if you are expecting the easy drive of a modern-day car you will be disappointed.

It has often been said among car specialists that the Mercedes S-Class is an example of the near future of car design. In its time, the 126 was one of the safest vehicles ever made, with its pyrotechnically operated seatbelt tensioners, ABS anti-lock braking system, driver's airbag and ASR, to name just a few of the innovations featured. It is often described as having 'soul' and it is certainly one of those cars that will give back what its owner puts into it. Whether driving at 100mph-plus on a German *autobahn* or creeping through snow at a careful 10mph, winding up and down curving mountain roads or sitting in a traffic jam, it seems to eat up both time and distance.

# CHAPTER THREE

# GETTING STARTED: BUYING A CAR

First, which version will suit you best? As far as fuel economy goes, none is particularly frugal and in reality there is little more than 5 to 10 miles per gallon difference between them all. If you want to follow the advice to buy the best you can afford, the six-cylinder models tend to offer better value for money. It would be as foolish to pass up a 'good' car for the sake of air conditioning as it would be to buy a 'bad' one just because it had rare side curtains. Common sense must be a big part of the decision-making process.

The car-buying process is a very time-consuming one, even when you know what you want, so narrowing down your requirements will save a lot of time and expense in the long run. For example, there really is no point in going to look at a straight-six 300SE if you crave a throaty V8, or in viewing a car

with a velour interior if you desire leather. You might be able to convince yourself that it is a lovely car and a good purchase, but you will probably regret it later.

It is also worth remembering that the 260, 280 and 300 were entry-level S-Classes, and the 380 and the later 420 were the entry-level V8s, which means that generally their options levels are quite low. There are always exceptions though and just occasionally you may come across a car on the market that was bought new by someone who wanted only a 300 six-cylinder, and chose to pay more to load it with optional extras.

If you are unsure exactly what you want, treat it as though it were a new car purchase. There are plenty of original 126 sales brochures still available to buy on auction sites and at car shows; for around £20, you will be able to see exactly what was available in

*Original sales brochures may help you decide which 126 would suit you.*

the option lists as well as model types. It is better to do it beforehand than to have to start trawling the internet after your purchase, looking for that elusive option.

## VIEWING AND ASSESSING CARS

### FIRST CONTACT

Once you have done your research online and else-where, and drawn up a short list of vehicles that have ticked your boxes, the time has come to put it all into practice and make the first contact. Although it is very simple today to contact people more or less anonymously by email or text, there is no substitute for a personal phone call. Not only do you get more information via the spoken word, but you should also get a better feel for the seller.

However you chose to make contact, rule number one is 'be prepared'; the seller will be assessing you as much as you will be assessing them. Have a separate sheet of paper for each prospective car, so you can make notes on the following:

• Is it a private or trade sale?
• Where is the car? It is always preferable to be able to view the car at the business address or, for a private sale, at the home of the seller. Details should correspond with the vehicle documents. If they do not, why not?
• If you decide to buy it, will you be able to drive it away? If it cannot be driven, how can it be trans-ported?
• What are the logistical and cost implications of checking out and collecting the car? What about insurance and road tax?

There are a number of specific questions you need to ask during your first contact with the seller (try to sound confident and informed, but not arrogant):

• What is the condition of the car? Ask the seller directly to be straight, honest and specific. You do not want to travel for hours on a train to see a car

**TIP:** Before you go to view a car, ask for the engine not to be started beforehand, if at all possible. Check that the engine is cold when you get there and if it is not, ask why.

that the seller has described as 'fantastic', only to discover that it is a heap.
• What are the reasons for the sale? If it is a private sale, do not be too shy to ask why the seller is selling and how long he or she has owned the car.
• Ask questions about servicing and maintenance. What kind of service record does it have? What sort of work has the seller done or had done, and are there receipts and invoices? A stamped 'Maintenance Book' is good but it is not conclusive proof of the work. If the stamps show the name of the garage or mechanic, give them a call and ask if they know the car. A full MBD service history will have been recorded centrally and if therefore accessible.

### GOING TO VIEW A CAR

If you are not 100 per cent sure of what to look for, take someone who is….

When you go to view a car, it is useful to take a 'buyer's kit', consisting of the following:

• Take this book with you because the moment you see the 126 your brain will turn to mush.
• Put a weak magnet in a cloth and use it to check any suspect areas for filler. Get used to the 'pull' of the magnet as you touch the surface and you will soon be able to detect any weakening.
• Jumping into a pair of overalls will enable you to confidently crawl around the lower edges of the car.
• If you have rubber gloves you will be able to have a proper rummage without the worry of having to wash up or putting dirty hands on the nice, clean interior.
• A decent torch will enable you to see all around the engine bay and up underneath (make sure it has fresh batteries).

- A digital camera of decent quality (with fresh batteries) is especially useful if you are looking at a number of vehicles. Take as many photos as you can, zooming in where you need to. You may see something when you get home that you missed during the visit.
- A pad and pen are essential for making notes. It is impossible to remember everything, especially if you are looking at a number of vehicles over a number of days. Keep a separate page or section for each car.
- Have a small tool kit handy. You will need to ask permission of the seller before you use any tools, but, depending on how confident you feel, you may be able to pull a spark plug or lift the distributor cap just to have a look. Include in the kit a plastic filler knife (not a sharp one).
- Consider taking out a temporary open insurance policy, explaining to the insurer that you plan to test drive a number of potential purchases. It will be money well spent – the seller may refuse to allow you to drive the car unless you are covered, and of course you will need insurance if you do decide to buy the car on the spot and wish to drive it straight home.

## MAKING YOUR ASSESSMENT

It is very easy to give advice on how to make buying decisions, but in reality it very rarely works the same way. You may have narrowed your choice to three or four vehicles and, finding the first one to be absolutely perfect, choose to snap it up before someone else does. (However, be wary of the seller who insists on telling you that 'someone else is coming to see the vehicle in an hour or so'. It may be a ploy to pressure you.) If you feel you might be inclined to make a quick decision like this, look at the best option first; that way, if you do decide to buy at that first viewing, at least you will not have the nagging feeling that you may have missed out on something better.

If you miss out on a car, do not fret; there will always be another one somewhere. While there is no unseen hand guiding you – you are buying a car, not having a spiritual experience – in the end you will probably be going with your gut instinct.

## FIRST IMPRESSIONS

The first fifteen-minute period of any visit is the most important, and will probably dictate whether you decide to shake hands and walk away or delve further. You will inevitably be making a judgement first about the person selling the car. If it is a private sale, does he or she talk affectionately and enthusiastically about the car? Is the seller chatting incessantly to introduce you to the car or trying to distract you? If you are talking to a trader, do they seem to know the car properly?

The way the car is presented will tell you a great deal about the way it has been cared for. It is quite easy to tell whether it has been washed especially for the occasion, or whether it has been generally well looked after. Have a look under the wheel arches to check whether they are clean or caked in road grime. How deep is that shine? A regularly polished car has a deeper shine than a spur-of-the-moment rub can achieve. Open the doors and check the closing panels, which should be as clean and shiny as the outer panels on a fastidiously prepared car.

Take a quick look at minor items, such as the wiper blades on the headlights as well as those on the windscreen. Run your fingers over the rubber seals; on cars that have been sitting around they often turn a dusty green/grey.

There are a number of important items to look at that will need a more in-depth analysis later, but this initial cursory inspection should be enough to help you decide whether to go further.

## CLOSER INSPECTION: RUST CORROSION

The 126 is generally not known for severe rust problems other than in exceptional circumstances but does have a number of common areas. At this stage of the purchasing process you will only be able to make a cursory inspection, but if even one of the items mentioned below has a severe case of rust, you can probably make the assumption that some or all of the others will be similarly affected.

For more in-depth reference to corrosion issues, see the 'Living With' section.

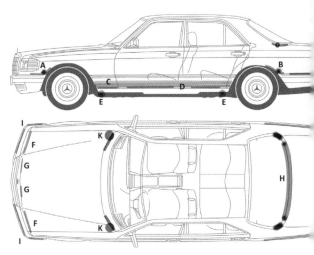

*A 126 that has spent its life in close proximity to the coast.*

The rear screen is the most important item on the list; especially around the bottom radii and towards the centre (H). It is a very common rust point throughout the 126 range, but always seems worse on the SEC Coupé.

There are a few tell-tale signs which should flag up the problem:

- Condensation on the inside of the rear screen.
- Water stains on the rear hat/parcel shelf.
- Curling up of the shelf box lids on the saloon models.
- Flopping in the middle of the rear screen to headlining trim.
- A musty and damp smell when you open the boot.
- Damp or even wet patches in the side wells in the boot.
- Water stains under the main boot mat.
- Rear screens 'delaminating' around the edges, leaving cloudy white marks.

Using the plastic filler knife from your small tool kit, lift the rubber seal around the bottom corners; if you hear a crunching sound or see a hole you can be sure it will have gone further.

Depending on the severity of the rust, be prepared to walk away. Repair panels are available and not very

*A: the rubber seal mounting point between bumper and front wing. B: the point where the bumper ends can touch the bodywork. C: inner wing and wing-mounting bolts behind cladding. D: rubber seal lip. E: jack-mounting sockets. F: bonnet lip above headlamps. G: front grille mounting bolts. H: lower radii of rear screen inside and outside. I: front chrome bumper embellishers. J: rear chrome bumper embellishers.*

expensive in themselves, but the job requires extensive labour time and could cost upwards of £800.

Rusty arches are usually caused by untreated accident damage. Run your fingers around all four of the wheel-arch rims. You should feel a continuous line; if you can feel bumps or lumps, that could be what remains of untrimmed filler.

The lower lip on each door where the rubber seal is held in can collect water and grit (D), so needs to be checked.

Bumper chromes tend to corrode on Generation 2 cars (I and J) more than they do on Generation 1 cars and they are becoming a rare item to source second-hand. They do remain available from MBD directly but, at approximately £1000 for the full kit, they are not cheap.

In certain circumstances rust can accumulate around the upper door frames however it can hide under the plastic facing cover. Although it is difficult to assess during a pre-purchase examination, running

ABOVE: *This area is also visible if you open the boot lid. Ask the owner if you can climb in the boot and take a proper look under the parcel shelf area; use your torch and aim the camera through the panel holes too.*

*Front wings: where the bumper touches the bottom edge is also where the inner plastic wheel-arch liner meets on the inside, causing an accumulation of grit and water.*

your fingers around the plastic trim can help you to detect it, via any crunchy rust sounds.

Kneel down at the rear and 'eye' down the panels to see if there are any dimples or creases. Filler under a panel may not be visible straight on but you may notice 'puddles' where light does not reflect in the same way.

The front grille outer shell is mild steel and nickel-chromed; its quality has saved it in the majority of cases but it is still worth checking around the rim for bubbles (G). Originals are very expensive and pattern parts tend to be of such poor quality that they do not last.

Anodized aluminium became a popular alternative to chrome and stainless-steel trim in the 1980s and 90s and even the S-Class Mercedes did not escape, with all the main door trim bright-work being finished in anodized aluminium. Normal aluminium is soft and requires continual polishing. To make it more

durable, it is put through an acid-bath process, which hardens the exterior shell, creating a polished finish that needs only minor care. The problem is that as it gets old it starts to go a milky colour and this is not removable without serious work.

If you can find new old stock it will be very expensive; it may not be a deal breaker but it is a consideration.

## ASSESSING THE ENGINE

By this point, you should have some instinct as to whether you should carry on with your assessment, or walk away. Trust your instinct! If it is telling you to keep looking, it is now time to inspect and start the engine.

The act of popping the bonnet is very important. If you fumble around searching for the catch, the seller with have the impression that you do not know what you are doing. The lever is on the vertical panel in the left foot well – familiarize yourself with the action before you go to visit a car. The safety latch holding the bonnet after release will 'pop out' of the plastic grille on the saloon versions. Pull the tab with one hand as you lift the bonnet from under the grille with the other.

*Anodized aluminium goes milky with age ('A' and 'B') and proprietary polishes will do little to improve it.*

The C126 has two safety releases adjacent to the latch; with a hand on either side of the grille, use your fingers to lift the latch as you lift the bonnet.

Check whether the engine is warm; it is not always possible to have a cold engine to inspect, as cars sometimes need to be moved around, but it is much better if possible.

First, make a visual inspection. Shine your torch all around and make a note of anything you feel to be important. Does it look clean and tidy or like it has not been touched in years? Newly detailed is not always a good sign, but it is not difficult to tell a nicely looked after engine bay from a recently jet-washed one. Pay particular attention to all the recesses around the second bulkhead.

Check the battery – a brand-new one could indicate the recommissioning of a vehicle that has been sitting inactive for a while.

The washer bottles pull up and out very easily without the need to disconnect the hoses or pumps, although you will have to uncouple the cable tie holding the cables tight; have a look underneath it for any signs of rust. This is also somewhere you will need to look when you get a 126 home, by removing the battery tray.

Check the oil on the dipstick; is it clean and to level? Undo the oil filler cap to see whether it is clean; it should not be black or contain any creamy sludge, especially on the M103 300 engine, which can suffer from minor gasket failure if not well cared for.

Check the fluid in the gearbox by unclipping and removing the dipstick, holding a cloth under the end so it does not drip. It should be a translucent straw-berry juice colour, not brown, and should not smell acidic or burnt.

If the owner/seller is cooperative, ask them to get in and start the car for you; you will learn a lot by watching them rather than the engine. Do they confidently start the car or fumble around like they do not know what they are doing? The engine should turn over and start almost instantly. Listen for any rattling or tinkling in the first 5 seconds. This is not necessarily always a bad thing if the car has been sitting a while, as it will pull the oil up very quickly, but it could be a sign of a lazy oil pump, sticking valve lifters or a rattling timing chain if the noise carries on for more

than 5 seconds. It is quite normal to see a little grey smoke from the exhaust.

All MBD KE Jetronic-powered injection models rev up to 900rpm for about 10–15 seconds then drop down to 650–700rpm but a common fault is that they rev up to 1000–1200rpm and stay there for an extended period. This is something that will need addressing and could be a bargaining tool.

These engines are so smooth in good condition that you should be able to stand a glass on the air box without it falling off. Anything but smooth will need work.

Shine a torch up under the engine to check for leaks and to assess its general condition.

The engine sits on rubber mounts with a little secondary shock absorber on either side. If these are looking compressed they will need to be replaced as soon as possible. They can cause all manner of vibrations and problems with the drive. In serious cases, the fan will damage the radiator and the gearbox mount, being under a lot of extra pressure, could fail. The necessary work would not take very long, but again it would be costly enough to be taken into consideration.

Check the oil sump pan for damage. If it is badly dented, this can cause oil pick-up problems; there was a skid pan available when new, although it was always an optional extra and not a very popular one.

## IN THE DRIVER'S SEAT

Now it is time for you to get in the driver's seat – but resist concentrating on the interior just for the moment. Turn the steering wheel from lock to lock with the engine running; it will hiss and might make a little squawk on full lock, but this is fine. It should not knock or clunk, however.

Put the hand/foot brake on and keep your foot on the brake. Move the gear lever out of park and into reverse and drive; it should not snatch, although you will feel a small clonk as it engages. The engine note will change slightly too, but you should not feel any vibration through the wheel or your seat. Put the lever back into park. Turn off the engine and leave it for a few seconds.

When you turn on the ignition again, you should see all the warning lights and hear the fuel pumps buzz for 2–3 seconds. Then, when you start the

*Cluster dials at idle.*

*The rear bench seat has two small red levers along the bottom corner edge; pull each one towards you and you will hear a click as the bench seat releases.*

engine again, it should start instantly, and all the lights should go out. The oil-pressure gauge (C) should be sitting firmly at 3bar when cold; after a run, this could settle to around 1.5 to 2bar at idle. As long as it returns to 3bar as soon as you accelerate, all is well.

The economy gauge (B) should swing to the left.

Depending on water temperature, the gauge (A) should read no more than 80/85 degrees once warm.

Now test the controls: indicators, wipers, washer, lights, horn (after giving a warning). Check the windows go fully up and down and try all the various switches in the centre console. For electrically adjustable seating, make sure that the switches work the corresponding items correctly.

Check the operation of the climate-control system; there are three types:

• Manual no air conditioning.
• Manual with air conditioning.
• Fully auto climate control.

Familiarize yourself with the operation of the systems – if these features are not working, they can be very expensive to repair, especially the automatic climate control.

Check the radio and aerial operation, and the dual operation of the sunroof, both back and forth and rear-end rise and fall.

All MBD switches, although robust, suffer from dirty contacts so if something is not working, it is sensible to suspect this first.

## THE INTERIOR

The MBD interiors are of the highest quality and are extremely durable if they are looked after properly. The main question to ask is, does the wear correspond with the mileage?

Make a visual inspection of the cloth, whether it is velour or leather, the pedal rubbers and steering wheel, the buttons, and the carpet. Interiors are expensive to replace and second-hand items are becoming increasingly scarce. Leather is an easier repair than material as some of the velours are hard to find now.

Mercedes seating has 'old-school' springs and horsehair matting and can seem a little more compliant than hard, modern-day foam-based seating. Each seat is individually sprung to match the suspension type, giving a smoother ride. With this in mind, sit yourself comfortably and in the correct manner and sway your legs from side to side. If the front corners of the seating give way, it is usually a sign of broken springs. It is not an expensive job, but it does involve dismantling the seat. Sit in the back seat too, checking the window switches in the rear doors, and trying out any reclining rear seating, which was a feature on some of the SEL models.

The main front floor mats can be removed to expose the floor area and to check for any ingress of water. Pull the mat up and look underneath. It should have a black insulation mat, a few sticky sweets and the odd coin or two, but it should not be wet or damp or smell musty or mouldy. If it is; suspect a leaking sunroof drain or tray.

Check the boot lining material in the side wells for wetness or dampness. Lift the black spare-wheel housing lid. It is manufactured from an MDF (medium-density fibreboard), so if the boot space has ever been damp it may have warped or twisted to some degree. Unscrew the bin that holds the spare wheel in place and lift it out to check the condition of the wheel and, more importantly, look out for any signs of damp or dents in the wheel well. There should be a deep red tool roll and a jack in the boot too.

## THE EXTERIOR

Apart from visual checks of the bodywork and trim you also need to check the operation of the doors. They have a double check stop but these are known to grind and squawk as they dry out; in the worst-case scenario, they can lock up. Replacement check strap units are about £40 each and require the removal of the door panel.

Check that the central locking system works correctly.

If the car has hydraulic suspension; get someone to start the engine while you watch the rear end to see that it rises as it should. If it does not rise, or sits high and solid, you will need to investigate further. More often than not, the culprit will be hydraulic spheres.

## THE TEST DRIVE

The last thing you need to do, if you still have not walked away, is the test drive. There are two ways to go about it: if you do not have any temporary insurance to show you are protected, the seller has every right to refuse you a drive. This is not always a bad thing, though. The 126 is incredibly smooth and comfortable and it is not always easy for the uninitiated to identify any niggles. Being a passenger will give you a chance to sit and listen and 'feel' the ride without having to concentrate on actually driving.

Ideally, the route of the test drive will take in a long straight road, where you can cruise along for a couple of miles, a couple of roundabouts, a place where you can do two tight circles, one left and one right, and a motorway or dual carriageway where you can put your foot down. If possible, the 'mechanically minded' friend who has accompanied you should follow you on the test drive. (Preferably, you should keep in contact by phone or walkie-talkie so you

can warn of any impending acceleration or stopping movements. It would be very embarrassing if your friend were to rear-end your potential purchase....) Their role is to note what is happening out of the exhaust. The 126 is a big car and it takes a while for the exhaust to warm up and dry out. There may be a small amount of light grey smoke for the first 5 minutes.

Assuming your helper can keep up with you... he or she will need to pay particular attention to the exhaust when going downhill or lifting off for a junction, and watch carefully what happens as the vehicle accelerates away again. Puffs of blue smoke, depending on severity, could either mean valve stem seals are in need of renewal or, worse, indicate the need for a cylinder-head revision.

The final check for your helper is when the accelerator is floored to overtake. Excessive amounts of blue smoke are not ideal, but a puff of black is normal, as the exhaust is cleared of a bit of soot.

If you have already had a bit of practice in a good 126, you will know what to expect. In general, it is a very smooth and fast car and if it is not working as it should it will be very noticeable. Although the gearboxes are smooth, the gear change is always noticeable, but it should not snatch. The engine revolutions should not flare between change-ups. There should be no hesitation of the engine at any range, even though, when the accelerator is floored, the 126 naturally takes a deep breath as it changes down and then shoots off like a rocket.

There are two kick-downs. If you smoothly snap the accelerator pedal it will drop one gear but, depending on the speed of the car, it is possible to get it to drop two gears by snapping your foot to the floor fully (there is a button under the accelerator). It is something you should consider important enough to practise every once in a while if you have a V8 and you are in a tunnel.

Keep a close eye on the way a seller drives a car to make sure they are not trying to hide something. For example; if they seem to be reluctant to brake, ask yourself why; better still, ask the seller why. There is no substitute for driving the car yourself to get the real feel.

# CHAPTER FOUR

# GETTING SERIOUS

This may sound a bit long-winded in theory but, if you prepare well, it should be seamless and confirm to the seller that you are a serious buyer. These are perfectly reasonable assessments to carry out on a potential purchase and should not really take much more than 30 minutes. They will suffice for the moment if your aim is to move on to assess the next vehicle on your list. You will not appear too eager and the seller should respect you as a serious purchaser and not just a 'tyre kicker'.

## WHAT IS IT WORTH?

Do not allow yourself to be pressured into a purchase at this stage. If you do decide to buy on the spot, make sure that it is because the car is exactly what you want, and not just because the seller has convinced you that you are in competition with another person, or any other reason.

One of the anomalies of the 126 is that, because it does not have solid 'classic' status at the moment, the asking price for the same car in various conditions can be anything between £800 for a non-runner and £8,000 for a pristine, pampered example. Unlike a regular vehicle, it is impossible to have a reliable figure for guidance. It is up to the seller to decide what they think it is worth and to set an asking price. This does not mean to say that it is indeed worth this amount – of course, ultimately, the final decision lies with the buyer not the seller. However, it is not a good idea to antagonise the seller by laughing at the price; instead, ask them to clarify why they think it is worth that amount.

Rather than focusing on how cheap you can get it, you need to concentrate on what the car is worth to you, taking into consideration of course the other vehicles on your list. When all is said and done and you are driving your 126 home, you want to know that you have picked the best car for the right price at the right time, and have nothing to regret. All this may sound rather philosophical, but it does play a big part in what is right and wrong with the car.

If the seller says, 'This car is worth £8,000 because it is spotless and has every option,' make sure that it is. If it is not, point it out. In the same way, if the car is £800, you have to be realistic. You are not going to be able to negotiate a discount for uneven panel gaps. The final evaluation is about making the offer and getting the price as close to what you think the car is worth.

## FINAL CHECKS

Hopefully by this point you will have narrowed down your options and are returning to do one final check and make a deal. If you have still not quite made your decision, it is worth running through things in a little more depth, looking at the following areas:

### PAINTWORK AND BRIGHT-WORK

Paintwork should be a very serious consideration in your purchase decision. It is very rarely a DIY job thus making it an expensive repair, especially if it is to be done properly. Does the existing paintwork meet your standards? Will it need work or maybe just a couple of good polishes? It is at this point that you need to check gaps and shut lines, which could point to some unseen accident damage. Get close to the panels and run your fingers around the edges; swage lines are notoriously difficult to correct and you should be able to feel any filler or damage this way.

Is the paintwork original or are there signs of a respray; if so, was it a good one? Check around the rubber seals or panel edges for signs of masking. Have a look underneath the car; very often, painters do not bother masking at sill level and any overspray will attach itself to protruding areas under the floor.

Poorly repaired dents will have been corrected with copious amounts of filler. These are generally easy to spot with a trained eye but it is also a good idea to get that magnet and cloth out again.

Bright-work parts are becoming extremely difficult to find now as some are no longer available. When they do come up as new old stock they are always very expensive. The anodized-aluminium bright-work pieces are next to impossible to re-polish once they have started to go 'milky'. Remember, the car is twenty-plus years old and nothing is going to be absolutely perfect. There are companies that will re-anodize but it is an expensive option.

The small lines on the radiator grille are also anodized aluminium and at about £50 to replace they will not break the bank. The grey plastic grille insert is about the same price but pay attention to the chrome shell itself; new ones are extremely expensive and although pattern parts are available their quality is generally poor.

Finally, check the chrome finish behind the door handles. As the chrome is laid over 'Mazak', it does tend to 'pit' and can look unsightly.

Closely inspect the bumper chromes again, tapping the chrome with your fingernail. It should resonate slightly but if you get a dull click this might indicate corrosion in the steel below. Do not test it by pushing your finger on an area you suspect; if it gives way, the broken chrome will slice your finger like a knife.

## WHEELS AND TYRES

Although the MBD original wheels are very robust, they are also very expensive to replace. New, poor-quality aftermarket aluminium alloy wheels can buckle under the weight and load of such a heavy car. Has the seller put cheap replacement tyres on the car? This is sometimes an indication of poor maintenance all round. Such a fast heavy car needs good-quality tyres.

## EXTERIOR ITEMS

Are the indicators and lights all original equipment? There is a trend at the moment to replace direction indicators and tail-lights with a more modern-looking crystal-clear lens but many of these items are of poor-quality plastic, and seals very rarely fit as well as the originals.

The front headlight wiper arms have a plastic cup over the spindle bolt but these get brittle and can disintegrate. They are becoming very difficult to source and costly, too, reaching prices of around £80 on eBay. Gen1 are different from Gen2 also.

Lift the boot lid and remove the bulb-holder units to check behind the lights. The presence of any water is evidence that the seals are leaking.

Check the door mirrors are in good working order; although second-hand are available at the moment, new from MBD are very expensive.

Make sure that every door handle functions as it should, from the outside and the inside. They should function smoothly and return easily.

## INTERIOR ITEMS

Check the following:

- Interior door panels should be correctly fixed, and should not rattle or move.
- Rubber door seals – no splits or wear.
- Boot seal: any wear may let in fumes while driving. When closed, the boot lid should be firm and not rattle.
- Is the warning triangle still attached to the inside of the boot lid?
- Seatbelts.
- Seating – no wear or stitching damage.
- The woodwork: every piece is pattern- and colour-matched to each car so it is not easy to replace one piece without it sticking out like a sore thumb.
- The dash, especially around the speaker vents, is vulnerable to cracking.
- The headliner on the saloon models has no problems but water stains around the edges are a sign of leaking sunroof drains.
- The SEC Coupé has a solid headlining backing and the material can separate and sag.

- The rear-screen top trim panel tends to warp if damp.
- Lift the hat shelf box lids to check the first aid kit is still available.

## ENGINE AND ENGINE BAY ITEMS

Take a good look at the engine and the engine bay. Used-car salespeople sometimes clean the engine bay so that the car looks better maintained than it really is. Usually, such cleaning is undertaken with a steam cleaner or high-pressure hose, both of which can damage the sensitive and expensive electronic components of the car.

Most engines of the 126 series have a tendency to 'sweat' a little oil. This is quite normal. Even a small amount of oil around the valve covers is not unusual; most of the time the valve cover seals have dried out and have allowed small amounts of oil to escape.

More important at this early stage are engine noises. If a ticking sound can be heard when the engine is cold, but then goes away when the engine is warm, the hydraulic tappets are usually the cause. If the ticking does not go away, then the camshafts are the likely culprit.

All the Mercedes engines have timing chains, however, even though they are considered very durable, they do have a maximum lifespan. Both mileage and age will affect their durability. Chain stretch can cause synchronization problems between the camshaft and the crankshaft and is not unknown for the hard plastic chain guides to get brittle and break, with catastrophic damage to the engine. Regardless of the mileage a 126 has covered, the youngest example is now a quarter of a century old, and it is recommended that you replace the chain guide and tensioner at the earliest opportunity. It is better to be safe than sorry.

The power-steering pump is also prone to leakage. Usually this is recognizable by large amounts of oil residue present around the pump. Be sure to check the oil level in the pump reservoir.

## EXTRAS AND OPTIONS

There are numerous extras and option on the 126 list. It is no good a seller advertising a car as 'fully loaded with every option' if half of them do not work, so be fastidious and take the time to check them all. By their nature they are usually high-quality options, which means they will be expensive to replace or repair. This applies particularly to climate-control/air-conditioning systems.

Check that the sunroof still slides back and forth and tilts with ease. The rear blind should raise and lower silently and the cruise control should operate smoothly. If they do not work as they should, that should make a good bargaining point.

## LACK OF USE

It should be mentioned at this stage that these complicated cars need exercise. If you are considering purchasing one that has been 'sitting' for any length of time, there are a number of issues to take into consideration.

It might seem exciting when a low-mileage vehicle comes on to the market, but it can equate to a lack of use that will throw up all sorts of problems, and entail a recommissioning process that will be not only tedious but also potentially very expensive.

A number of problems may arise through lack of use:

- Dry rubber joints and seals: lack of movement through the vehicle will harden and dry door and window seals, to the point that they no longer keep water or air out of the interior. They will crack more easily and deteriorate very quickly if not treated.
- Dry, damaged tyres with irretrievable flat spots: a 2-tonne car sitting on the same part of the tyre will create flat spots that will not correct themselves with use. The side wall will dry out and ultimately become dangerous to use, especially at the speeds that the vehicle can attain. Over time, even wheels can lose their shape should the tyre go flat and not be attended to.
- Contaminated fuel and fuel lines: a couple of gallons of fuel in a tank will destabilize in a matter of months. The tank will sweat internally, creating moisture, which will further contaminate the fuel. The increased use of E10 ethanol fuels in most

*Ensure the VIN
stamp on the rear
bulkhead matches
the VIN plate on
the bonnet closing
panel.*

countries does not help, as they tend to encourage moisture. Without careful recommissioning of a laid-up vehicle, any attempt at starting the engine could pull contaminated fuel into the very sensitive metering head and injectors.

- Dry auto gearbox: auto boxes have a very intricate network of oil-ways and valves and need this immersion for longevity.
- Engine gaskets, vacuum hoses and internal seals will dry out: the MBD engines rely on many vacuum pipes and unions for engine-running control and tracing a culprit is not easy. Valve stem seal can dry out and cause heavy smoking or oil use. Dry gaskets can lead to leakage.
- Suspension squeaks and squawks: whether the car has hydraulic or standard suspension, dry joints can be heard squawking as the car is driven slowly over undulating ground. This is not only unseemly in an S-Class but will quickly wear out the offending joints.
- Electrical gremlins: in use, MBD connectors, cabling, terminals and switches are extremely robust but one of their few failings is corrosion. The surface area of a connector is such that moisture creeps in and disrupts its ability to perform and can create all manner of starting and running issues as well as gremlins in switches and motors.

- Cooling and fuel-system hoses: all rubber will dry out over time, even in normal use; lack of normal use exacerbates the drying-out process, which, if not caught in time, can cause leaks. The results can be catastrophic, especially where fuel lines are concerned.

## PAPERWORK

It goes without saying that it is essential to check the registration documents against the owner's and maybe even undertake a proper VIN check. More importantly, ensure you check that the VIN on the closing panel matches that of the bulkhead stamp just behind the gearbox dipstick; if something does not look right, do not touch it.

In this day and age, with number-plate recognition and all details being logged centrally, it is not hard to check the legitimacy of a vehicle.

When you receive your documents back from the DVLA the most recent owner's name and address will be written on them and if you purchased from a dealer, you might consider contacting them to glean some helpful history. It is also possible to request information on all previous owners from the DVLA for a small fee.

# PART III

# LIVING WITH A 126

First, do not be put off. A book such as this will inevitably highlight the negative, having a tendency to paint the model in a bad light. Most problems can be put down, however, to misuse, bad maintenance and lack of care by owners and garages over many years. Not everything you read and see in the photos will apply to every single 126. It is simply a list of common faults and failings that more often than not occur to a126 at some point, to some degree.

If you find a 126 that has been garaged all its life by one owner, who has had it serviced every 5,000 miles, you will not find a better car. Unfortunately, such examples are extremely rare, and this is why you need this book. Above all, be realistic – if you understand what you are getting yourself into, you are less likely to end up with a 126 that you do not use, which will eventually become a money pit.

When new, the flagship 126, the 560SEL, cost about the same as a small suburban house in the UK. Now, you can pick up the same car for a couple of thousand pounds; this juxtaposition can have the effect of making it feel like a cheap runabout that does not deserve to have any money spent on it. This is incorrect on every level: it was an expensive car to make, an expensive car to buy and it will always be an expensive car to maintain and repair on a yearly basis. Having to recommission one after a lengthy lay-up could very easily break the bank.

It is not a fuel-efficient car by today's standards, giving you no more than around 450 miles from a 90-litre tank. On the other hand, your insurance will be cheap on a 'classic' policy. Most 126 owners see their car as more than just a means of transportation, but you should not be frightened of using it, and using it to its fullest. The 126 is one of those classics that you have to use if you are to get the best from it; you will find that the more you drive it, the better it will become.

# CHAPTER FIVE

# GETTING TO KNOW YOUR CAR

## THE DRIVE HOME

Now is the time to forget everything you think you already know about your newly purchased Mercedes 126 S-Class. Ignore what the seller or trader has told you; there is always a reason behind selling a car. Some of the reasons may be genuine and honest, but in the process of selling a car the truth can be mislaid. What they may not have told you is that the 'one careful lady owner' only ever drove two miles a week to her bridge club, so the engine never got up to operating temperatures and needs a de-coke.

The best thing to do is to buy yourself a small notepad – or a big one, depending on whether you are a pessimist or an optimist.

That first drive home is one of the most important times for getting to know your 126. Everything is new to you so you will be more aware of anything that is not quite right. Slight vibrations in the running gear or the odd noise will be more noticeable, so take the time to jot down a note as soon as you can (not while driving), so you do not forget once you are familiar with the way it drives. Even if you find out later that it was 'normal' it is at this point that you will notice it the most.

## PAPERWORK AND DOCUMENTATION

Once home, collect up all the paperwork you can find in the car, take it indoors, spread it out and read it through. Find out what has been done in the way of maintenance and servicing, and make a note of when the next service or MOT is due. Read through the 'Owner's Guide' to familiarize yourself with the functions and controls on the car. Start collating material and make up a folder immediately; start as you mean to go on.

Any classic-car collector will tell you about the importance of paperwork and documentation. It is surprising that a buyer will insist on a full service history and then accept a dozen stamps in a book as proof; on the other hand, a seller will often assume that the buyer will be happy with a few crumpled invoices.

Paperwork is not the be all and end all of maintenance but there is a connection. This is an area so often disregarded as non-essential but, actually, through association, it can mean a huge difference to the end value of a car. When you sell a treasured vehicle, sharing your enthusiasm for the marque and the vehicle will always help the process along. There is no better way of doing this than getting a file of information out on the table, to show a prospective purchaser how well you have looked after the car. Collated paperwork goes a long way to prove the effort that has been put in to its care.

By way of an example, this is a true story. I had a Jaguar XJ12 that was badly damaged in an incident by a drunk Volvo driver. Without my knowledge, an assessor visited the vehicle at the yard where it had been towed, and within days I received an offer of a settlement as a write-off, which failed to take into consideration the condition of the car and amount of work that had been done to get it close to concours condition. I demanded an assessor visit the car with me and assess it properly. My file full of paperwork and information not only got the car repaired, but also motivated the assessor to specify that it should be repaired by a Jaguar main dealer, which entailed a full bare-metal respray.

*The 126 was originally supplied with a clear polyurethane folder containing all the factory-supplied documentation. A number of the documents were 'option-related', but they always included the user manual and dealer network information. Some main dealers supplied a more refined folder.*

Keeping records and invoices is doubly important if you do all your own work; although I do not put a stamp in the maintenance book, I do mark it with a reference to the relevant section in the folder where proof of work done can be found.

In the grand scheme of things, such factors may not seem to be very important, but classic-car fanatics set a lot of store by them. It is about preserving the car's originality. If a 'For Sale' advert states that a car still has its original First Aid kit, it is not because the seller thinks that you may need to use the kit! As the car moves into the 'classic' phase, such items become increasingly important, as well as more expensive, so make sure you have yours now. It is also worth collecting the original sales brochures for the correct year, as well as any other factory information you can get hold of.

## FIRST WASH AND POLISH

For me, the second most important activity after bringing a new car home is giving it a good wash, polish and clean-up. This does not mean the local car wash or a quick Sunday-afternoon hose-down, but a proper job, which will probably take you a whole weekend if not a good long day.

There is no better way to check out the bodywork than by getting down and dirty with buckets, sponges, Chamois leather and polishing cloth. You should find every blemish, rust spot, scratch and paint chip and become intimate with door shuts, hinges, door seals and catches.

Do not ignore the interior. Take out any mats and vacuum the carpet, front back and boot. You might even want to remove all the boot linings at this point and take the opportunity to check the side and spare wheel wells properly.

Have that notepad handy and write down exactly what you find as you find it. Whether you plan to do anything about it is up to you, but knowing about it is the first step towards getting the car right.

Before moving on to look at corrosion, there are a couple of items that apply to cleaning maintenance. If they remain unaddressed, they may well end up in

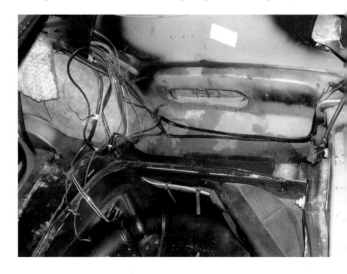

*Removing the boot carpet lining may help to reveal issues that would otherwise have gone unnoticed.*

the corrosion chapter in their own right. These items should be checked on a six-monthly basis without fail, or maybe even every three months if the car is often parked in the vicinity of deciduous trees.

The Mercedes designers created a false bulkhead area behind the engine and in front of the firewall. The idea was to create a separate, secure compartment to house the battery, the washer-bottle unit, and the brake master cylinder and fuse panel, to shield these items as well as the cabin from heat, vibration and noise. On that level it worked a treat, however; it also created an area where foliage and grit could collect.

*My own car when I first acquired it. Coming from southern Spain, it had not suffered too much from damp, but there was still a blush of rust around the panel joins.*

On one side is a battery and screen-wash reservoir. Even a good battery will sweat acid, which will eat paint and create a foothold for corrosion. Couple this with badly aimed top-ups of the washer reservoir, leaking washer-pump seals and damp foliage hidden underneath, and disaster looms large.

On the other side there are two potential problem areas. The first one involves brake fluid dripped during fluid changes, top-ups or brake-pad changes, which will dissolve paint down to the bare metal. Again, if this is combined with damp foliage in a very difficult place to access, the result will be a rust trap.

The second area has the potential to lead to disaster. Even though the fuse board sits in an enclosed box, it is surprising how much debris finds its way in over the years. Dry foliage also settles in the confined space under the fuse board, and this, sitting close to warm wires or an overloaded fuse, could lead to a fire.

Below both of these areas are the 'front anti-roll bar bushes' and it does not take much to rust out the mounting points. If this does happen, the only way to remedy it is to remove everything from that scuttle area – in itself not an easy job – and cut out and repair the metal.

Fortunately, it is not too difficult to keep on top of these potentially problematic areas. The damage will only happen when it has been left alone for many months or even years. The easiest section to maintain is the battery side. Unplug the power to the pumps and the water-level sensor and pull the washer reservoir upwards. It is easier to ease the pumps out of their seal seats than to try and pull the hoses off the pumps – if there is any washer fluid remaining it will want to escape, so tip the reservoir on its back. Now is a good to time to clean it up and get rid of any jellifying washer fluid that may block up the jets.

Remove the battery and set it aside carefully. This area could have a residue of battery acid so the first thing to do, regardless of how it looks, is to give everything a good clean. In order to neutralize acid, you need an alkali, which is most easily available in the form of baking powder or bicarbonate of soda. Before you make any attempt to remove dirt and leaves, mix a teaspoon of baking powder or bicarb in a small cup of hot water and brush the dissolved

*Removing the battery tray: there are two 10mm bolts into the firewall (A) and two 10mm nuts, one on the front corner of the tray and one in an extended leg supporting the other corner (B). The tray will lift right out.*

mixture over everything in the area. Any debris can then be removed, either by hand or with a vacuum.

There is a plastic infill piece beside the anti-roll bar clamp that can be pulled out to allow you to brush or wash down the area with what is left of the baking soda mix, and then with a detergent. Dry and then treat any surface rust and make a note of anything that may need further attention.

Clean up and check the battery tray and consider a repaint should it show any signs of corrosion. Before you reinstate it all, make sure the wiring loom is secure and out of the way and not nipped. As well as the ground/negative terminal for the battery, there are many earth wires all meeting under the battery and any acid corrosion could have undermined this 'ground nest'.

The opposite side is not as easy to maintain as there is very little space under and around the brake master cylinder and fuse box. It is potentially much more disastrous if left unattended.

A combination of an air line with a long nose blow gun with a tube attached and a vacuum will usually be enough, however if you see impacted

*Remove the bolt and clean up all the terminals with wire wool, then reinstall the bolt nice and tight, and smear with a little Vaseline.*

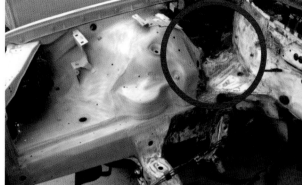

*The fuse panel was designed to swing up out of the box.*

*The stripped-out engine bay, showing the two vulnerable areas more clearly.*

grit or soil it may need a careful wash-down. Ensure you put a dust sheet over the engine and blow this end out before you reinstate the battery tray in the other, so you do not need to unbolt it again and clear all the blown-in debris. Unplugging the ABS ECU and removing it from its cradle will give you a little more access. Undo the two screws at the front edge and pull this end upwards. Get a vacuum cleaner nozzle on the inside of the box to suck up all the dry debris.

# CHAPTER SIX

# CORROSION

A proud 126 owner will want his or her car always to look beautiful, and grubby alloys can let down its appearance considerably. When it comes to corrosion, however, the home mechanic is entering a different realm. Many will have tools for much of the mechanical work, but welders, compressors and spray guns are usually last on the list of purchases. Even if they do decide to acquire such items, they are often too nervous to attempt anything beyond spraying something under the wheel arch, which will not be staring them in the face for all time.

Compared with other cars of the time, the 126 body was subject to a wide-ranging, complicated and advanced multi-layer paint system, including electro-plated-zinc steel, a primer immersion dipping process and a very thorough and high-quality underfloor stone-chip protection and cavity-wax application. Considering even the youngest 126 is now twenty-five years old, all this protection has proved its worth, and the majority of rust issues are usually the result of badly repaired or ignored accident damage.

Even taking all this into consideration, corrosion is probably close to the top of the list – if not at the top of the list – as the principal killer of the 126. In the majority of cases, the corrosion is not necessarily terminal, but becomes what is generally referred to in the trade as an 'uneconomical repair'. A quality job will always cost good money and, even though the overall value of a 126 is increasing, at this moment in time the expenditure is not likely to be recouped.

## REAR SCREEN

The number-one corrosion issue on all 126s involves the rear screen. What makes this issue worse is that early signs are almost impossible to spot without

*Even if there are no visible signs of a problem, it is a good idea to remove the screen to check.*

*All 126 bodies suffer the same fate, however the coupé's lack of a full B-post support exacerbates the problem in the SEC.*

actually removing the screen and the rubber. Rust can nibble away unseen at the screen lip and it is not until it has reached the point at which it has perforated enough of the metal to let water through, or when it has reached a visible section beyond the seal, that you know you are in trouble. By this time there will be a job to do.

The main reason for the rust in this area is a slight body flex at the join (B) in the panel where the single skin of the exterior C post meets the bottom of the screen panel. It is at this point that the skin overlaps (A) and can encourage moisture to travel between the layers. Once that corner seam begins to flex under the rubber, the moisture that manages to squeeze behind the seal starts to travel via capillary action between the double skins, flowing to the lowest point. It then rusts through from the inside.

A new, fairly inexpensive panel skin is available for this bottom screen section, but the inner section is not available and will have to be 'remade' if the rust has taken hold. A body shop will probably charge

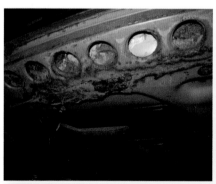

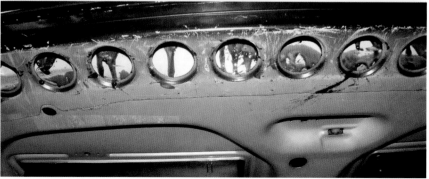

*Top and middle: a considerable amount of corrosion that went unnoticed until someone climbed in with a torch. Bottom: my own vehicle after being liberally coated with cavity wax.*

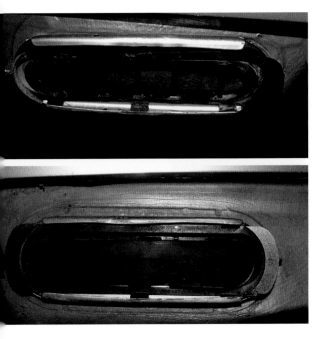

*The slider vent has been broken (A) and is also missing its rubber draught/water shield. It should be as it looks in (B).*

*To remove the rear bumper, undo the two large nuts from each side and pull the bumper backwards evenly.*

between £1250 and £1500, including a repaint and new screen rubber. Add another £700 if you or they break the screen taking it out – they are laminated, not toughened, and will crack very easily.

A close look at the panel underneath the screen from inside the boot may reveal rust developing between the seams. Keep a close eye out for this, or for rusty drip marks on the carpet.

Not all cases will be equally bad, but it is important not to ignore any signs. Once moisture gets into this area it will create condensation on the inside of the rear screen, which will aggravate the situation. Damp in the boot area will then go on to play havoc with the rear light units, causing the terminals and bulb bases to corrode and interfering with contact.

## BOOT AREA

There are a number of rust traps in the boot area and it will be necessary to remove all the carpet in order to investigate. There are two side wells and a spare-wheel well and any water finding its way into

*Check all along the bottom edge of the recess (A) and the mounting points (B) for any rubbed areas and hints of corrosion.*

the boot usually gets in via one or all of these low-lying sections.

Both side wells have a boot vent/bumper mounting point. If at some point the bumper has been swiped, the seal can be cracked and start letting in water washed up from the road by the wheels. The

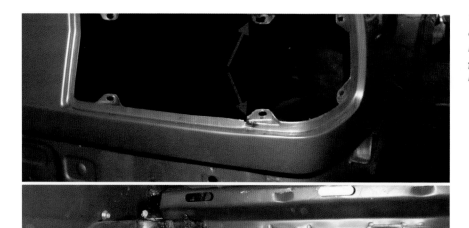

*These panel seams easily attract rust as moisture squeezes past loose or dry rubber seals.*

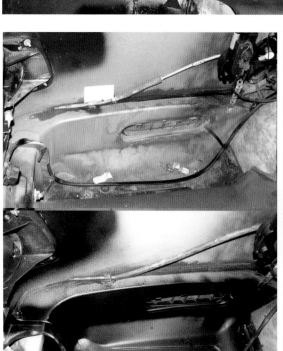

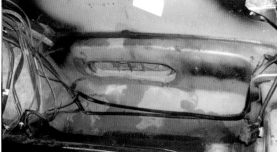

**Take the opportunity to clean up the side wells and check that the drain grommets are intact and clear of debris, and that there is no damage or corrosion.**

ABOVE: *The boot should be satin black, clean and rust-free.*

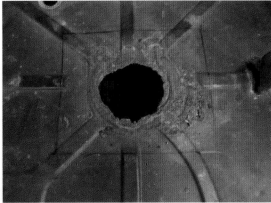

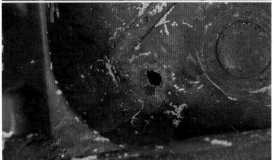

RIGHT: *With water leaking into the wheel-well area or external damage, the first place to go is often the centre post that holds the spare wheel in place.*

bumper-mount vents can only be inspected properly by removing the bumper, which is much easier with two people. Once the bumper has been removed, check the recess for any corrosion and around the mounting-bolt area for any bare metal or rust starting to take hold.

The slightest bump may have deformed the bumper sufficiently to cause body damage.

Water can also find its way past the tail-light seals if they are old and dry and usually this will find its way into the side wells.

The left-hand well can quickly become a mini swimming pool if the electric aerial seal lets water past; the original Hirschman aerials had a drain pipe in the bottom of the aerial motor with a small pipe attached, which directed water to one of the well-drain grommets.

The spare-wheel well hangs quite low at the back, especially on the first-generation cars, on which the bumper depth was a good deal shallower than on later models. It is very easy to catch it on high pavements and road humps and, once the under seal has been scratched, rust will take hold very quickly.

## DOORS

Generally, the doors survive very well, however, as with any vehicle, this is often dependant on the location of the vehicle. One common issue involves the rubber seal lip along the bottom of the door; grit seems to get trapped in between the rubber and the lip, and subsequently wears through the paint (A). It is very easy to pull out the seal and clean this track, and regular checks should save the door from creeping corrosion.

The door drain holes do not usually cause any corrosion problems, but checking these to ensure they are not blocked will guard against a build-up of moisture inside.

As the 126 ages, the area behind the interior plastic trim door lining may become problematic. The top half of the door is just a simple frame; over time, the flexing that occurs when opening and closing the doors may crack the spot-welded sections, allowing ingress of moisture and encouraging corrosion (B). To check this, you will need to remove the top half of the door rubber. The plastic covers are simply pushed and clicked into position, so it is not too difficult to take a quick look.

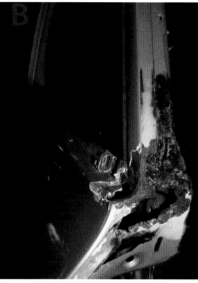

*Overall the doors are good at resisting corrosion, but you should check the bottom seal channel (A) and behind the interior trim (B).*

## PLASTIC CLADDING

The exterior plastic cladding is intended to protect the lower parts of the bodywork from day-to-day knocks bumps and scrapes. As a result, it is unlikely that you will find it all to be perfect but it could also be hiding unseen damage or corrosion. A part of it could easily have been scraped by another car's bumper, creasing the metal behind before 'popping' back into place.

For more information on removing the cladding, see the relevant section later in the book. It is advisable that, at least once in your ownership, if not bi-yearly, you remove it for maintenance.

Before attempting to remove a panel, ensure you have a selection of replacement clips; you may also want to replace the clip recess gaskets that help to keep the metal clips from rubbing the bodywork.

Another good reason to remove the lower sill covers (Generation 2 cars only) is to have a good look at the jack mounting points. The sills were fairly well protected externally with stone-chip protection paint and cavity wax on the interior, but water and grit can get thrown up into the sill cover and find its way into the mounting tube. If the jack is never used, that debris can just sit there until the damp eats its way out. An incorrectly inserted stock jack or even attempts to lift the car with a misplaced trolley jack insert can crease the surrounding area and thus cause weaknesses, which will inevitably allow rust to start.

*Fine dirt and grit can corrode the metal clips, which, over time, will lead to rust around the clip recesses.*

*There are many plastic clips per section and they can get brittle and snap.*

*A good reason to remove the sill cladding on the Generation 2 cars; the damage is usually caused by an incorrectly placed jack.*

*An incorrectly placed jack puts pressure on the tube and can crease the surrounding sill material, causing rust to develop on the lower lip.*

## CHROME BRIGHT-WORK

Predominantly, Daimler used anodized aluminium for the bright-work. The only chrome-finished parts on a 126 were the radiator grille, the door-handle back plates and the bumper blades.

In normal use, the radiator grilles survive really well, testament to the quality of the copper and chrome-plating at the factory. However, it is a large adornment on the front of the car and fairly vulner-able to accident damage, which can crack the plating and allow it to rust.

The chrome-finished door-handle back plates were cast in a material commonly used in the 1970s and 80s called 'Mazak'. Although it is not generally known for its durability, the Daimler product seemed to have lasted exceptionally well. Most re-chroming companies will refuse to refinish it, so if yours have started to show marks, your only option is new or good second-hand.

*'Mazak' corrodes internally and bubbles up from under the chrome finish, showing pock marks (B). Nickel chrome is porous and requires polishing to protect; sometimes if it is neglected it will start to peel too (A).*

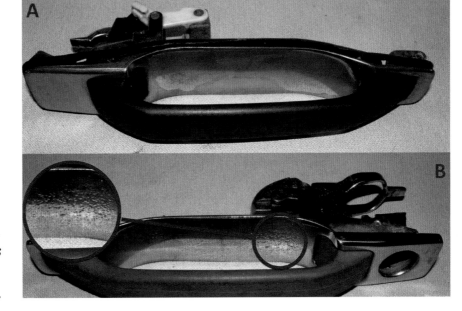

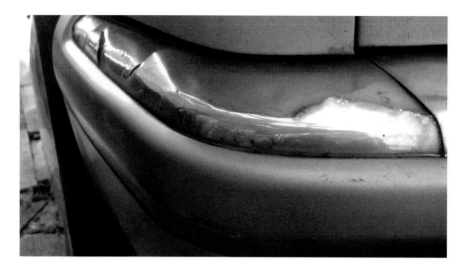

*Even though the quality of the chroming process was excellent; the Achilles heel for the chrome bumper blades was the steel base.*

The chrome bumper blades are another matter. The exact reason is 'unknown', but it is rumoured that, during the steel production crisis of the mid-1980s most automotive steel came from the USSR. That steel had a lower carbon content. What is known is that Generation 1 cars suffered much less than as Generation 2 cars. With no interchangeability between the two generations or US/Canadian versions, second-hand sets are quite rare now. A complete bumper set will cost between £250 and £400 from auction sites and they may still even have some rust or use marks. The blades are still available from Daimler but cost around £650 a set for the fronts and £800 for the rears, including the special fittings. New fixings are also expensive, at about £50 per bumper, but they are worth considering. Not only will new ones stop the rust creeping from the fixing to the blade but dismantling the blades from the casing will provide you with the opportunity to thoroughly recoat and protect the backs.

It must be remembered too that, even though the chrome blades are 'cosmetic', when it is badly corroded the plated chrome is as sharp as a razor and will cause an MOT test failure as a pedestrian hazard.

*This will fail an MOT/safety check in most European countries due to razor-sharp edges.*

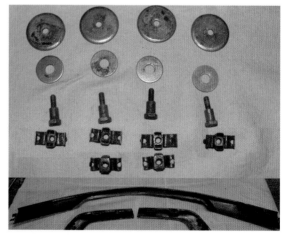

*If your blades are in good order they are well worth protecting, which means removing the bumpers to check and address even the slightest rust issue.*

## ANODIZED ALUMINIUM BRIGHT-WORK

The majority of bright-work on the 126 is anodized aluminium. Anodizing is not a coating applied to the surface of the metal but the result of an electrolytic process, which transforms the surface of the aluminium into a hard oxide layer integral with the metal itself.

Although its finish is more durable than that of the original 'raw' aluminium, anodized aluminium still needs looking after. The problem arises when the anodized surface starts to lose its lustre and starts to look as though it has milky water stains. If it were raw aluminium it could be brought back with a bit of rubbing; however, the anodized surface is hard and porous and the staining goes deep so no amount of rubbing will bring it back 100 per cent.

If you want your car to look concours-perfect, your only real option is to remove all trim and have it re-anodized professionally. There are a number of 'magic solutions' on the internet but they all have a very limited result; the only other option is to polish it as best you can and look around for 'better' second-hand trim as most of these parts are NLA.

Oddly enough, the embellisher in the plastic side-body mouldings is stainless steel. It is a real shame that Daimler did not extend this to the other bright-work, as it is one of the only features that will really let a good-looking car down.

## WINGS/FENDERS AND WHEEL ARCHES

### THE FRONT

The front wings do not generally suffer from inherent rust problems but there are a couple of common areas where careful maintenance will save the panel. Removing the complete wing is fairly straightforward, so doing it periodically will pay dividends in curbing any corrosion and most probably save it. For information on doing this, see the section later in the book.

Although it does a good job of neatening that join line and stops water flowing in between the gap, the rubber seal does have a tendency to be a grit trap.

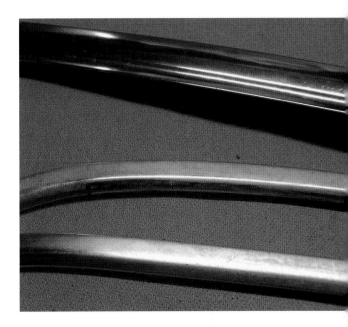

*Anodized aluminium was never as bright as nickel chrome and as it ages it starts to lose its lustre.*

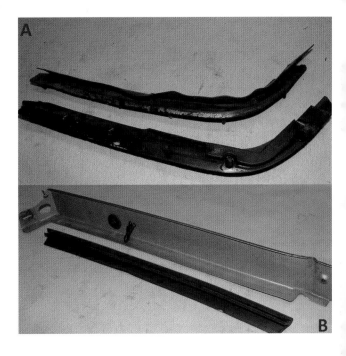

*Just below the indicator, where the bumper meets the wing, there is a rubber seal which pegs to the inner edge (B) The seal continues along the small valance under the headlight too (A).*

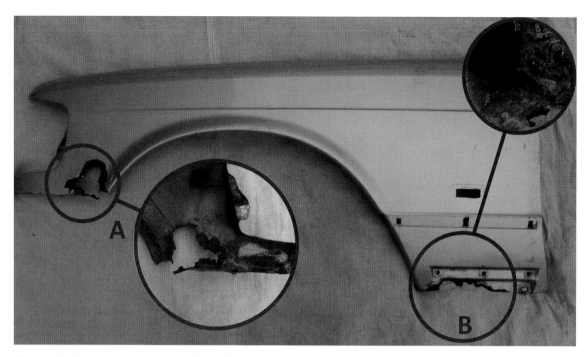

*Years of vibration or movement from the bumper edge will wear away the paint and bare the metal, with inevitable results (A). Soil and moisture can also gather behind the inner wheel-arch protector, eventually corroding the bottom edge of the wing (B).*

*Water travels from the scuttle flange (A) and exits at the suspension mount (C), via the rubber tubes (B). Soil and grit can build up in this compact area and remain damp, which will eventually rot out the bottom of the sill or wing (D).*

*Any signs of rust around this area should be cleaned and treated as soon as possible, as it will creep unseen under the fixings and into the chassis rails if left.*

If you do not feel inclined to remove the wing completely, next time you take the wheel off, poke your head up inside the wing to locate the plastic inner wheel-arch liner. It is fitted only with 8mm hex-head screws and well worth removing, to allow a good look around inside. It is not as good as removing the wing but at least it will enable you to clean the area behind the bumper seal (A) and the lower edge of the wing (B). This is a common area for soil to gather, especially if the scuttle-drain tube has split. This rubber tube (A), which transports the water from the wiper scuttle, is fairly thin and apt to dry out and crack. This then allows gritty water to leak unseen behind the inner arch protector

The scuttle-drain tube exits above the point where the guide rod mount (also known as the 'dog bone') attaches to the chassis (A). The rear mount is an unusual-looking trumpet-shaped box section, which is already vulnerable to grit and water. With the drain tube exiting at this point, this vulnerability is exacerbated.

If it is still clean and rust-free, take the time to add some cavity wax into the holes. This will not only

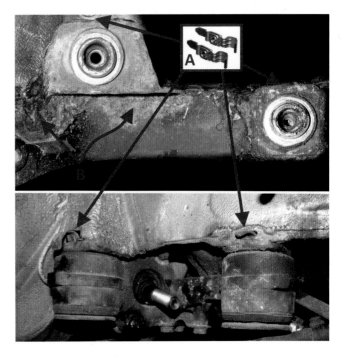

*The captive nut cage tabs (A) rust so badly that, when it comes to removing the mount, the nut will merely spin. You will then need to cut the frame to fit in a pair of grips to hold it.*

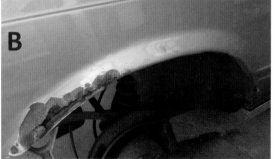

*What may just appear as bubbling under the surface will invariably need an extensive repair.*

protect the frame from rusting out from the inside but will also help to preserve the tab fixings on the inside. Check between the 'dog bone' and the chassis for corrosion too (B).

## THE REAR

The majority of 126s will have had or will need some work done on the rear wheel arches at some point. Structurally, this is the point at which the outer-side panel skin is joined to the inner wheel enclosure. Although it is welded and sealed, there are a number of issues that can disturb the seam sealer and allow water to ingress.

There was a popular trend in the 1980s and 90s to fit additional chrome arch covers. Although they can look good on certain colours, they can trap moisture and in most cases they were attached using small screws, which will immediately begin the rust process. Excessively wide wheels and tyres could have rubbed the edge too.

Rear-arch repair panels are available, but fitting them is generally a costly exercise as it will necessitate at least a half-side re-paint to blend in any metallic colour.

While you are having a poke around these various areas, have a couple of cans of cavity wax with a long nozzle handy, to inject wax into places not previously reached. This wheel-arch area is easily visible when you have the boot interior trim out.

*Removing the battery tray once in a while will stop this happening.*

*Once the covering has been removed you will see the scuttle drain holes in each corner (A); make sure these are clear of debris and that water runs freely to the exit at the guide mount. Look up under the screen edge (B) too, as this is a common rust area and any build-up of water will leak into the cabin and possibly on to relays and ECU on the inside of the firewall.*

## UNDER THE BONNET

Due to its restricted access, the area around the false bulkhead is one of the areas that is most vulnerable to corrosion, mainly because it goes unseen. Simply adding it to this yearly maintenance schedule, you should be able to keep any creeping corrosion at bay. It will involve the removal of a number of parts to gain access but it is well worth the effort considering the consequences if it is left unattended.

Just above the false bulkhead area there is an area referred to as the 'wiper scuttle'. For a step-by-step guide to removing the covering panel and wiper motor to gain access to the wiper scuttle, see the information on wiper overhaul later in the book. Set the bonnet on its vertical position, as this makes it much easier to investigate the area thoroughly.

## SUNROOF

The unit that houses the sliding roof mechanism is generally referred to as the 'cassette'. It is basically a pressed-steel pan fixed to the inside of the roof and is hidden behind the headlining. When closed, the sliding lid sits in a recess in the roof with a rubber perimeter seal. This seal is not meant to be 100 per cent waterproof so the cassette has a drain outlet in each corner; any water finding its way into the pan should find its way out via these outlets and down a rubber tube to the exterior.

The cassette drain tubes are simply inserts welded into place, which leaves a vulnerable join once rust takes hold. The rear ones especially can very easily get blocked with grit and silt, leaving only the front ones to dispose of the water.

It is recommended that you make regular checks of these drains to make sure they are clear from blockages (see the section on sunroof maintenance). The best way is to remove the sunroof trim panel and, using a flexible wire, locate the rear corner drains and have a poke around. If you encounter resistance, your only other option is to lower the outer edges of the headlining; it is a little time-consuming as you have to remove the side trims but it is well worth it just to check. Do not rely solely on water stains to tell you there is a leak, as the headlining is a plasticized cloth and any water will find its way to the edges down the A, B or C post and on to the floor. The first place you may notice water is under the rear bench seat.

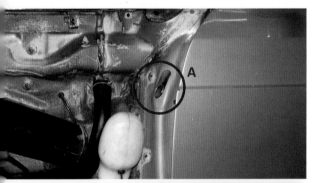

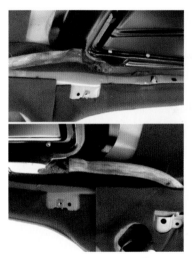

*Neglecting the sunroof drains can lead to serious corrosion in the cassette, necessitating a great deal of work to remove and repair.*

*The front tubes exit in the small recess behind the door hinges (A). The rear tubes exit just behind the trailing edge of the rear bumper (B).*

# CHAPTER SEVEN

# INTERIOR

## UPHOLSTERY

Over the twelve-year period of 126 manufacture, there were five options in covering material in eight different colours for all except the velour, which had nine. There were variations in colour names for different markets and years, and Daimler offered recommended dual-colour contrasts for certain body colours.

The basic main colours offered were as follows:

- In MBTex vinyl, Leather, Amaretta (synthetic suede-look material similar to Alcantara), and Fabric/ Velour: Black, Blue, Brazil (dark brown), Light Brown, Crème Beige, Fir Green, Medium Red and Grey
- In velour: Anthracite, Blue, Brazil (dark brown), Light Brown, Crème Beige, Fir Green, Medium Red and Blue Grey

As far as quality is concerned it would be difficult to find better. The materials are robust and durable, as long as they are well cared for and that means deep cleaning and, for the leather, regular cleaning and feeding.

Although extremely hard-wearing, however, all the materials have their negative points. Fabrics and velours are known to fade or, in some cases, completely change colour. Red covers fade to pink but, unusually, the Fir Green tends to fade to a lilac colour.

Most of the materials are still available from specialists and from MBD but they are getting harder to find.

In common with other high-end manufacturers, Daimler reared their own cattle to produce the

*Although extremely hard-wearing, its suede-like texture can look flat and soiled if it is not looked after. Like suede, it needs its nap brushing regularly.*

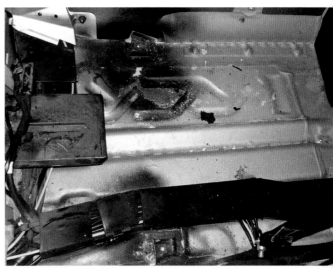

*Even a cream beige interior can look new again after a good clean.*

*Cable conduit also runs along the floor and seating electrics can be affected when damp gets in to the motors or relays, which are also nestled away under the seats.*

hide for their vehicle interiors. This allowed them to control the quality and look, and to avoid natural blemishes from barbed wire or trees. From the point of view of production, unlike the UK market hides they did not have a very deep grain, or even much of a leather fragrance; this is all very well for quality control but, when it comes to replacing a single panel, it may be difficult to locate a hide with a similar look.

As with the velour materials, some of the leathers suffered from colour leaching and fading. Both the Grey and the Palomino had a propensity to leach the red in the dye, giving them a pink hue, while the Reds would tend to fade to an orangey colour and the Crème Beige would fade to a dirty white over time.

The synthetic suede-look material Amaretta has the 'wow factor' in any 126 and is an extremely rare option for cars of the 1980s; more recently, a similar fabric called Alcantara has been used on equally high-end vehicles.

By far the most durable material, but probably the least desired, is Daimler's trademark vinyl MBTex. Even seats that have been dragged out of a collapsed interior, that has been sitting in a damp garage, can be made to look pristine again with nothing more than a wipe.

## CARPETS

The 126's carpets are made from a very hard-wearing polyester fibre called Anso IV, which was at the time an extremely high- quality and expensive covering. It has a thick plastic backing, which makes it extremely robust – resilient enough to withstand cleaning with a jet-washer, although the polyester can be damaged by hot steam cleaners.

The plastic backing can be a hindrance, though, when it comes to minor leaks around the sunroof cassette, for example. Seat mounting points can rust very quickly when water sits under the carpet unchecked.

## SEATING

Sitting in a 126 may take a bit of getting used to for those who are more familiar with the solid foam feel of modern vehicle seating. The seats' frames were upholstered in a more traditional way, albeit with a slightly modern twist. The actual seat covering material panels were stitched to layers of foam and wadding material to give the extra form.

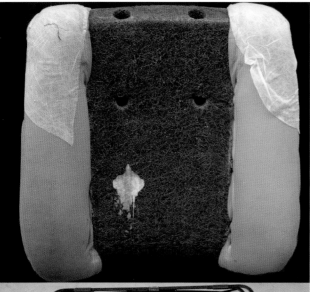

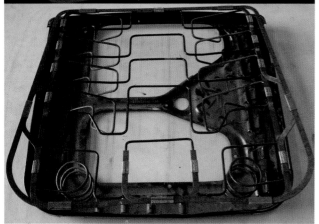

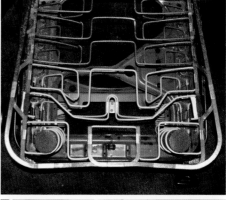

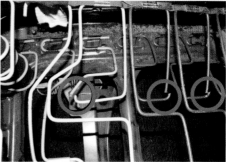

*Once the springs have broken, the horsehair shaped former matting disintegrates very quickly, which in turn puts strain on the material covering.*

*The bases were made from pressed steel, which supported a bed of traditional springs topped by a steel border which held a pressed horsehair-style pad to give the beginnings of the seat shape.*

Although the seats are very robust, there are a couple of age-related issues that may manifest themselves. The edge panel and the back-bolster panel on the driver's seat suffer the most. The effect of the driver getting in and out of the vehicle over many years tends to weaken the springs along the edge and they may eventually snap. The material, whether it be velour or leather, is very tightly stretched to shape over the back support bolster and the constant chafing it receives can wear it thin enough to create a hole or tear.

It is possible to use a swimming 'noodle' (a length of closed-cell foam) to provide extra support along the inside perimeter of the seat instead of repairing the springs, but this should not be considered as a permanent repair. Spring packs are commonly available for repair and it is a fairly easy job. However, it will take a good amount of time as it is necessary first to remove the seating from the vehicle, then to dismantle the seat and remove the covering completely. The full electric seats are extremely heavy to manoeuvre and trying to do it alone could cause damage, either to yourself or to the car.

Unless someone has already repaired them, the cargo-net-style pockets on the backs of the pre-1987 seats will be looking saggy, baggy and untidy. This can usually be sorted by replacing the elasticated cord along the top edge. The elasticated bands in the later leather or velour pockets suffer a similar fate, but it never really looks as bad.

*Denim jeans with bronze pocket studs were always one of the biggest culprits of scratched and worn bolsters.*

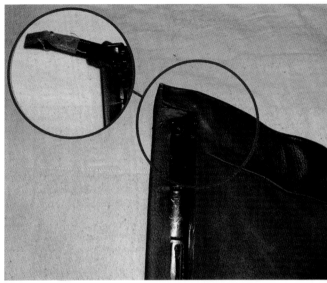

*On the solid rear pocket it is necessary to de-stitch the top corners to replace the elastic but it is a DIY job.*

## INTERIOR CLADDING AND PANELLING

At some point in the future, in the act of taking care of your prized possession, you are going to find it necessary to remove some, if not all, of the trim and interior panelling. Interior cladding and panelling in a 126 are of the highest of quality – and so are the clips that hold them fast. It takes a bit of care and thought to remove most parts; if they are thoughtlessly pulled and levered, they may snap.

Very often parts are located sequentially, so you will need to familiarize yourself with the sequence as you take them apart. For example, to remove the rear-screen top cover it is first necessary to remove the seat squab, the back squab and the C post covers.

### REAR-SCREEN VALANCE

Since it is made of thin hardboard, any problems with damp in the interior will cause the rear-screen valance to warp and droop (A). If yours is still holding its shape it is a good idea to remove it and varnish it, to keep it this way. If it has already sagged, twisted or drooped, dry it out first, while keeping the centre

*To assist with holding the shape it may be necessary to glue a thin steel rod along the inside front edge (B). Once reinstalled it should have a nice neat line along the front edge (C).*

*An untidy B-post cover spoils the whole interior. Consider covering in leather as an alternative to the original vinyl it isn't original but a considerable improvement.*

section flat to see if you can bring the shape back. Very often the fixings drop off the back boards so it may be necessary to re-glue them back into place

## DOOR PANELS

Door-panel tabs break off when the panel is forced by pulling forwards instead of lifting up and out. More often than not, this leaves the panel free to vibrate, squeak and rattle.

For the correct procedure when removing the door panels, see later.

## THE B POST

The B-post covering is a thin vinyl with a very thin foam backing, which disintegrates with age. The glue stops holding along the edges and the vinyl shrinks back, leaving a very baggy untidy mess. To remove the complete frame, undo the screws on the plastic sill plinth and pull it downwards to unlatch the top clip; you will need to remove the bottom seatbelt bolt before you can take out the cover completely from the vehicle.

## CREAKS AND SQUEAKS

Certainly not conducive to the luxurious ride that you will be expecting in the 126 are the squeaks and creaks from which you will no doubt suffer at some point.

Leather creaks can usually be sorted out by a good clean and hide food conditioning, but particularly troublesome are the areas where the door panel meets the sill plate. It may also help to some extent if you remove the sill plates and clean all the dirt and grit out of the underside.

Spray conditioners for interior vinyl can give limited results, but they are short term only. By far the best solution is simply a roll of 20mm wide self-adhesive, anti-squeak felt tape, applied along the bottom edge of each door panel.

*Daimler themselves used anti-squeak tape behind a lot of the plastic trim so ensure you have a decent roll of it and every time you remove a piece of trim, replace what was there previously or add it where friction might cause noise.*

## WOOD TRIM

The wood trims in a 126 were either Burl Walnut or Zebrano veneered items. Any manhandling of these veneered trim panels can result in a cracking of the lacquer finish, so be ultra-careful not to flex them when removing them from their original position.

Over the years it will start to look dull and lose its lustre but 99 per cent of the time the damage is only superficial. It should be possible to bring it back to its glossy best by using a good car-paint cutting polish.

Even though there are second-hand veneered parts around, you must remember that all items are mirror-matched across doors, and so on. If you are changing only one or two items, you may have trouble matching grain and colour.

Although it is rare for veneer to separate from its aluminium backing, it is not unheard of, especially when the interior has become damp. Unfortunately, this can only really be put right by a specialist. The trim also has shape infill sections cut from timber to take fixing screws and so on. Sometimes the glue dries out and they drop off, but these can be replaced by re-gluing and clamping gently.

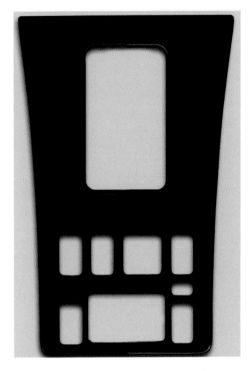

*You will have either burl walnut or Zebrano-veneered trim.*

## DASHBOARD

The 126 dashboard was, like many other safety dashboards of the time, constructed from a polyurethane foam interior and covered in a PVC/ABS mixed vinyl. Over time, the polymer oils leach and the finish starts to shrink and dry out, resulting in cracks around the weakest areas. These usually develop first around the front speaker mounts and near the screen vents. In hotter countries they will crack anywhere. It seems that some colours are worse than others, and blue and red seem especially susceptible.

If you have a good one, try to keep the sun off it and use a good-quality plastics conditioner; light mineral oils are said to help, but might leave a residue.

Dashboards can still be bought from Daimler but at over £800 they are not cheap. The only other alternative is to get an upholsterer to cover it in leather, but, although it will look superb when new, it must be said that leather will actually shrink and dry out a lot faster than the original PVC.

*The seat-belt buttons are fairly easily replaced but it will be necessary to remove the seat first.*

## SEATBELT BUTTONS

It might sound pedantic but sometimes the smallest of items can make the biggest difference. The seatbelt buttons are a case in point – if they do not look good, they make an otherwise perfectly tidy interior look very shabby.

The front seatbelt buttons point upwards, facing both the front and side screens where the sun streams through. Over time, the red 'PUSH' buttons tend to fade to an unpleasant powdery pink.

Some owners have attempted to paint them but the best bet is to find a couple of rear belt latches from your favourite auction site or scrapyard and change them.

## HEADLINING MATERIAL

The headlining material in the saloon versions is a plasticized fabric held in place with stretcher bars. The edges are clipped under the door perimeter piping trim. There are times when it may be necessary to remove it, for example, when you need to inspect the sunroof cassette or wish to clean it. Luckily, it is fairly easy to remove and, more importantly, to replace without wrinkles and creases appearing.

The headlining on the coupé version is equally easy to remove – the material is stuck to a sound-

*The plasticized headlining material is excellent in quality and will even take a good scrubbing to clean it.*

deadening fibre board so it comes down in one unit. It is necessary to point out that the material of the coupé version is known to sag as the glue lets go. A good-quality heat-resistant contact adhesive will sort this out.

## CENTRAL-LOCKING SYSTEM

The central-locking system works via its own vacuum system. In all but the very early 126s, the pump is in the boot and each door has its own actuator. The pipework is in yellow nylon.

It is a robust and secure system, but tracing faults can be a little troublesome as the pipework weaves in and out of the door and upholstery.

*Central-locking vacuum.*

# First Generation

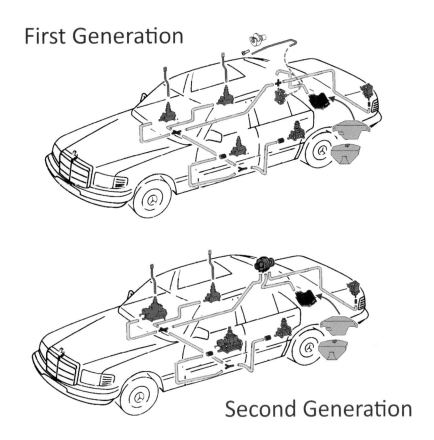

# Second Generation

## INTERIOR ELECTRICS

### SWITCHES

When most car manufacturers were venturing into sealed-for-life, moulded-plastic switch gear, thin foil contacts and crimped terminals, Daimler held on to the belief that chunky and robust was the way to go. They even had a robotic set-up in the factory with the single task of switching a switch on then off millions of times, to make sure they were getting it right.

An upside to this is that it is rare for a 126 switch to need replacing; they very rarely break apart and, even when they do, they can usually be put back together quite simply. A downside to large, robust contacts is that they require maintaining; due to the large surface area they will statically attract dust and grime and, if in an exposed area, they might be vulnerable to moisture corrosion. The most vulnerable are the horizontally set rocker switches in the centre

*Do not just throw away your switches if they stop working: take them out, pull them apart and clean them up.*

console, which attract dust, crumbs and even the odd spilt sticky drink. The window switches in the doors are known to fail too, especially if the plastic sheeting has not been replaced behind the door panels.

A gummed-up switch from any other vehicle would usually need to be replaced, but a 126 switch can be dismantled and have its metal rocker, springs and ball bearings cleaned, and 99 per cent of the time it will be as good as new again. It is very fiddly removing all those bits and pieces from all the switches, but it is well worth doing if you are experiencing electrical issues.

The connector pins also need to be kept clean. As the connectors are usually tucked away in 'colder' areas of the car, their large surface area is susceptible to damp corrosion deposits. Get into the habit of always having a can of contact cleaner and a small brass wire brush handy, and every time you disconnect a plug give it a spray and a clean-up.

## CONNECTOR BLOCKS

Everything in a Mercedes has a connector block, to connect power to an item or as a mid-wiring loom connector. Single connectors, such as spade or bullet connectors, are very rare, and even simple twin connections have a robust plug of some sort.

The positive aspect of this is that every plug is easily dismantled. Some come apart completely, while others are hinged and fitted with click tabs, with the connecting pins, whether male or female, being soldered and the pins just fitted in holes.

*A tin of contact cleaner and a small brass suede brush will bring these up a treat and very often correct all manner of intermittent problems.*

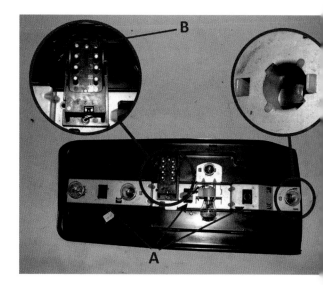

*The main metal plate is easily removable by squeezing and releasing tabs (A) and removing the small screw (B) in the connector.*

Take care when dismantling the connector in order to clean it thoroughly. The pins are loose and if they fall out before you have taken note of their position, you could be in trouble. This is when it is a good idea to use a camera.

## TAIL-LIGHT CLUSTER

Tail-light panel problems such as intermittent lights and warning lights on the cluster can be the result of an accumulation of all the common problems – damp from the boot, large connectors, metal contact surfaces and heat from the bulbs attracting corrosion.

The main bulb-holder plate provides the ground and relies on clean contact. The light housing back plate is not sealed in any way and can attract dust and road grime. Clean it regularly, including the copper bulb connectors, and spray with contact cleaner.

## SEATBELT BUTLER

The C126 has seatbelt 'butlers', which present the latch over the driver's or passenger's shoulder so they do not have to turn and twist in the seat to reach it. The stop limit micro switch is a weak point and when it fails this can overstretch the arm, which breaks the teeth; both items are easily available

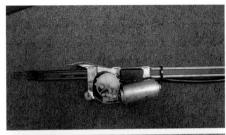

Broken teeth

Open Micro switch    Close Micro switch

*The cogs driving the presenter arm get brittle and break, especially when the micro switch fails to stop the arm correctly.*

to purchase online. The hardest part of the job is removing the side trim to access it all.

## COMBINATION STALK

The combination stalk on most 126 examples will have survived a good couple of decades without problems. It very rarely breaks apart physically, but it is difficult to understand why Daimler saw fit not to have a relay circuit on the main headlights. A relay is a remote electrical switch that allows a low-current circuit to control a high-current circuit. It allows thinner cable to be used on the control side and a shorter but thicker cable on the load side. This helps to preserve the switch from arcing, and also succeeds in reducing voltage drop. The consequence of not having a relay circuit on the 126 is an intermittently faulty combination stalk, caused by the heating up and arcing of the internal connectors. Of course,

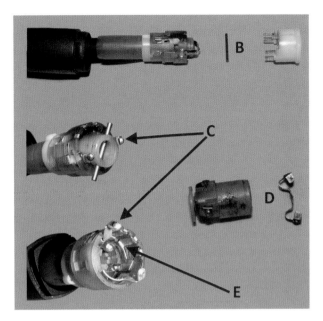

*Use a cotton bud on the internal parts and the suede brush on the external contacts. Do not use wire wool, as loose wire threads can cause internal shorts.*

the problem is exacerbated once the wiring has been operating for twenty years or more.

The main lighting and wiper controls are fairly easy to dismantle by removing the end cap (A). Take care, as the internal contact parts are loose. Clean up the contacts with a suede brush and contact cleaner (B to D)

## DIAL CLUSTER

For information on cluster removal and repairs, see the section on 'Interior Maintenance'.

### POD LIGHTING

If the instrument clusters seem to be badly lit, this is usually resolved by removing and replacing all the bulbs. There are between fifteen and twenty bulbs, depending on option list. The bulbs tend to go black before giving up completely so the dials will start to look dimmer than they should long before they go out. There could also be twenty-plus years' worth of dust in there.

It is always important to disconnect the battery when working on the 126 but this is especially the case when dealing with the cluster. There is a constant 12v to the clock even without the ignition key on, so if you attempt to pull the cluster out with the battery connected, you run the risk of fusing part of the cluster's circuit board. The clock will definitely stop working.

Be careful not to touch the matt-black dial faces as grease from fingers can leave permanent marks.

Looking along the top edge of the cluster, you will see two white triangular strips that cover a clear channel of Perspex. This acts to transport the back lighting from the 3-watt bulb at the back of the unit to the display at the front. Sometimes, the 3-watt dash-illumination bulbs are erroneously replaced with 5-watt bulbs. This tends to cause the plastic strips and the white insert to heat up and either distort or burn, restricting their ability to direct any light to the face. Unfortunately, if this has happened there is nothing to be done, as they are glued into place. A replacement pod is the only answer.

## DIMMER RHEOSTAT

One common issue on the cluster is the dash lights suddenly going out, or working one minute and not the next. If none of the fuses has blown, the second place to look is the dimmer rheostat. Checking this

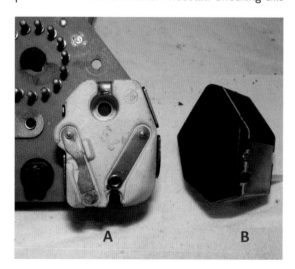

*There are two types of rheostat: the ceramic version (A) was replaced in around 1988 by a non-serviceable integrated circuit-board type (B).*

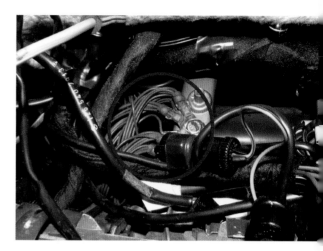

*Take the opportunity to clean and check the 'ground nest' any time you remove the cluster.*

will necessitate the removal of the cluster as it is fixed to the rear right corner of the cluster.

The earlier version has a very basic resistance spring, which can get dirty and corroded. Dismantling and cleaning should bring it back to life.

## SPEEDOMETER

If the speedometer has failed, this is most likely to be due to the small cogs on the side of the unit. They are made from a slightly pliable rubberized plastic that, over time and especially in a hotter climate, eventually becomes crumbly like a biscuit, causing the teeth to snap.

Repair kits are available for very little money and the job, although fiddly, is manageable with just a little skill.

## THE CLOCK

If the dash-pod clock is not keeping time or not working at all, it is a fairly simple fix if you are handy with a soldering iron – or you know someone who is.

## DIAL NEEDLES

The dial needles have a tendency to fade to a dull yellow, so, while the cluster is dismantled, it is worth taking the time to do bit of careful painting.

100uF/35v
Capacitors

*Depending on the year of the car it is usually a matter of replacing either a single 100uF/35-volt capacitor or two.*

*Brighten up the faded needles using a model shop fluorescent orange paint, such as Revell 32125 matt, or similar.*

## CLIMATE CONTROL

There are generally three types of interior climate control available for the 126:

1 A manually adjustable but thermostatically controlled heating and ventilation system, known as 'Heatmatic', with the ability to adjust the temperature independently on the left and right sides of the car. Once the temperature had been set via the thumb roller, a thermostat in the car maintained it, regardless of any change in outside conditions.

2 A semi-automatic air-conditioning system. The facia looked similar to the manual version with the dual thumb roller for left and right control but with an air-conditioning compressor supplying the cool air.

3 The fully automatic 'climate control', which had a push-button controller with a single thumb roller to set the temperature.

All systems were excellent, with their own limitations, but they all suffered from one main Achilles heel – the flow direction control for the flaps and vents was reliant on a good vacuum supply and the integrity of vacuum control pods. Most of these pods are hidden away behind the dash and a real pain to get to if they fail.

*A: fully automatic climate-control system. B: manually controlled system for each side of the vehicle.*

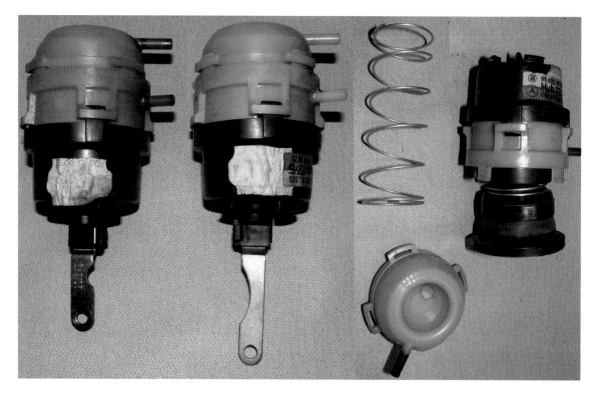

*Most vacuum pods are hidden away under the dash and over time suffer fatigue from the ambient heat.*

The climate-conditioning system push-button controller can suffer with dry solder joints, but it is a fairly easy fix with a good soldering iron. Alternatively, if you are not circuit-board confident, you should be able to find an electronic board repair company that will do it and check it for you for a relatively low cost.

Like any other air-conditioning compressor, the 126 compressors will benefit from regular use, even in the winter, and regular gas and lubrication changes will also extend their life.

## BLOWER MOTOR

There are two motors under the knee-roll carpet in the passenger foot well. One is a small 'sniffer'-type motor that draws in air to control interior temperature and the other is the main blower motor, which controls air flow to the vents. The 'sniffer' motor is wrapped in foam and clipped to the side wall with a pipe line that runs to the temperature sensor in the

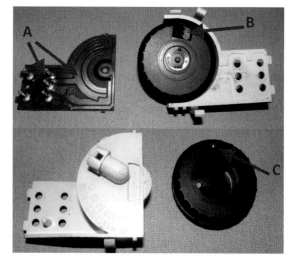

*If you ever have cause to remove the horizontal wood facia, take the time to clean the thumb rollers. They are easily dismantled with care and you will be able to clean the contact board (A) and contact points (B). Take care not to lose the ball bearing (C) as you withdraw the thumb roller from the casing.*

*The two blower motors work very hard in their lifetime. If you hear a squeaking or screeching sound from under the passenger side of the dash, it is very likely it will be one of these.*

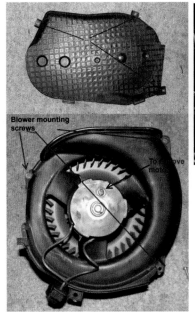

courtesy-light housing. If you are sitting in the car and you hear a high-pitched cheeping sound, it will more than likely be this motor; it is an easy replacement.

The main blower motor sits vertically in its housing and works very hard. The bottom bearing can dry out and, although the housing cover has a little oiler pad to assist with periodical lubrication, it will very rarely have had any attention. Both remain available but ensure that you buy original, especially with the large blower motor, as there are some abysmal-quality aftermarket units around that are not balanced and will vibrate badly.

## IGNITION/STEERING LOCK

The ignition lock/key is not inherently bad, but it needs a mention as it causes all manner of problems if it jams up. The classic symptoms to look out for are a notchiness in inserting and withdrawing the key, followed closely by a difficulty in turning it without the need to 'wiggle' it. Why does the lock wear out? It seems to be a combination of things, but a heavy bunch of keys will certainly not help matters. When in the column, any key-ring weight is transferred along the length of the key but when it's horizontally out of the dash the key-ring weight forces the tip of

the key upwards and vibrations allow it to wear the internals.

If you feel any kind of notchiness in the barrel when inserting, removing or turning the key, get yourself a new barrel from MBD. Do not buy them from any other source as they will not be good enough; all

*The only correct thing to put on the 126 key. The purpose-made pouch looks much more dignified than a bunch of house keys and a teddy bear.*

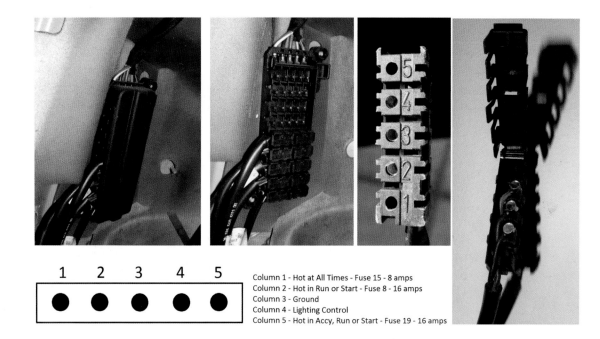

| 1 | 2 | 3 | 4 | 5 |
|---|---|---|---|---|
| ● | ● | ● | ● | ● |

Column 1 - Hot at All Times - Fuse 15 - 8 amps
Column 2 - Hot in Run or Start - Fuse 8 - 16 amps
Column 3 - Ground
Column 4 - Lighting Control
Column 5 - Hot in Accy, Run or Start - Fuse 19 - 16 amps

*The X30 is ideal if you want to add any accessories and it negates the need of those horrid scotch block connectors.*

you have to do is give your VIN to the parts department and they will get you a lock that was meant for your particular car. It is a ten-minute job to replace a barrel but a ten-hour job and a lot of butchering to remove it once it has locked up.

## X30 ACCESSORY BLOCK

Most 126 had extras fitted and to facilitate this MBD very cleverly fitted a handy item called the 'X30 accessory block'. Not every car has one, but many do. To find it you need to undo the bonnet-release handle and remove the left side-wall carpet, and it will be tucked up close to the firewall. The blocks and pins can be purchased from MBD and wired in whatever combination you require.

## INTERIOR LED LIGHTS

The interior of a 126 has a number of lighting systems for safety and convenience, but the yellow haze of an incandescent bulb looks oddly inadequate now, com-

pared with the quality of the bright-white light given off by an LED. LEDs make it much safer and easier to see what you are doing when entering and exiting the vehicle, and when fumbling around looking for something that has rolled out of view.

Another reason to consider using LEDs is that they use a tenth of the power of an incandescent bulb. If the boot light gets left on, an incandescent bulb will drain a battery in a few days; with an LED it would take a month or so. They do not get as hot as incandescent bulbs, so are less likely to burn or scorch the surrounding housing. They are also a lot less fragile and generally a change of bulbs will last for many, many years.

When buying LED bulbs, be aware that, if it does not mention that they are dual-pole, they are likely to be single-pole and will rely on the correct positioning of the positive and negative terminals.

# CHAPTER EIGHT

# EXTERIOR

## GENERAL BODY

As you would expect from any Mercedes, the original panel work on the 126s was of the highest quality but it is still metal and you just never know what might have happened to your car in the past two decades. Repairs could have been done badly or with inferior panels. Pattern-part wings might look acceptable from a distance, but to an untrained eye they would not stand the test of time.

Take your time and use all your senses to familiarize yourself with everything. A thorough wash and polish will help you identify the three Fs: fit, finish and faults.

## THE BOOT

The boot-lid top panel should fit flush and even to the surrounding bodywork. When you press the button it should click open and feel almost weightless to lift. The C126 boot lid should spring open under the power of its lifting springs, unless it has a heavy spoiler attached. No one knows why only the SECs do this, but it might be because their lids are aluminium and not steel.

Closing the boot lid should take no more than just a firm click with the fingertips; it should never need to be slammed.

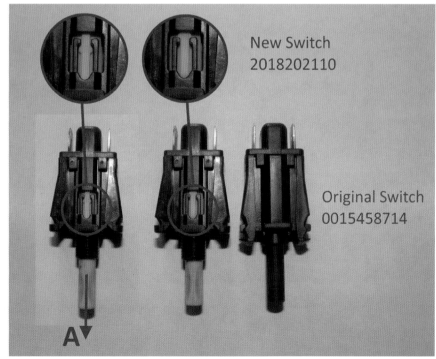

New Switch
2018202110

Original Switch
0015458714

*To turn the boot light off when the lid is open, just pull the plunger (A) until it clicks.*

A▼

## REAR BUMPER WHEEL ARCH INSERT

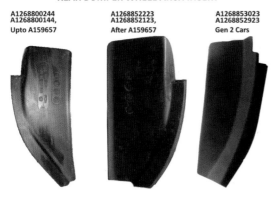

| A1268800244 A1268800144, Upto A159657 | A1268852223 A1268852123, After A159657 | A1268853023 A1268852923 Gen 2 Cars |
|---|---|---|

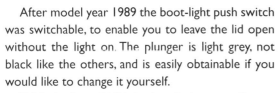

*The bumper to body rear wheel-arch inserts changed shape three times.*

*Without the rubber insert, fumes can be drawn through the side vent (A).*

After model year 1989 the boot-light push switch was switchable, to enable you to leave the lid open without the light on. The plunger is light grey, not black like the others, and is easily obtainable if you would like to change it yourself.

With the boot lid firmly closed, place your fingers under the rear lip and joggle it up and down slightly to see if it moves on the latch. If it does, it means that the rubber seal is not doing its job and might need replacing. Most importantly, if the seal is not doing its job properly, exhaust fumes can be drawn in to the interior. Of course, this is not pleasant on short journeys but it could even be dangerous over a longer period of time. Sometimes, opening a window or the sunroof will actually make matter worse as the through-draught will draw in even more fumes.

Incidentally, fumes may also be drawn in to the interior via the side fresh-air vents. There should be rubber blanking pieces at the point where the bumper side sections meet the rear inner wheel arch. Poke your head into the rear wheel arch; if all you see is a hole, then the blanking pieces are missing. Although they are very simple pieces of rubber, they serve to keep water kicked up by the wheels from entering the side fresh-air vents, and prevent fumes being drawn in to the same vents and finding their way into the interior.

Before the 124 came along, with its carpet-lined boot lid, Mercedes were of the opinion that plain and simple was best and the S-Class was no different. The inside of the lid was painted in a dark grey satin finish and had the warning triangle neatly clipped away in the centre. One sign of corrosion and/or leaks from seals into the boot space will be considerable amounts of condensation forming on this surface. This condensation will not be completely stopped until a full repair has been made, but the problem may be temporarily alleviated by removing the little rubber bungs in the lid framework. This stops moisture building up in the framework and also adds a small amount of air to circulate in the frame.

Moisture getting in to the boot area can also cause corrosion under the hinge where it attaches to the

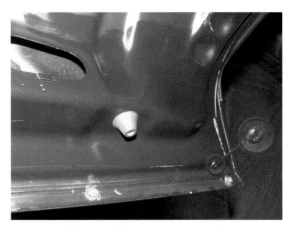

*Remove this bung as a temporary fix to reduce water collecting in the boot lid.*

*Unless you have a reason to remove the boot lid, the first you will know about it is when the corrosion has spread beyond the hinge.*

*Once the latch has popped, put your right hand under the grille (B), pull the tongue out of the grille with your left hand (A) and lift past the safety latch.*

boot. It is a shame that, by the time the underside of the boot lid was painted at the factory with dark grey satin, the hinge had already been attached, so it did not get that extra protection.

## THE BONNET

You may protest that you do not need someone to tell you how to open a bonnet, but experience shows that many people do not realize that this one opens vertically. Also, it is an extremely heavy panel and doing it incorrectly can cause all sorts of problems in the long term. The bonnet should never be lifted by the 'tongue', as it is not strong enough and will eventually break.

The diesel-powered 126s and some of the 560 cars have bonnets that are pressed from aluminium. They may be lifted from the edges above the head-light housing but both sides must be lifted evenly; lifting from just one side can put pressure on one

hinge or twist the bonnet. It is a very heavy item to balance and the assisting springs stay under stretched tension when the bonnet is shut. If something is not quite right with the hinges, it will show in the way in which it sits between the wings; sometimes, the end closest to the windscreen will not want to 'fall into place'.

There are three main issues to keep an eye out for (for more information, see the 'Maintenance' section).

A weak assisting spring will not be able to keep the bonnet raised to its first position. The first time you may notice this is when you try and hold the hinge latch out in preparation for setting it into its upright position; normally the tongue latch will hold out of position but, if the springs are weak, the tongue will keep slipping back into its first lock slot. As you lift the bonnet, the two large springs should assist, making it feel almost weightless.

The second and third issues are caused by a lack of lubrication. There are seven pivot points per hinge, including two sleeved roller pins. Ideally, they need lubricating every year, but in reality they may have been done a couple of times in the last twenty-five years – if you are lucky. The multiple pivot points are known to rust and when they do, they bind; if they are left too long, they will shear. To test for this, slowly lift the bonnet from the middle of the bottom of the

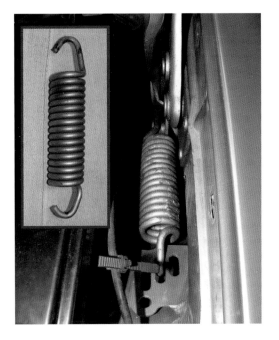

*Once the bonnet is lifted into its vertical position, the spring releases and becomes easily removable.*

*Periodically loosen the cable, disconnect it and blow light oil down the line.*

main grille with one hand and try to feel whether it is lifting evenly or binding.

There are two latches holding the bonnet in place when it is shut. The action of pulling the bonnet release should feel solid but smooth and both latches should release simultaneously with an audible click. It is quite common for only one to release but usually it is only a matter of freeing up the latch and/or adjusting the cable.

Consider cleaning out all the old grease from the latch mechanisms using something like a bottle brush and plenty of WD40, but make sure it is re-greased afterwards. If it does not improve after that, you may need to remove it completely. It involves removing the headlight units but it is well worth the effort, and it also gives you the opportunity to blow oil into the latch cable.

The underside of the bonnet should have an insulation panel about 10mm thick over the single sheet surface. The original one looks like a potato waffle in texture and it does have a propensity to disintegrate all over the engine once it has been

*There are aftermarket versions with a variety of finishes available, but none has the class of the original waffle look, which is sadly available only for the SEC.*

contaminated with oils; if you still have yours intact, treat it with respect as this particular finish is only available for the SEC. The SE/L bonnet pad supplied by Daimler as a replacement is a multi-use unit that will fit all 126s, including the turbo-diesel versions with the foil heat pad.

## LIGHTS

### TAIL-LIGHTS

The tail-lights of a Mercedes have remained one of the most recognizable features of any vehicle in the world, however there was more to them than just a contribution to brand recognition. The deep horizontal fluting profile of the plastic lenses was purposely designed this way for safety – even in the muddiest of conditions, there was always at least 50 per cent of the lens free from dirt, and consequently visible.

The lenses on a 126 can start to look a little 'washed out' over time and the clear, reversing-light part of the lens tends to yellow with age too. Dust settling on to the prismatic grid on the inside can also dim the light output. Like most MBD items, however, they can be easily taken apart for maintenance. The lenses themselves are held on to their frame with 5.5mm hex-head screws.

Using a clay bar on the exterior helps to brighten the plastic, and it is surprising how much difference a good wash of the interior and a good cutting polish on the smooth exterior will make.

Check and replace the seal, too, it is a simple 3.5mm closed-cell tubular seal that can be purchased from MBD by the metre. It will stop any water creeping in and contributing to dampness in the boot.

### NUMBER-PLATE LIGHTS

The number-plate lights do not appear to be an issue of much importance, however, when they are not working correctly, they can very easily attract unwanted attention from 'the law'. You certainly do not want to encourage them to stop you, and end up paying a fine.

The lenses have little inbuilt clips that hold the bulb and push it against little strip terminals. These terminals can get easily corroded, so make sure they and the lenses are clean. Also consider using LED replacements for a cleaner, crisper light.

### HEADLIGHTS

The Euro headlights on the saloon are the largest of the 126 range, as they also incorporate the front fog

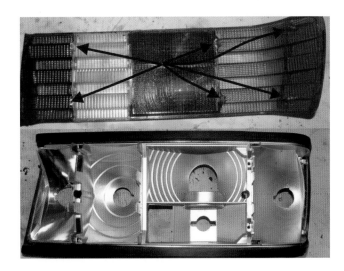

*Separate the housings and clean them well with a good detergent. Do not use thinners.*

*The left-hand lens and contact strips have simply been cleaned, nothing more, but the light intensity is vastly improved.*

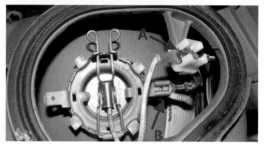

*A wash/wipe makes a significant difference, in terms of both appearance and light intensity.*

*Cleaning all the metalwork to enable a good ground connection (B) and the positive terminals (A) will help to get the full electrical supply to the bulb.*

units. Their only real shortcomings are age-related. Fine dust can get into the interior and sit in the directional ridges of the glass and on the mirrored reflectors, dimming their light output. Also, seals can shrink, allowing moisture behind the lens.

As a matter of course once in a while, strip the light units down and give them a good clean, especially in dusty areas. Use a damp cloth to wipe the reflectors; never use any chemicals, as the mirror finish is very fine. If they are at all corroded your only course of action is to replace them or get them re-silvered.

The wiring and connections can contribute to dim or inefficient lighting just as much as dusty or dirty reflectors.

The US/Canada-specification D.O.T headlights are sealed units, so if the silvering has corroded, the only option is to replace the complete unit. The outer lens is made from a hard translucent ABS plastic, which can yellow in the sunlight and look unsightly, as well as reducing light output.

The headlight has a height-adjustment facility, which works using engine vacuum accumulated in a reservoir under the wheel arch. The actuating pods inside the lights rarely fail but the switch attached to the dash and the one-way valve behind it can develop leaks. Again, the only option is replacement.

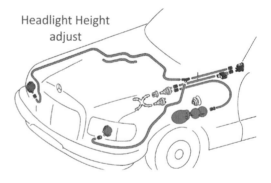

Headlight Height adjust

*The headlight-adjust vacuum system.*

## MAIN DOORS

Some preventive maintenance work requires the removal of the interior door panels. (See the information on door-panel removal in the 'Maintenance' section.) Do not be frightened of this job; once you have completed it once or twice, it is only a ten-minute job and well worth the effort. For most people, the typical 'thunk' of a Mercedes door shutting means quality, especially when compared with the insipid click and clang of most modern car doors. The

*The rear hinge nipple (B) is on the back edge so it is accessed by opening the front doors.*

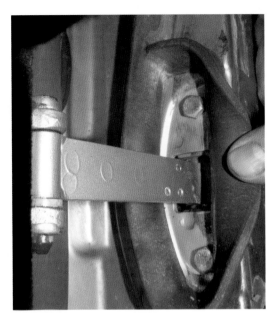

*The only way to grease the check-strap mechanism satisfactorily is by removing it.*

upside of this is that it is possible to hear if something is not quite right – a change in the sound may indicate a problem such as a dropping hinge, latches not perfectly aligned, side skirts or door panels being loose, even something loose on the inside, such as a window runner.

Check all around the door shuts and rubber door seals to make sure they seat correctly and there are no cuts or missing chunks.

## HINGES

Open each door so that it is about 30cm (12in) free of the latch and attempt to lift and lower it vertically, to see if there is any play in the hinges. If there is, they will need replacing completely, as there are no service-able parts. They do have a little grease nipple however to allow lubrication; you need a domed grease-gun nozzle or a universal pointed nozzle to dislodge the bearing. It is very satisfactory to watch all the black-ened grease being replaced by clean grease.

## CHECK STRAPS

While opening and closing the doors, is there an audible squawking sound like metal grinding on metal? Each door has an internal double-stop check

strap and these have a pair of ball bearings that run in a greased track. The grease dries out and the cage and ball bearings start to rust, causing the dry grind-ing sound.

Be aware that, once you hear that horrible sound, it will only get worse and the straps will eventually fail if not attended to. Most of the time they will fail in the fully open position, and your only option then will be to remove the door panel and remove them from the inside – not a great thing to do in a busy car park.

They are cheap enough to buy from MBD at about £50 apiece; cheaper versions are always available elsewhere, but they are usually of dubious quality. They are not complicated items and, as long as the cage is not too worn, it is possible to dismantle and rebuild them using new high-quality 15mm ball bear-ings (see how to do this in the 'Maintenance' section).

## MAIN LATCHES

The internal latches look extremely complicated but very rarely need anything other than cleaning and lubricating. As always, the grease dries out and leaves a hard lump that just picks up grit and dust.

They are not easy to remove completely due to restricted space but there is enough room to clean

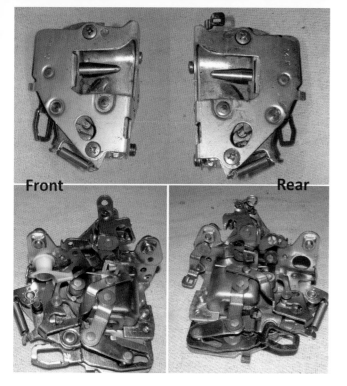

Front    Rear

*Complicated mechanisms generally only need a thorough clean.*

them up using a can of WD40 and a paintbrush. Always re-grease them properly afterwards, using a quality lithium-based grease.

## DOOR HANDLES

Removing the door handles is simply a matter of undoing two machine screws while the door panel is off (A), so take the time to clean, check and lubricate them. If the black plastic perimeter gaskets are in good order, do not attempt to remove them completely without dipping them in hot water first as they will simply break apart.

One point of note for the front door handles is that they can only be released fully for removal by using the key to turn the lock as the handle is withdrawn, to release the lock spindle (B). The spindle is made of cast aluminium and a little heavy-handedness can break it.

There is also a return spring in each handle, so make sure these are free and working correctly.

## WINDOW REGULATORS

Previous checks should have given some indication as to how the windows are performing. Even if you found them perfectly smooth, it is a good idea to check out the movement of the window regulators from the business end.

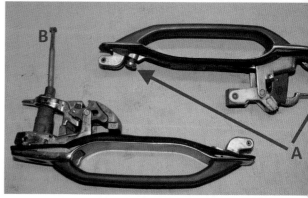

*Door handles are extremely expensive to purchase direct from Daimler and second-hand ones are becoming few and far between, so regular cleaning and lubrication of anything that moves or pivots could save a great deal of heartache in the future.*

*Clean and re-grease the main drive (A) and sliders (B).*

*The regulator becomes brittle with age and when it breaks apart the side glass will be left in the bottom of the door.*

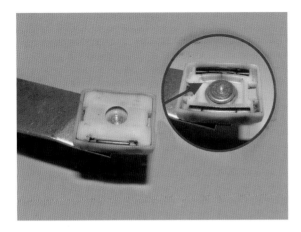

*The only way to check properly is to remove the regulator – even though it may look all right, the slider bush might still be cracked.*

Run the windows up and down and watch the regulator. Any juddering, twisting or movement from the frame could indicate a problem. When it comes to re-greasing do not be tempted just to apply more over the dried-out, biscuit-coloured blobs left behind from twenty years ago. Remove it and brush the actuating rack with fresh lithium-based grease.

Check the white nylon slide bush that joins the main arm to the glass runner. The bushes are easily obtainable and inexpensive to buy (part number A1267200142), but they were originally riveted on to the arm so will need to be ground off before the new one is pressed into place. There are so-called 'upgraded' versions available, which have been made from solid polypropylene as opposed to the original Daimler version, which is made up from two separate halves. Although the thinking behind it is sound, the original is constructed in such a way that it cushions some of the action of the bush as it stops and starts, moves along the track and changes direction. A solid version, with no give, would put a great deal of strain directly on the mechanism and the fixings. It has been said that the original part is too flimsy, but it has lasted twenty years, and more in some cases!

Before you reattach the battery after removing the door panels, make sure that there are no bare wires or terminals touching metal.

## SIDE CLADDING AND BUMPERS

The plastic side cladding acts as protection for minor scrapes and knocks, but it is also an important part of the aesthetic of the 126. When it is damaged or not in good order generally, it can very easily ruin the lines of the car. A visual check is the best way of telling if anything is not right but it is also wise to go around them with your fist closed and lightly bang along it, to see if there are any loose sections. The plastic clips are very easily broken once they get brittle with age and a rattle when opening and closing the door can become extremely irritating.

The bright-work trim strip is in stainless steel. If it has been rubbed too hard or scuffed by another vehicle it will make the whole cladding panel look oddly positioned. (For advice on its removal, see later.)

## WHEELS

The first-generation 126s came with 14in steel wheels (D) and plastic wheel trims (C) or Fuchs alloy wheels, often referred to as 'Mexican Hat' or 'Baroque' alloys (A). The second generation came with 15in steel

*All Daimler wheels were excellent quality and even now command a higher premium second-hand than other makes.*

*Attempting to remove broken lug bolts can result in serious damage to the wheel.*

*As a cosmetic issue, the end caps are removable and either replaceable with new, or easily cleaned up as they are made from aluminium.*

wheels or a 15-hole flat dish alloy (B). There are always other types in the mix, especially with the number of 'tuners' who were active at the time.

At some point, it might be worth checking each individual rim for 'true' as buckled wheels can cause all manner of vibrations as well as can exacerbate wear and tear on bearings and joints.

One feature that is worth a mention is the 'wheel lug bolt'. Tyre fitters will use an air wrench to tighten the lug bolts and rarely pay much attention to torque settings in their haste to get your new tyres on. It is not until you try to remove them yourself at some later day that you find them so tight you have to use a breaker bar. The problem is that the Generation 2 flat alloys had 17mm nut lug bolts on an extended shaft, so that they would sit flush with the face of the wheel; this extended shaft can become a weak point after repeated over-tightening. If this is coupled with its susceptibility to corrosion, it can mean a broken bolt.

Remove the bolts and check for any stress or stretch marks in the shaft. If they look anything more than blushed with rust, replace them.

## SUNROOF

The early sunroof for the 126s were slide-open only, but from the last year of the Generation 1 models and all of the Generation 2 models they had a 'lift and tilt' mechanism. In good working order, it is a silent and smooth unit, but it not only needs a bit of looking after, it needs looking after correctly.

The control motor is in the boot behind the left-hand carpet panel but, unless you are doing anything major such as replacing the cable or motor itself, you do not really need to do anything with this.

The biggest problem is that, all too often, with the best intentions, the wrong grease is used. There is a combination of plastics, rubber and metal in the one unit and very quickly any type of petroleum-based grease can swell rubber and make the ABS plastic brittle. It also attracts dirt and grit, which just adds to wear and tear.

*It might be expensive but the only grease recommended for the 126 sunroof is Gleitpaste, Part number A001 989 14 51.*

Gleitpaste is the only suitable product, available from Daimler in a 500-gram pot at a cost of about £60. Quite a few companies are also selling 50-gram pots now. Although it is expensive, it is amazing stuff that can render the sunroof all but silent in its operation.

A full sunroof overhaul will take around three hours and it is best to remove the under-lid lining to gain access to the mechanism. (For more information, see the 'Maintenance' section.)

## PAINT DATA

### MAIN BODY

Although MBD officially offered only twenty-four body colours, there was a palette of more than fifty other colours in total available as a special order.

The original colour code for a particular 126 can easily be found on the data card in the back of the

## STANDARD COLOURS

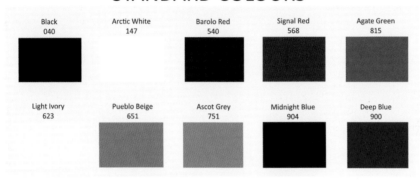

## METALLIC COLOURS

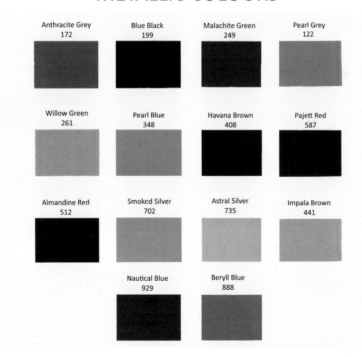

*The colour chart detailing the main twenty-four colours provided is only to assist with cross-referencing the codes; do not rely on the shades being accurate after printing.*

```
10 Kunde   Z WARTUNGSHEFT
------------------------
1 FAHRZEUGDATEN (Mercedes star)
2 Fg.-Nr.  Vehicle Chassis Number
WDB  126034  2A  585594  1        11 Reifen vorn 1  PIRELLI   Tyre FLH      21 Achse vorn 1   Axle FLH           31 Lack/L.-Zus.1  199
3 Motor-Nr.  Engine Number 22 087138   12 Reifen vorn 2            Tyre FRH      22 Achse vorn 2   Axle FRH           32 Lack/L.-Zus.2
                                       13 Reifen hint.1           Tyre RLH      23 Achse hint.1   Axle RLH           33 Lack/L.-Zus.3   Colours
4 Typ   420 SE  Model Type             14 Reifen hint.2           Tyre RRH      24 Achse hint.2   Axle RRH           34 Lack/L.-Zus.4
5 Auftrags-Nr.  Order Number 97881     15 Heizung   Heater                     25 Aufbau/Fahrerhaus 00302  Construction Number  35 Lack/L.-Zus.5
6 Produkt.-Nr. 5559688 6 Product Number 16 Felgen   Wheel Rims                 26 Pritsche   Truck Bed Number        36 Türschloß  Door Locks
7 Getriebe 722355 Transmission Number  17 Leuchten  BOSCH  Headlamps           27 VIN   Vehicle Identification Number 37 Lenkschloß Steering Lock
8 Vert. Getriebe                       18 Scheibenwisch. Windscreen Wipers     28 Anh.-Kuppl.  Tow Bar               38 Getriebeschloß Transmission Lock
9 Nebenantrieb  Transfer Case Number (4x4) 19 Seilwinde  Cable Winch           29 Lenkung   Steering                39 Tankschloß  Fuel Tank Lock
                                       20 Wegdrehz.-A. Speedometer             30 Ausstattung 265  Interior Trim Code 40 Retarder

412  461  524  543  571  592  600  615  640  664  341  362  731
             These 3 digit numbers refer to options list.
```

*Data card details are also available online or from a Mercedes Daimler dealership.*

handbook up until October 1989, or on the data plate attached to the closing panel under the bonnet, to the right of the Vehicle Identification Plate.

## SIDE CLADDING

The corresponding side-cladding colour has always been a confusing topic, not helped in recent times by the trend for the exterior side cladding to be painted in the same colour as the body. Originally, the side cladding would have been a semi-matt, slightly complementary contrasting colour, which gave the 126 a less bulky look. It also eliminated the reflection and movement of the dark road, which would have spoilt the lines from the onlooker's point of view.

## GENERATION 1 (1979–1985)

The following is a summary of all contrasting finishes and how they correspond to their respective vehicle paint finishes, metallic and solid (body colour codes in parentheses) to enable you to find your original combination.

### Saloon Version

From 1979 through to 1985 the bumpers and side panels were supplied to match the exterior paint in three contrasting colours.

DB 7174 Matt Anthracite Grey
(Previous version 7172)
(172, 473, 476, 479, 480, 482, 501, 504, 540, 568, 581, 587, 618, 623, 673, 680, 681, 684, 702, 803, 822, 875, 876, 880, 881)
DB 7175 Matt Grey
(Previous version 7007)
(040, 199, 312, 355, 735, 737, 740, 751, 877, 900, 904, 929, 930, 932, 934, 940)
DB 8414 Matt Brown
(427, 444, 459, 585)

### Coupé Version

At the introduction of the SEC types in 1980, only two contrasting colours were initially available: 7172 Matt Anthracite Grey and 7007 Matt Grey. These were then supplemented from about 09/1981 with 8414 Matt Brown.

From about 09/1982 they matched the three contrasting finishes of the Saloon version to the end of the construction of the Generation 1 vehicles.

## GENERATION 2 (1985–1988), ALL VEHICLES

Five contrasting colours were offered from September 1985.
DB7176 Muschel Grau
(172, 540, 568A (to A 281435), 587, 623, 651, 684, 702, 803, 822, 876, 881)
DB 7177 Stratus Grau
(040, 122, 147, 199, 254, 261, 568B (from A 281436), 735, 751, 815, 877)
DB 8477 Chinchilla
(432, 441, 444, 459, 473, 480, 690)
DB 5944 Fregattblau
(355, 900, 904, 929)
G8081 Silver
All MBD silver alloy wheels.

## GENERATION 2 (1988–1991), ALL VEHICLES

In September 1988 twelve new contrasting colours were offered, making the W126 even more elegant. This added up to sixteen contrast colours in total in the period 09/1988 until the end of production; some have been replaced by other colours.

DB 1611 Sina Beige
(623A – until A 485 221)
DB 1631 Safari Beige
(623B – from A 485222)
DB 3521 Navarrarot
(512, 540, 587)
DB 3526 Korsarrot
(568A – until A 485 221)
DB 3515 Tartanrot
(568B – from A 485222)
DB 5301 Andorblau
(348, 355, 900, 929)
DB 5309 Rioblau
(904)
DB 6211 Kiwi Grun
(249, 254, 261, 815)
DB 6212 Taxusgrün
(877)
DB 6250 Lago
(888)
DB 7166 Violet Grau
(481)
DB 7176 Muschel Grau
(172, 651, 702)
DB 7177 Stratus Grau
(735, 744, 751)
DB 7700 Alto Grau
(040, 122, 199)
DB 7738 Sato Grau
(147)
DB 8477 Chinchilla
(432, 441)

| Trunk and Hood interior colour | | |
|---|---|---|
| Colour Code | Designation | Application Period |
| Generation One | | |
| DB7129 | Galinit Grey Satin Finish | 1979-1985 |
| Generation Two | | |
| DB7129 | Galinit Grey Satin Finish | 1985- 09/1989 |
| DB7167 | Deep Dark Grey Matt Finish | 10/1989-04/1991 |

| Exterior Mirror covers | | |
|---|---|---|
| Colour Code | Designation | Application Period |
| Saloon/Sedan | | |
| DB7175 | Matt Grey Metallic | Generation One |
| DB7177 | Stratus Grey | Generation Two |
| Coupé | | |
| | Follows side skirt colours | 1981-1992 |

| Alloy Wheel colour | | |
|---|---|---|
| Colour Code | Designation | Application Period |
| Generation One | | |
| Bundt Wheels | 735 Astral Silver | 1979-1985 |
| Generation Two | | |
| 15 Hole Alloy | 744 Brilliant Silver | 1985-1991 |
| | | |

*For those who are interested in originality: a table of original colour codes for parts that are not painted in the full body colour.*

# CHAPTER NINE

# UNDER THE BONNET

## KEEPING IT CLEAN

With modern cars, everything under the bonnet is hidden away under a plastic shroud, but this is not the case with the 126 S-Class Mercedes; this is 'old-school' beautiful, made in the days when the aesthetics of an engine were almost as important as its performance. Because everything is on show, it is very important that this area is kept clean and tidy. It is so vast that, if it is unkempt, it will look abused and uncared for.

*There have been many discussions in the past concerning the relevance of keeping an engine bay clean. Which one would you buy?*

With a clean and tidy engine bay it is possible to see at a glance if there has been any kind of fluid leak or if something looks out of place; also, you will not be transferring dust, grit and grease from one place to another. This is not a suggestion that everything has to be artificially shiny – that can almost be as bad as a dirty engine bay, as it looks false – but clean and well laid out is essential. The pancake air-filter lid is a prime example; it is pressed from plain aluminium and, although it never originally had a mirror finish, many owners like to polish it up until they can see their face in it. However, as long as it does not look corroded and powdery, this does not really matter in the grand scheme of things. It is quite easily kept clean with a bit of metal paste cleaner and fine wire wool; it is also good to see the correct sticker at '6 o'clock'.

When it comes to a good clean in the engine bay, the only correct way is with a small washing-up brush and good old elbow grease. Do not be tempted to use either a jet wash or steam-cleaning machine as the damage it could do to sensitive electrical components could become extremely costly. Once it has been done properly, it will be easy to keep it clean with just a small amount of work.

## ELECTRICAL TERMINALS

Many 126s today are brought out only on weekends, high days and holidays. This lack of regular usage tends to create damp and condensation under the bonnet, exacerbating the build-up of corrosion around terminals and 'connector blocks'.

One of the most important jobs to carry out on a newly purchased 126 is to buy yourself a can of electrical contact cleaner and a little brass suede brush, disconnect the battery and go around every plug and terminal in the engine bay. As tedious as it may seem, this will save many niggling problems in the future and may also prevent a future breakdown.

Overall there is nothing fragile about the wiring or the terminals (that came later, with the W140 S-Class), but, because of their large surface area and robust size, they do benefit from being kept clean.

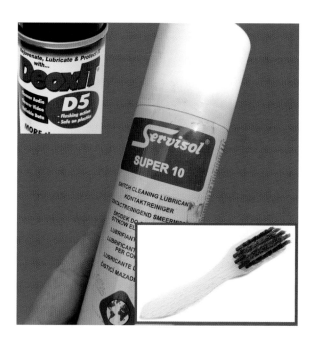

*An essential part of your toolkit when you own a Mercedes 126.*

## BATTERY TERMINALS

Most of the time, a good 126 engine should start almost as soon as you turn the key, but occasionally it will start only after a few turns or it will seem to crank more slowly than normal. More often than not, this is a battery cable issue. The hefty cables are prone to attack from moisture, oxygen, vibration and even UV to some degree. The crimped and soldered terminals are the weakest area and, should damp get into the PVC sleeve, the copper strands will oxidize and create a higher rate of electrical resistance. If the resistance increases by just 0.01 ohms there can be as much as a 1-volt drop in battery power.

At some point, make sure you remove the high power cables and inspect the terminal and the copper strands. If you see any internal corrosion or bluing on the cables, they will benefit from being replaced.

## ALTERNATOR REGULATOR

The alternator is not, in general, something you think about until the dreaded battery light starts to flicker, or you find you have a dead battery one cold frosty

*If the above faults do not fully show themselves, or they are ignored, the regulator will at some point let you down.*

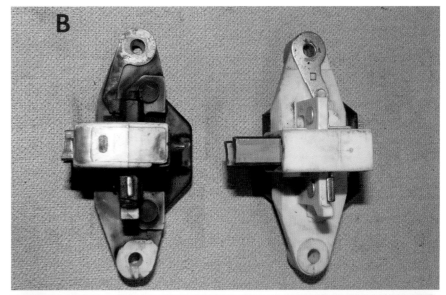

morning. However, it is one of the first items you should check when recommissioning a 126. The 126 is very 'electrically dependent' and, as the alternator is the main source of power, it is one that needs checking if you have never done it before.

Luckily, it is not the alternator itself that may need replacing, but the 'regulator brush box' on the back, a small unit that will cost you no more than around £25 and thirty minutes of your time. Sorting it out could potentially save you hours trying to solve a niggling problem that you would not immediately recognize as an alternator fault, but could ultimately leave you on the side of the road waiting for a truck to take you home. When the 'brush box' starts to fail, the car can develop odd faults such as inconsistent and high engine idle, hesitation on acceleration, blown fuses, warning

lights lighting up for no reason, as well as dim headlights and slow wipers.

The regulator is bolted to the rear of the alternator with a couple of Philips dome-head machine screws. Its position on the engine means that even removing the belt does not fully allow comfortable access for a screwdriver. This is not a bad thing, as it encourages you to remove the alternator completely and check it over.

If the brush box has never been changed, the carbon contacts (B) will be very worn and there will be carbon dust inside too. Blow this out using a compressor air gun and check the copper stator rings (A) and bearing for any play.

If you fit 7mm hex-head bolts instead of the Philips-head screws, you will not need to remove the whole alternator the next time it needs doing.

## FUSE BOX

After years of classic-car ownership and restoration, one thing remains constant: there is always one baffling thing about the way a car has been designed. On the 126, it is a simple fuse. Why on earth did Daimler think that putting aluminium alloy fuses in a fuse board with bronze terminals was a good idea? How come no one raised the question about dissimilar metal corrosion?

If, like many people, you think that a fuse that has not broken or blown is fine, think again. There is nothing in the service manual to suggest that they need maintaining but, on any vehicle, the ability of the fuses to work correctly diminishes with the passage of time and current. This, coupled this dissimilar metals, damp and heat, creates a recipe for corrosion and electrical gremlins. If the fuses are left unattended, it can lead to a number of common faults:

• Intermittent faults on motors.
• Over-heating fuses and/or wiring.
• Rough running and engine idling issues.
• Intermittent dash lights.
• ABS/ASR issues.
• Issues with engine starting.

This is not about being pedantic; you can see from the image the extent to which corrosion can take hold (A). Both fuses (B) were working but causing intermittent problems.

If you still have the alloy fuses, change them for copper or brass as soon as conveniently possible (D). Make sure you clean up all the bronze terminals with a brass brush, or better still a 'Dremel-style' tool until they look like they do in the illustration (C).

## HIGH IDLE

There are numerous sites, documents and books explaining the ins and outs of the Bosch KE Jetronic system, so there is no point going into minute detail about the workings of the system. However, there is a common 'high-idle' issue, which needs attention if the engine is to continue running as smooth as silk. When running correctly, the engine should start almost

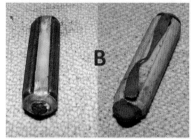

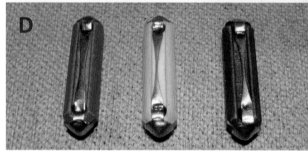

**Why did no one ask the question about dissimilar metal corrosion?**

immediately from cold, run up to around 900rpm for around 10–20 seconds and then drop back down to around 750. When the car is put into gear to pull away, the load takes the RPM to around 600.

There are so many reasons why the idle could fluctuate and the only way to rectify it is to work through it systematically. Unless you are 100 per cent certain you are competent enough to work on the system, it should be left to a professional as it is easy to create other problems. However, there are a few straightforward items that you can check yourself, as follows.

### IDLE AIR CONTROL VALVE

If you are experiencing idle issues, the IACV or 'idle air control valve' should be your first port of call. Although it is essentially a dual-outlet solenoid valve, it is not just an 'on-off' affair; the input voltage range

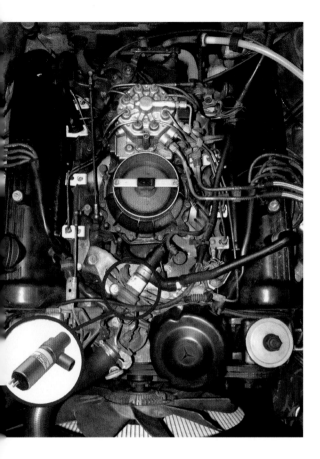

ABOVE: *The cold-start injector mount body needs cleaning periodically.*

LEFT: *Dismantle the valve and check the connecting hoses and body units; soak in petrol to clean away any carbon or oil deposits.*

controls the amount of air flowing into the plenum chamber by varying the opening position.

The valve can be cleaned in a brake and carburettor cleaner to make sure the valve seals are seating correctly. Even though it may seem to be working correctly on test, it may still be faulty, in which case the only thing to do is to replace it completely.

Check that all hoses are tight-fitting and replace as necessary if they show any signs of age.

One of the connections to the ICV is the cold-start injector mount (A). In the top of the unit is an engine breather union (B) with a little hole that has a tendency to clog up with carbon. This will benefit from a periodic clean.

## THE EZL

The ignition module sits on the right-hand side of the engine bay on the wheel-arch hump. Although it is not a particularly fragile part, it does send a variety of signals to the ECU, one of which involves idle speed. When it does cause problems it is not an easy fix, as it is sealed for life. Really the only way to test it your-

*The six-cylinder version (A) and the post-1988 version for the V8 engines (B), generally known as the eight-pin version due to the eight-pin plugs. The pre-1988 version (C) had four-pin plugs.*

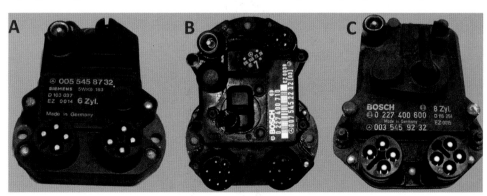

*Check the EHA visually for any signs of fuel leaks, but only attempt to*
*adjust it if you are certain you understand the way it works.*

self is to find a spare one that you know is working and swap them over.

The biggest issue is that it is an extremely expensive item to buy new, at around £1600. It might even be prudent to buy a couple when they come up on auction sites.

## THE EHA

The 'electro-hydraulic actuator' is the little black box attached to the side of the fuel distributor. By variations in current it controls the final adjustments to the mixture. Adjusting it correctly requires some knowledge and even the slightest of adjustments to the external screw can change the way the car behaves. Do not attempt it if you do not have some knowledge of how these items work. Even replacing with a new item will entail a certain amount of adjustment.

## VACUUM LINES

The vacuum lines in the engine bay can become brittle and fracture in the heat. The rubber connectors can dry out and split, or even become loose, which in turn can cause engine-idle and running issues. Most are hidden from view and will involve the removal of certain items to gain proper access.

## FUEL-PUMP RELAY AND OVER-VOLTAGE PROTECTION RELAY

Both the fuel-pump relay and the over-voltage protection relay can affect the smooth running of the engine. Because the engine relies heavily on stable electrics, they can, coupled with other items, contribute to idle issues.

Both these items can also cause niggling electrical problems due to dry solder joints. Should you be proficient with a soldering iron you may have some success dismantling and re-soldering, but this is not always the case.

On the top of the OVP relay there is a 10-amp fuse (sometimes 2) which should be clean and in perfect order. Keep a spare of each in the boot, as the engine will cut out when it goes bad.

*The fuel-pump relay (A) and the over-voltage protection relay (B) in position.*

## ALTERNATOR REGULATOR

The alternator regulator (see above) should always be suspected in the event of any problems.

The Bosch KE Jetronic system relies on a sealed system to meter fuel correctly; any unregulated air ingress due to failure of seals and air hoses will have the effect of running the engine too lean, which in itself can cause a build-up of heat.

*The injector seals (A), injector seats (B) and air tubing (C) nestle neatly in the V section of the engine and become brittle and loose with heat and age.*

*This is what a dry joint looks like when it causes problems.*

## ACCELERATOR/ THROTTLE LINKAGE

At first glance, the linkage system used to control the throttle looks bizarrely, even unnecessarily, complicated, however this is not the case. MBD much preferred hard linkage over cable, not only for control and safety but also, just as importantly, for the feel of the power delivery. The linkage behaves like a gearing system, responding to the weight of the foot, rather like the electronics in a modern car controlling throttle response.

The 126 was made for the executive, and that rather complicated linkage system immediately justified itself in the way the 126 could accelerate smoothly and evenly from idle without jostling its passengers, and could maintain position with consummate ease both at very slow speeds and at fast, constant motorway speeds. Even under foot-to-the-floor acceleration, the power is evenly damped in such a way that it is not necessary for the driver to plant their foot down so hard that they lose concentration on the act of driving.

Multiple linkages may be great for pedal feel, however they do need to be kept clean and lubricated. If they are left unattended, they will start to stick and react slowly, and eventually they can lock up.

Remove the air-filter housing to expose the link bars, pivots and ball joints. They are mainly ball and socket so will just lever off – take one off at a time and clean thoroughly. (For more on this, see the 'Maintenance' section.)

Something else that should be checked is the throttle pedal, which made of hard plastic and has a removable rubber-sleeved tread grip. It is connected to the main linkage rod via a flexible tab on the rear of the pedal (B) and over time this joint can weaken and detach (A).

If you feel movement or hear a click in the top half of the pedal during use yours may have detached. The part is still available at a reasonable price from MBD and it is a simple two-minute job to replace it, so do not leave it as it could become dangerously stuck in position.

## POWER STEERING

Although robust in themselves, both pump and gear units suffer from leaking seals. On the pump this tends to be the rear seal, most probably because it is directly attached to one of the hottest parts of the engine. The recirculating-ball steering gear box can suffer from a leaking main-shaft seal, which tends to drop all its fluid directly on to the suspension unit. They can also develop

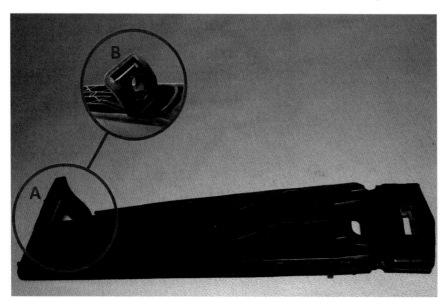

*Over time the connector tab breaks away from the linkage, leaving the accelerator pedal loose.*

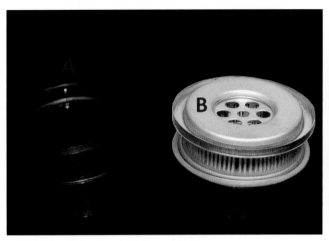

*Although it has a strong tube, the power-steering cooler can suffer from dents and rust.*

*The non-disposable power-steering filter (A) was superseded by a throwaway cartridge version (B). They are interchangeable.*

play in the straight-ahead position, although this can be adjusted to some degree.

This is one of the easiest units to keep serviced but for some reason it tends to be forgotten. The fluid should be a rose-wine colour but if the unit is left unattended, the fluid will look as black as treacle.

There is a filter in the base of the pump. Pre-1987 this was a non-disposable item that could be dismantled and cleaned in petrol, but after this it was similar to an air filter, with a throwaway paper cartridge. The two items are interchangeable. The fluid system

runs through a cooler tube (coloured green on the illustration). It sits in front of the radiator and behind the front bumper, to pick up cool air, and it is fairly vulnerable to attack by road debris or even front-end bumps; if holed, it will drain the power-steering fluid all over the road.

The steering damper sits horizontally behind the cross member under the engine sump. Although a simple gas strut, it dampens both the steering action and the feel of the road. As the unit fails, it tends to leak so slowly that you get used to the way it feels.

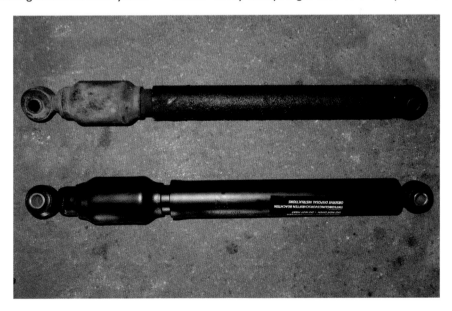

*It is not until you replace the damper that you realize its importance.*

*First of all, buy yourself a handheld vacuum test tool – cheap as chips and ideal for the 126 owner due to the number of vacuum-related items on the car.*

You may eventually hear a rattle or notice the wheels tracking the road before you realize it has lost its ability to act as a damper.

## VACUUM PIPES

Every Mercedes model of the period had a vast network of vacuum pipes, with many permutations (diagrams are fairly easy to come by online). There are four main systems:

- central locking;
- gearbox vacuum;
- engine vacuum; and
- headlight height adjustment.

The important thing is the integrity of the nylon pipework, rubber unions and valves; as the cars age, everything starts to get brittle.

## THE PETROL ENGINES

All internal combustion engines are complicated in their own way but they all work using the same principles. As with anything mechanical there will always be strengths and weaknesses, and the Mercedes engines are no exception, even allowing for the over-used

terms of 'bullet-proof and over-engineered'. To deal with every ailment that has ever reared its head on a Mercedes engine over the last thirty-five years would demand a book of its own, but there are a number of issues that can be covered to give an understanding of the basics.

### V8 M116/117 ENGINE

The V8 engines in the 126 are MBD-coded as M116 for the 380 and 420 and M117 for the 500 and the 560. Not only have they proved themselves to be among the smoothest and most reliable engines of their time, they were also good-looking, enhanced by an aluminium air-filter pan on top. Like all engines, they benefit from good servicing but, more importantly, they thrive when used regularly and well.

When other cars of the time were using the dreaded 'Nikasil' bore liners and suffering from all the problems associated with them, MBD had their own 'Alusil' system. Unlike the Nikasil, this has proved to be almost indestructible in normal use; the rest of the car will probably fall apart before the liners wear.

The early M116 had cast-iron blocks and aluminium heads for the first generation of 380 126s, but when the second-generation 420 came out, it was all aluminium.

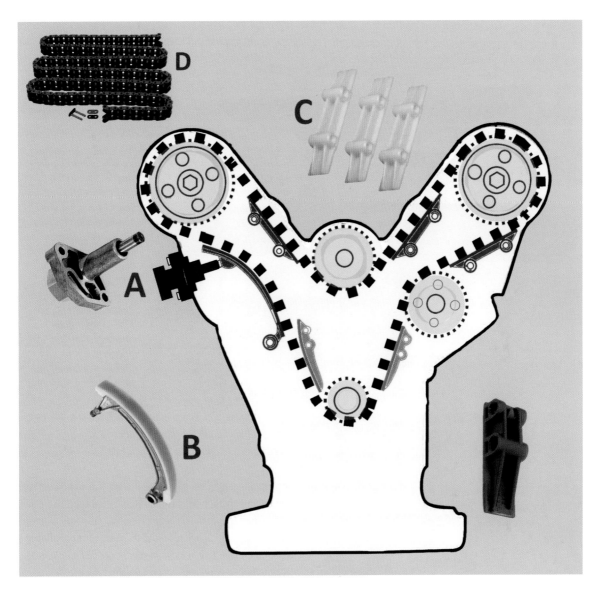

*A simplified timing-gear drawing of the front of an M116/7 engine:*
*(A) chain tensioner, (B) main tensioner guide, (C) top guides, (D) chain.*

The Achilles heel of the M116/117 is the timing chain set-up. Pardon the pun, but there is usually a 'chain of events' that leads up to its demise and learning to recognize the symptoms will probably save you from potential catastrophic engine damage. With the camshaft holding the valves open, the piston rises on its stroke and batters them.

There are three items that need to be considered:

• The duplex timing chain (D) has a long way to travel and over time it will eventually stretch enough to allow it to flex slightly and throw the ignition timing out a few degrees.

• There is only a single, oil-pressure-fed tensioner (A) on the side of the engine and, should this become weak, that small amount of flexing will turn into a full slap.

LEFT: *Colour is usually a good indication of fragility.*

BELOW LEFT: *On an early 3.8, from 1979 to 1982, check the timing of the chain immediately. Because it was only a single-row chain and not a duplex like all the other V8s, it suffered from excessive stretch. The single-row chains also had the propensity to eat their way into the tensioner guide rail.*

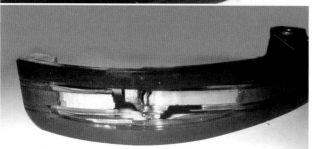

- The guides (C) are constructed from a hard nylon material and, although they do not wear to any great extent, they do become brittle with age.

Although a slight rattle is normal for the first few seconds on start-up, especially if the engine has been left dormant for a while, an extended rattle from start-up could spell trouble. It is not unheard of for the chain to slap to such a degree that it breaks through the top of the cam cover

If you know your chain has never been replaced, consider doing it, regardless of mileage. Take off the valve covers and have a look to see what colour the top two guides are; if they are dark brown, it is definitely time to replace them. This will be an important job on your list.

Original MBD parts will cost around £450, but they should be used, as pattern parts have proved to be of unreliable quality. The most expensive part is the chain tensioner, at just over £200. A good, independent MBD garage will charge around £200 for the four- to five-hour job, but the work is not beyond the realms of a competent DIYer with care.

*The oiler tubes are connected to the cam carriers via nylon holders, which generally snap when old. Buy new ones before attempting to remove them.*

*As the mounts sink there will be a noticeable amount of vibration through the body. This should not be ignored, as the engine can lose as much as 20mm (¾in) in height, and very soon after the viscous fan blade will grind its way into the bottom lip of the radiator.*

Having done the job twice now, it takes me around eight hours – usually carrying other minor jobs at the same time, including cleaning parts before they go back on.

While the cam covers are off, it is also prudent to check the oiler tubes. If the car has suffered from infrequent oil changes, these can block and starve the cams of oil spray, resulting in worn cam lobes and followers.

The oiler tube connectors are only about £12 for a full set, and replacing them allows you to remove the tubes, clean them out and check the pinholes are all clear.

## ENGINE MOUNTS

It is important to keep an eye on the engine mounts. The main motor mounts sit on either side of the engine on the top of the front mainframe structure;

*Vibration mounts lose pressure and the rubber mounts go soft from oil contamination.*

there is also a pair of small gas-filled damper struts just along the front edge of this cross member, which assist as vibration dampers.

The mounting bushes for these tend to go soft, especially if they have been contaminated with engine oil, which puts extra strain on the main mounts. If these have gone flat, the gearbox mount should be checked too; worn engine mounts will tip the engine forward, which in turn will put a huge amount of twist upon this rear mount. You will probably find that it has cracked away from its mounting and also needs replacing.

Oil leaks are not necessarily prevalent on the M116/7 but the engines are known to sweat oil a little. It also seems to be a common occurrence to have a small oil leak from the rear of the head-gasket edge, due to high pressure oil ways close to the outer edge. While this is not a problem generally, oil residue can build up around the starter motor and cause minor issues.

## STRAIGHT-SIX M110 ENGINE

There are two types of straight-six engine in the 126. The M110 2.8-litre is the good-looking twin-cam engine used between 1973 and 1986 on most Mercedes, so it was already a proven engine by the time it went into the 126, from 1980 and until 1985. The M110 was a very reliable unit if well looked after and regularly serviced, and was capable of very high mileages – I know of a W123 280TE with over 800,000km on it!

Looking after the engine means the following:

• Flushing and changing the cooling system every two years. If this is not done, the cooling passages close to the outside edges of the block could corrode and leak close to the head gasket.
• An oil change every 3000 miles – highly recommended to keep the oil ways clear.
• Tappet adjustment is essential on a yearly basis.
• Correct spark plugs are essential for smooth running.
• Regular checking for leaks from the complicated gasket on the top camshaft-housing section.

## STRAIGHT-SIX M103 ENGINE

In the 1985 second-generation 126 the M110 was superseded by the 2.6- and a 3-litre M103. Although it was not originally considered to be as reliable as the M110, thirty years on, the M103 has proved itself – as long as it had a regular and good service record. However, it is still known for two main problems:

*A new upgraded head gasket usually sorts out the common problems on the M103 engine.*

- Head-gasket problems at around 100,000 miles, usually around piston number 6 at the back, now easily rectified with an upgraded gasket.
- Excessive valve-guide wear, which is not so easily repaired, but a lot easier if you do it at the same time as the head gasket.

There are a number of other minor problems. The ignition distributor fits horizontally on the front of the camshaft and just underneath this is a rubber oil seal that continues from the cam-cover gasket; these have a propensity to weep. The M103 distributor also suffers from condensation, which can cause misfires and even stalling. The best way to remedy this is to change the cap and O-ring every two years, using only original MBD parts.

Mercedes-Benz were a little too clever in the use of plastic under-bonnet parts and some early plastic thermostat housings failed, leading potentially to a cooked engine. The hose neck in the plastic radiator header tank could collapse, resulting in a terminal loss of coolant. The fix was a metal reinforcement collar or later header tanks, which came with the upgrade.

## THE DIESEL ENGINES

### SALES NUMBERS

Oddly, even with the increasing market for diesel vehicles in Europe during the 1980s, MBD only ever sold the diesel-engine 126 for the US and Canadian markets. In more recent years, the diesel versions have come up for sale via a number of 'specialists' in Europe.

The first-generation five-cylinder diesels took nearly 9 per cent of the overall 126 market, selling over 78,000 units, making it third in line over the 280SE and the 300SE. In the late 1980s, however, the oil burner began losing favour on the other side of the Atlantic, and the Generation 2 350SD, 350SDL and 300SDL could only manage just short of 18,000 units in total, making those second, third and fifth respectively from the bottom of the model sales list.

### FIVE-CYLINDER OM617 DIESEL ENGINE

The OM617 engine is probably one of the main reasons why MBD got their reputation for producing 'bullet-proof' engines; if any are deserving of this accolade it might be this one. It certainly ranks as one of the most reliable diesel engines of the 1970s and the 1980s and many have returned hundreds of thousands of kilometres.

One 123 estate I know has achieved 1.3 million kilometres; bought new by a sales rep, the car has travelled throughout Europe and, although tatty cosmetically, it still runs like a clock on the same engine with which it was delivered. My own G-Wagen, with the very same engine, albeit non-turbo, has never let me down in fifteen years of ownership. As with any engine, however, achieving these huge mileages is highly dependent on an impeccable service record. This particular car had been serviced religiously every 5000km as well as having had a full service yearly from new. The only major work it had to have done was two new timing chains due to stretch, and the replacement of valve guides.

This is typical of the OM617. It was already a robust, high-torque engine as a naturally aspirated version in the 123 and G-Wagen 4x4. When it was fitted in the 126, it was further upgraded to withstand the stresses of a turbo.

It is also interesting to note that, due to its old-style Bosch pump, it will run happily on many 'alternative' fuels such as waste or straight vegetable oil, or even central heating oil. This is not recommended, however, without careful consideration – great care must be taken with regard to the processing of waste oils, otherwise damage is likely.

## SIX-CYLINDER OM603 DIESEL ENGINE

The OM603 was a giant leap forward in diesel-engine technology and held a lot of promise for Mercedes. In Europe the new engine was proving to be a reasonably reliable unit in other models in its naturally aspirated version, however, there were problems with the US versions.

The 126 was offered in the US market with the turbocharged version of the OM603 engine. Due to restrictive emission controls, it became necessary to add a 'trap oxidizer' or particulate filter. At first, the trap was set too close to the engine and the heat generated by it caused damage to the cylinder heads, left, right and centre. Later 3.0-litre engines did have

*MBD removed the 'trap oxidizer' completely on a recall, thinking this would take care of the problem. However, the cylinder heads were inherently weak and problems persisted.*

an upgraded cylinder head, which seemed to cure the problem.

The later 3.5-litre versions were basically the same as the 3.0-litre but with a larger turbocharger and larger bore cylinders. The higher pressures and extra torque created problems with erosion of the cylinder-head gasket, which in turn let oil into the number-one cylinder. Elevated oil consumption is an early warning of this problem.

There is also some evidence, yet unproved, that the piston connecting rods were weak and would cause 'ovaling' of the cylinder bore. Generally, these problems seemed to manifest themselves early on in the life of the vehicle so it could have been an intermittent production fault.

Another problem common to all the OM60X series engines involved the engine mounts. If these were left to deteriorate, the vibration created internally could loosen tiny internal screws that then worked their way into the oil passages and the oil pump, with catastrophic results, including thrown rods and cracked blocks. This can be prevented now simply by maintaining the engine mounts.

MBD did replace a number of these engines under warranty – and sometimes even after the warranty had expired for the original owners – although no liability was accepted and there was never a formal recall.

# CHAPTER TEN

# THE DRIVE TRAIN

## REAR SUSPENSION AND DRIVE UNIT

The rear suspension was based on the same semi-trailing arm independent system that MBD had developed for the 116 range, although it had been upgraded to suit the compliant nature of the S-Class limousine.

The Mercedes numbering system took into consideration every possible optional extra and model configuration, and the suspension was tweaked for each 126 model so that every one felt correctly balanced.

The original supplied dampers were high-quality gas/oil Bilstein units and were critical to the handling and ride of the S-Class. They are quite difficult to check visually and, if you suspect a problem with

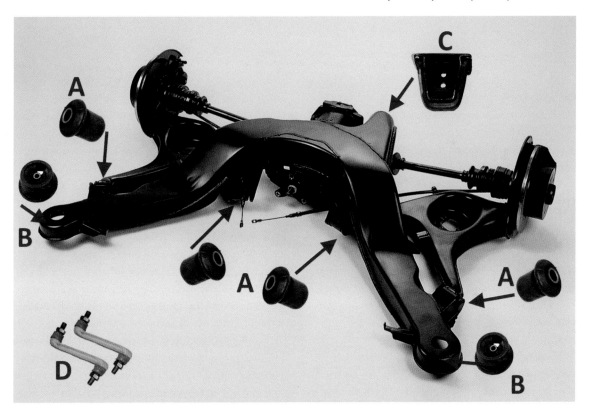

*MBDs used the tried and trusted semi-trailing arm set-up, upgraded from the previous 116 S-Class.*

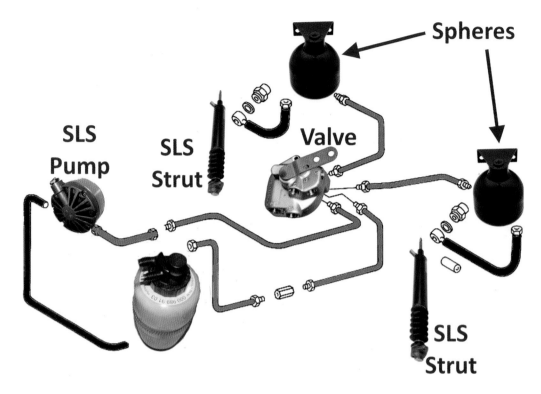

**Spheres**

**SLS Pump**

**SLS Strut**

**Valve**

**SLS Strut**

*Mercedes' version of the hydraulic rear-suspension system was a simple one.*

them, the only real way to identify it is to remove them. Keep a close eye on the large sub-frame mounting bushes (B), too. Wear on these can manifest itself in uneven tyre wear, and in excessive cases, in rear-end instability and crabbing and sagging. There are two rear trailing-arm bushes (A) on each side, which can cause similar problems when worn. However, by far the most common reason for a sagging rear end or 'bottoming out' on acceleration is the centre diff mount (C).

Choice of tyre is critical to a smooth ride and to avoid excessive roar on road surfaces. Make sure tyres are V-rated.

On the 'non-SLS' system, check the sway/anti-roll bar links (D) for any play.

The rear self-levelling system is a fairly simple one, run via a pump on the front of the engine below the ignition distributor. Very often, when it goes wrong, the best option is to swap over to the manual system, but this can be more about a fear of the likely expense than actually looking for the problem. More often than not, simply renewing the nitrogen spheres or just correcting a leaky joint will bring it back again.

It is unusual for the pump to give up completely, although failure of the rear radial seal is common. When it does fail, hydraulic fluid will find its way back into the engine, diluting the oil, which could cause damage. There is a warning light on the dash indicating loss of fluid and pressure.

The adjustable struts have a general work life of around ten years or 100,000 miles. The most common failure with these is worn or weak nylon seals and rubber O-rings. These endure quite severe heating and cooling cycles as the struts compress and extend, and gradually lose their elasticity.

Finally, the 'accumulator spheres' may fail. Their job is to act as dampers to the spring. When they fail you will notice the suspension either bobs around like you are at sea or goes as hard as a board. They are not serviceable once this has happened and your only option is to replace them with new units. They need changing in pairs.

*There are two flexible coupling discs, one at gearbox end of the propshaft and the other at the final drive end.*

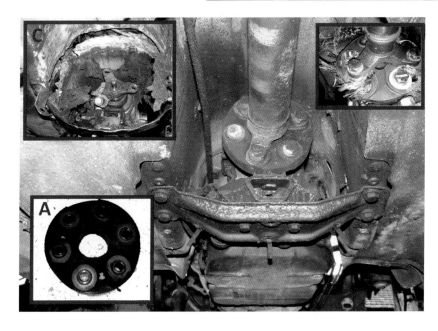

*You may notice a vibration through your seat before the 'doughnuts' get too bad, but do not leave it – suspect these first before anything else.*

Finally, keeping the fluid and the filter clean and making regular checks on the rubber boots, with periodic cleaning, can greatly extend their life. If there are any tears in the rubber gaiters, they should be changed as soon as possible.

The final-drive unit is a good-quality item but it can suffer from neglect. An oil change every couple of years can work wonders and should help to preserve it for the life of the car. Any internal wear will be easily noticeable by a constant whine but you should also look out for signs of oil leaks at the output driveshafts. Remember there is a special oil for the LSD version.

Last, and perhaps most important, are the propshaft flexible discs (also called 'doughnuts'). It is imperative to check these yearly; when the structure starts to become more flexible you may spot what appear to be dark bruises in the rubber. These stresses will turn into cracks (A). If you notice even the slightest elongation of bolt holes or what appears to be twine coming to the surface edges (B), refrain from driving the car and get them replaced immediately. If one of these flexible discs disintegrates at speed, a huge amount of damage may be caused by the propshaft breaking free (see the illustration, C). It is rare to get this far and frankly inexcusable, so check your doughnuts!

## FRONT SUSPENSION

The front suspension of the 126 is a complicated system of joints and pivot points. Although it is not particularly difficult to repair and well within the range of a home mechanic with the right equipment, it will still be expensive to put right an abused set-up due mostly to the number of individual parts needed.

What often happens is that one part wears and needs replacing. If it is left unattended, this puts excessive stress and strain on other connected parts, speeding up wear and tear there. If any wear is identified and corrected promptly, the whole unit should retain its integrity.

The most common wear point however is the brake control joint and bush, also known as the 'dog bone', due to its shape. When the ball joint inside the bushing starts to wear, you will begin to hear a sharp clunking sound on both braking and acceleration. A visual check or even shaking parts by hand is not good enough; the tensions and stresses are such that it will need a machine that can oscillate the wheel in multiple directions to be able to see any movement in the parts.

The only other part worthy of note is the front anti-roll bar. It seems like a very minimal part of the suspension system – and in one way it is – however, it has a vulnerability that needs to be checked and

# Front Suspension Components

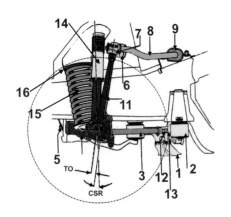
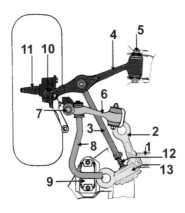
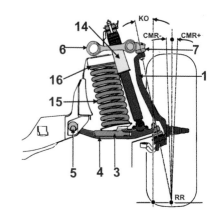

| | |
|---|---|
| TO = Toe-in Offset | 1 = Cross member |
| CSR = Caster | 2 = Brake control yoke (dog bone) |
| KO = King pin Offset | 3 = Support tube |
| CMR = Camber | 4 = Lower control arm |
| RR = Roll Radius | 5 = Eccentric bolt caster adjustment |
| | 6 = Upper control arm |
| | 7 = Upper control arm ball joint |
| | 8 = Torsion (anti roll) bar |

9 = Torsion bar bush to chassis
10 = Lower ball joint
11 = Steering knuckle hub unit
12 = Ball pin caster adjustment
13 = Brake control arm support
14 = Shock absorber unit
15 = Front coil spring
16 = Coil spring support adjustment pad

*Although complicated in appearance, the front suspension set-up is a very strong reliable system – if it is well cared for.*

*The purpose of the rod is to prevent the front suspension from moving aft under heavy braking, while the rubber bushing isolates vibration and road noise from the suspension attached to this rod.*

*It is not until you come to replace the bushes that you realize how bad it can be.*

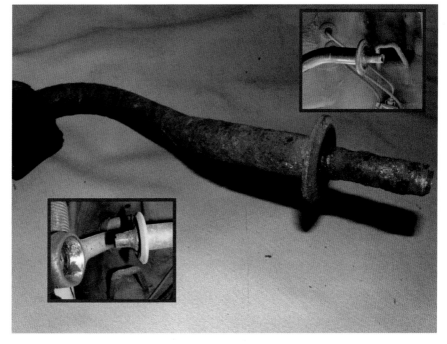

controlled in order to save a whole pile of work. Rust seems sometimes to take hold of the spindle, under the two rubber bushes where it meets the upper control arm.

*Removing the bar to replace it is a massive job, but there is now a sleeve-over kit available to repair it, without having to remove it completely. It does need to be done by a competent welder.*

## AUTOMATIC GEARBOX

The Mercedes 722.3 and 722.4 gearboxes used in a 126 work very hard, especially with the high-torque V8s. They are perfectly capable of high mileages, especially with a fluid and filter change every couple of years. The problem is that they are complicated items and generally beyond the realms of the DIYer. Many owners, very fearful of something going wrong, will hand the car over to a specialist who will willingly charge hundreds of pounds to overhaul it when all it really needs is a little tweaking.

I was once given a 126 because the gearbox was snatching and high-revving before up-changes, and the owner thought that was it for his beloved car. In fact, all it needed was a new upgraded modulating vacuum valve (A), at a cost of about £25, a filter and fluid change and all was perfect again, albeit after a slight adjustment, made a lot simpler by the newly designed turnkey provided. The vehicle was soon returned to its owner….

The gear-linkage bushes may also cause problems as the car ages. There are two, one at the bottom of the lever and the other along a selector rod. They are made of a rubbery plastic compound that becomes brittle with age and contamination, and disintegrates. Gear changes become sloppy and accurate selection is all but impossible, which can cause all sorts of problems.

Many 126 owners do not realize that the auto box only ever pulls from second gear in normal use. If you want a first-gear start, pull the lever down to the bottom of its gate, move over to the B setting and back up to drive. Get yourself comfortable in the seat, strap everything down and floor the accelerator. You will not regret it!

## BRAKES

The brakes on the 126 are often accused of being quite poor and certainly not capable of stopping the car efficiently at speed. If the system has not been well looked after, or has been neglected, any lack of efficiency will certainly feel exaggerated with such a heavy car. However, this is certainly not the case with a well-maintained system; if yours does not feel right, you should take a good look at it.

Although discs are considered 'low-maintenance' items compared to drums, it is constantly surprising that some owners largely ignore their brakes until they start to make a grinding noise or a warning light comes on. While it does take a bit of effort to check the brakes regularly – jacking up the car four times and removing the wheels – there is probably nothing more important. The next day you have saved for car maintenance, do yourself a favour and get to know your brakes.

ABOVE: *Changing the vacuum-modulating valve first could save you the cost of a gearbox rebuild.*

RIGHT: *It is a DIY job, but getting the bush and clip back on is very fiddly in the confined space under the lever. The gearbox selector can be easily removed and replaced intact.*

They are notorious for creating a fair amount of dust and blackening the alloy wheels but, if you make a point of cleaning the dust off every time you remove the wheels, you will not end up with excessive dust build-up on the calipers themselves. Replacing the pads with the new ceramic-based friction linings also helps.

The brake fluid should not be forgotten either. Mineral oil-based brake fluid is hygroscopic, in other words it will absorb moisture. This moisture will then just sit in the pipework or in the calipers and cause rust. This is why the 126 is known for sticking caliper pistons. Keep the system in good order, changing the fluid every two years, and all should be well.

For more information and advice, see the 'Brake Overhaul' section later.

## PARKING BRAKE

One of the things about having an automatic gearbox in the car is that the 'Park' setting is taken literally and is often the only thing used to hold the car when it is stationary – at least until the MOT or safety check is done and the tester finds that the parking brake is seized or inefficient.

If it feels as if the parking brake is getting stiff to apply, take the time to remove the rear discs and inspect the shoes.

## ABS

The ABS system has three sensors, one on each front hub and one on the final drive unit. The sensors need to be kept clean as does the reluctor ring, which is a part of the hub, not a separate item as on more modern cars. Very often, illuminated ABS warning lights are the result of brake dust caked on the rear of the bearing hub. The OVP relay can also give a false ABS warning, as can faulty alternators.

The ABS pump unit has a plastic cover under which are two relays, very often missed when trying to diagnose warning lights.

ABOVE: *The shoes are in a confined space and dust can build up to such an extent that it hardens like concrete, causing the parking brake eventually to lock up and refuse to release.*

LEFT: *The UK version is a hand-pull brake, while all other versions have a foot pedal with a hand release.*

## WHEEL BEARINGS

Wheel bearings are worth a mention as regular checks and maintenance will increase their lifespan significantly. The front hub has an inner and an outer roller and taper bearing set supported by a stub axle in the front leg; in original condition, they go through a great deal of stress while supporting a heavy car. If the car has larger, aftermarket wheels, they may need more regular checks. They will benefit from a regular regime of a clean and re-grease but be very precise with the amount of grease used; do not overfill the bearing cap.

Should they become noisy or exhibit excessive play, they must be replaced quickly. The stub axle can easily be damaged by disintegrating bearings and then it will be necessary to change the complete front leg.

The rear bearing units are a different matter. They are fitted from the rear of the hub and tightened to the correct torque with a special nut. They cannot be serviced without dismantling a great deal of the rear suspension unit.

# PART IV

# MAINTAINING A 126

If you feel nervous about doing your own servicing on a 126, because it has the reputation of being a complicated machine, remember it is fundamentally just an assembly of parts. It was designed and put together by human beings using common materials; it did not drop from the sky ready-made. The hardest part of any job on a 126 is summoning the confidence to do it; if you start with the easy jobs, it will give you the impetus, enthusiasm and courage to continue and you will soon be tackling the bigger jobs.

Even the most fastidious-looking 'servicing record' may reflect just the minimum required in order to keep the car on the road; add to that the 'If it ain't broke don't fix it' attitude of many garages, and you are going to have no choice but to get involved if you want your car to be one of the best. Whether your car is five or fifty years old, your starting point will have to be 'deferred maintenance' – catching up with all the jobs that should have been done over the years but have most likely been neglected.

## PREPARATIONS

• Equip yourself: there are all sorts of tools, gadgets and gizmos for the home mechanic. Make sure that your family and friends know what you need at Christmas and birthday times, and start collecting.
• Take your time: garage mechanics are constrained by time and working schedules, but you are not. While a mechanic will do the job you ask him to do, he will do nothing else. You on the other hand can clean up the area, spend time to look around and get to know the vehicle. You might see a rusty bolt or nut that needs replacing or a cable that needs clipping back up. If the person who works on

the car does not know it very well, things can get broken and forced. You can take as long as you like to remove a panel and no one will tell you off for having a cup of tea in the middle of the job when things are not going well.
• Be prepared: it is very annoying not to have the right tool to hand when you are already buried in the engine compartment or lying on your back. Gather tools and supplies needed for the job and lay them out on a tray where you can easily grab them without looking for them.
• Prepare the area: if you are going to be flushing fluids, put down a drop cloth. If you need to lie down under the car, a flattened, large cardboard box or a scrap of carpet can make all the difference for comfort and cleanliness. A mechanic's rolling

*Select the tools you might need and place them in a carry-all to save time.*

trolley is good if you have a perfectly flat garage floor. Otherwise, a sheet of thick plastic will help you to glide while on your back. If you don't have a solid work bench or the room for one, a couple of trestles and a piece of ply will work a treat as an area to clean up or dismantle a part. Add a couple of old dinner trays to stop things rolling off.
- Take pictures: if you are unsure about something and/or concerned you might forget something, take photographs and make notes.
- Keep records: everyone loves a 'service history' but your own work will not provide a garage stamp in the service manual. For your peace of mind, as well as any prospective purchaser in the future, keep detailed records, including receipts. This will also assist with any insurance claim in case you need to prove how your vehicle has been looked after.

## PARTS

Everyone loves a bargain but it is vital to ensure that you are not making buying decisions at the expense of common sense, quality or, more importantly, safety. It has never been easier to buy car parts but, as you look down a long list of similar parts at different prices, you might be tempted by the lowest price and delivery cost, rather than the best quality.

Companies and individuals always sell for maximum profit and, if that means buying cheap to beat the competition, most will do it. It is up to you to use your common sense as to what is right and most appropriate for your needs. They will always be a reason why a cheap part is cheap.

Like most manufacturers, Daimler-Mercedes sell their parts at a premium. There is no conspiracy to squeeze money from an unsuspecting public; instead, the parts have been designed and made to a specification worked out by the original designers and engineers. Buying main dealer parts is always going to be the best option and you can guarantee they will be of the same quality as the original, which will have probably lasted twenty years or more. If you cannot go for a main-dealer item, try looking for a real 'original equipment manufacturer' or OEM item. (The term 'OEM' is so often used now that it has lost

### The Battery
Get into the habit of disconnecting the battery every time you want to 'tinker' with the car (apart from washing and polishing), to avoid sparks, shorts, blown fuses, failed relays and ECUs. When you buy a new battery, make sure you save the little caps protecting the terminals. Keep them handy in the boot and use them to protect the terminals when you have disconnected the battery. Due to the thickness of the leads, they tend to find their original position and if it finds its way back to the exposed terminals, they will not make contact.

If you need to jump-start a 126, it is not recommended that you join 'Ground to Ground' as it can undermine the sensitive ECUs.

some meaning. It was originally used to denote parts not made by the vehicle manufacturer but outsourced by them, and chosen for their quality, or specially manufactured.) You may be able find the same part at a much lower price if it comes directly from the manufacturer or from an independent supplier.

Make sure you check internet forums or club members when researching the quality or the integrity of 'pattern' parts. Not all pattern or non-original parts are bad – in the end you tend to get what you pay for – but just because something looks similar does not mean that it is. New out of the box, a Lemforder engine mount costing over £150 from a main dealer might look almost identical to an item made in China costing £40. It is only in use that any difference in quality will become apparent – and by then it will be too late. There is always plenty of information available from individuals who have used parts that have failed or not stood up under test, so do your research.

## JACKING UP THE 126

On the Generation 2 cars the plastic sill covers hide the jack lift point holes but this is not the case on

Original Bosch          Bremi Aftermarket

Both the original Bosch distributor cap and the Bremi aftermarket version are considered to be of reasonable quality and neither is the cheapest option. The difference in the strength of the items is immediately obvious. The OEM version has external support ribs at all the vulnerable HT lead connectors, as well as an internal strengthening rib and extra support for the contact points. There is approximately a 50 per cent difference in the overall thickness of the body material.

ABOVE: Retain the terminal caps, as they make excellent protectors.

BELOW: Join the ground from the 'good' battery to a good metal point on the 126 IE Engine block or good exposed body/chassis point.

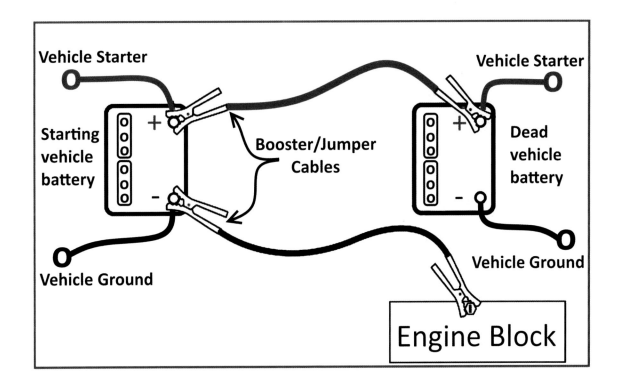

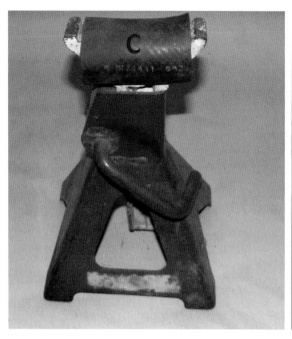

*If you have work to do on or under the car, only ever use a heavy-duty trolley jack and never rely on the jack only to keep the vehicle aloft. Always add axle stands.*

the first-generation cars. Although there are four factory jack lift points provided in the sills of the 126, it is not recommended that you use these for anything other than changing a wheel in an emergency situation.

When inserting the jack into the hole in the sill (B), ensure the jack has been inserted fully and hold it in this position until the foot bites the ground. Make certain that the leg is well positioned and there is no risk that it will collapse or slip – a badly positioned jack is the quickest way to crease the sill and/ or damage the tube, which will encourage rust to penetrate.

There is a rubber bung on each sill corner (A), which shows where you can position the jack cradle or lift arms, depending on what you are using. You

**TIP:** If you are removing a wheel, push it under the side of the car as an extra security against the vehicle slipping. It might be what saves your life.

Also, if you use a small length of coolant hose over the axle stand support head, it will prevent damage to the paint and the under-seal finish (C).

can see the chassis rails running the length of the car; these provide an ideal position to place the axle stands.

The only other recommended positions for lifting the car are the front cross member and the base of the rear-axle final-drive unit.

# CHAPTER ELEVEN

# ROUTINE MAINTENANCE SCHEDULES

The maintenance intervals given here are provided on the assumption that you, not the dealer, will be carrying out the work and that your car is used regularly. If you wish to keep your vehicle in peak condition at all times, you may wish to carry out some of the procedures more often. If the vehicle is driven in dusty areas, used to tow a trailer, or driven frequently at slow speeds (for example, idling in traffic), or mainly for short journeys, shorter maintenance intervals are recommended. Regular and frequent maintenance will enhance the efficiency, performance and resale value of your vehicle. Using the maintenance schedules as a guide, you will soon work out a comfortable routine of your own.

## WEEKLY CHECKLIST

### EXTERIOR INSPECTION (360 WALK-AROUND)

- Is the vehicle exterior free of visible damage?
- Do all four tyres look to be undamaged?
- Are all four tyres properly inflated by gauge?
- Is tyre tread depth and tread wearing acceptable?
- Are there any signs of fluid leakage underneath vehicle?
- Are wiper blades adequate?

### INTERIOR INSPECTION

- Is the vehicle's interior clean of debris?
- Are safety belts working properly?
- Is a first aid and emergency kit available?

- Are the vehicle registration documents easily accessible?
- Is a spare tyre available and inflated?
- Is there a jack system available?
- Is the owner's manual available?

## OPERATING INSPECTION

- Are the headlights working?
- Are the tail-lights working?
- Are the brake lights working?
- Are the interior lights working?
- Are the windscreen wipers working properly?
- Is the horn working?
- Are the rear-view mirrors undamaged?
- Is the handbrake/parking brake working?
- Do the turn signals work (independently of hazard switch)?
- Does the hazard light switch function correctly?

## UNDER-BONNET INSPECTION

- Is the engine oil within range?
- Is the windscreen-wiper fluid within range?
- Is the power-steering fluid within range?
- Is the transmission fluid within range and a reddish colour?
- Is the brake fluid within proper levels?
- Is the coolant within proper levels?
- Do all belts appear in good condition?

## WHEELS AND TYRES

- Check tyres for general condition and tread depth.

• Check correct tyre pressure.
• Retighten wheel bolts. Observe tightening torque!

## GENERAL BODY AND UNDERSIDE OF CAR

• Check for anything hanging or stuck.
• Check all water drains.

## ENGINE COMPARTMENT

• Check engine oil.
• Check condition and tension of V-belts.
• Check around dual bulkhead for leaves and debris.
• Check wiper blades (screen and headlights).
• Check fuse box for corrosion around terminals or blown fuses.

## CHECK AND CORRECT FLUID LEVELS

• Engine coolant.
• Automatic transmission fluid.
• Level control, ADS, ASD, SLS fluid.
• Brake fluid.
• Power-steering fluid.
• Battery electrolyte (if applicable).
• Windscreen-washer fluid.

## BOOT

• Check, correct tyre pressure (spare).
• Check, tools and emergency spare parts/bulbs.

## CHECK AND CORRECT FLUID LEVELS

• Engine coolant/antifreeze protection.
• Automatic transmission fluid.
• Level control, ADS, ASD, SLS fluid.
• Brake system.
• Power-steering fluid.
• Battery electrolyte (if applicable).
• Windscreen-washer fluid.

## GENERAL AND FLUIDS SERVICE

All models: Every 4000 miles/6400 km or every year.

## ENGINE COMPARTMENT

• Engine oil and filter change.
• Inspect, lubricate throttle linkage.
• Check and correct battery electrolyte level (if applicable).
• Lubricate bonnet hinges.
• Check condition and tension of V- and rib-belts.
• Check condition of air filter.
• Check spark plugs, replace if necessary.

## GENERAL INSPECTION SERVICE

All models, every 4000 miles/6400km or every year.
• Inspect, lubricate engine throttle linkage.
• Check A/C refrigerant charge.
• Inspect handbrake/parking-brake cables.
• Retighten steering gear bolts.

## GENERAL MAINTENANCE SERVICE

All models: Every 12,000 miles/18,000 km or every 2 years.

## ENGINE COMPARTMENT

• Change air filter.
• Change spark plugs.

## INTERIOR

• Check warning and indicator lights, horn.
• Clean cassette-deck tape head (if applicable).
• Interior console lights and courtesy lights.
• Heating and ventilation.
• Inspect seatbelts for movement/damage.
• Backrest lock, check operation.

• Seat adjustment operation.
• Heated rear screen.

## BODY

• Inspect headlights and exterior lights.
• Lubricate door hinges.
• Lubricate door locks.
• Clean antenna mast with cleaning cloth.
• Lubricate sunroof mechanism.
• Check condition of headlight wiper blades.
• Replace windscreen wiper insert(s).
• Inspect/test windscreen, rear window and headlight wiper/washer system.

## WHEELS, TYRES AND BRAKES

• Inspect, rotate wheels.
• Inspect tyres and record tread depth.
• Correct tyre pressure.
• Check brake pad/disc thickness, check condition of discs.
• Adjust handbrake/parking brake.
• Brake test, handbrake/parking brake check.
• Replace brake fluid.

## UNDERSIDE OF THE CAR

• Inspect condition, routing, leaks of components, lines and hoses.
• Rear axle oil.

• Check front-axle ball joints.
• Check steering play.
• Retighten steering-gear bolts.
• Inspect suspension and body structure.
• Check all water drains run clear.
• Check exhaust system and mountings.
• Check the condition of the driveshaft gaiters.

Additionally every 30,000 miles/48,000km

• Check clutch disc for wear (where applicable).
• Automatic transmission fluid and filter change.
• Inspect propshaft flex discs.
• Inspect handbrake/parking-brake cables.
• Retighten steering gear bolts.

Additionally every 60,000 miles/96,000km

• Replace fuel filter.
• Check front-axle ball joint free play.

## ENGINE COMPARTMENT

• Inspect condition, routing and any leaks of components, lines and hoses.
• Check valve clearance (M110 engine).

# CHAPTER TWELVE

# ROUTINE MAINTENANCE INFORMATION

To go through every routine service item on every 126 model and every engine would take a whole book. The following information highlights some of the issues that affect each particular model, but are not generally dealt with as a part of routine servicing.

There are also service manuals available online or in disc form, which will help you with some of the processes relating to your own model.

It is a common misconception that a yearly safety check or service by the garage is enough to keep a car running indefinitely. It may be acceptable for a daily runner that you might sell before anything gets too old, but it does not apply to a classic car. In general, keeping a regular check on your vehicle requires no particular skills or tools – regardless of whether you do the work yourself or pay a garage to do it for you, it could save you a great deal of expense and inconvenience in the future.

## TYRES

The 126 is a very heavy car and the only thing between you and the road surface are the tyres, constantly playing a game of balance and feel. Everything you do in the car involves the tyres: pulling away, stopping when and where you need to in all weathers and cruising on a motorway. Mercedes spent a significant amount of time on getting the correct combination between ride, comfort and safety, and got the combination spot on with the standard set-up. However, if something is not quite right, it is all compromised.

Generally speaking, the tyres are at their optimum once they have bedded in to their rim and settled to the dynamics of the car, at about 100 miles after fitting from new. After this point they will start to deteriorate naturally.

| Condition | Excessive wear at Shoulders | Excessive wear at Centre | Cracked & Crazed Tread | Excessive wear on One Side | Feathering | Bald Spots | Scalloped wear |
|---|---|---|---|---|---|---|---|
| Deterioration Effect | 1. 2. | | | | | | |
| Deterioration Cause | Under-Inflated | Over-Inflated | Under-inflated Age related Exceeding speed rating | Excessive Camber | Incorrect Toe | Unbalanced | Worn or Damaged Suspension Joints |

*Your regime of regular weekly checks will not only extend the life span of all the items on the car, but will also allow you to spot a potential problem early on, avoiding dangers and possibly extending your own life span.*

## CORRECT PRESSURE

There are three main reasons why the correct tyre pressure is important:

1) Safety: under-inflated tyres will overheat, which softens the material and exacerbates tyre roll and vehicle instability. Over-inflated tyres reduce the footprint of the tyre on the road and again will have a negative effect on road-holding.
2) Economy: uneven stress will wear certain areas more quickly, which will lead to replacement becoming necessary prematurely; under-inflation creates tyre drag, which will increase fuel consumption by 5 to 10 per cent.
3) Environment: recent research suggests that poor tyre-pressure maintenance is costing UK motorists more than £350 million, wasting more than 370 million litres of fuel and pumping an additional 1 million tonnes of carbon dioxide into the atmosphere.

## TREAD DEPTH

European law dictates that the minimum tyre tread depth must be 1.6mm over a minimum of 75 per cent

### Stopping distance relating to tread degradation

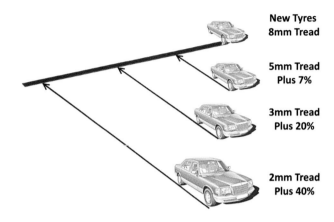

New Tyres
8mm Tread

5mm Tread
Plus 7%

3mm Tread
Plus 20%

2mm Tread
Plus 40%

*Stopping distances increase as tyres wear.*

of the tyre. Although most tyres now have a strip that indicates when the tyre has reached this limit, RoSPA (the Royal Society for Prevention of Accidents) suggests that tyres should be replaced when they reach the 3mm point of wear. At any time after this, the

*A guide to tread depth.*

| | | | |
|---|---|---|---|
| 8mm Tyre Tread | Your tyre is 0% worn | Good |
| 7mm Tyre Tread | Your tyre is 15% worn | Good |
| 6mm Tyre Tread | Your tyre is 31% worn | Good |
| 5mm Tyre Tread | Your tyre is 47% worn | Good |
| 4mm Tyre Tread | Your tyre is 62% worn | Okay |
| 3mm Tyre Tread | Your tyre is 78% worn | Inspect Monthly |
| 2mm Tyre Tread | Your tyre is 94% worn | Time to Replace |
| 1.6mm Tyre Tread | Your tyre is 100% worn | On Legal Limit |

low tread rate, especially in wet weather, will severely reduce grip and control.

## SPEED RATING

It is very important that you check your speed rating before buying tyres. Although it is not illegal to use a tyre with a lower speed/weight rating, choosing a tyre with a lower rating than is appropriate for your car can invalidate your insurance.

## BATTERY

Most vehicle batteries will last on average for around five years; you may be able to gain another year or so on a vehicle that is used every day but on a vehicle that is used less often, and allowed to discharge more often, the maximum age can easily be reduced by a couple of years. Most of the time, the 126 is used as a 'high days and holidays' car, so it tends to be left in the garage or on the drive for days if not weeks on end. If there is one thing a vehicle battery does not like, it is inactivity. Then, to make matters worse, the owner will jump in the car, put in the key and expect it to start every time.

Battery condition is everything on a 126. When the battery is not up to scratch, the car can experience slow starting, slow engine turning, inconsistent idle, dim headlights and slow screen wipers, to name just a few ailments that can rear their ugly head. These problems can occur because the different parts are drawing excessive voltage to compensate for the lack of battery power. If the issue is left unresolved, the charging system, starter motor or starter solenoid can be affected. You could even end up replacing expensive electrical parts such as relays and ECUs after suffering power surges from attempted jump-starting.

If the car is going to be left for any extended period, the battery should be disconnected. If it is in a garage, plug in a maintenance charger – there are many available on the market, some of which plug into the cigar-lighter socket so you will not even have to open the bonnet.

NB: do not use a boost charger on a 126.

A poor battery is more likely to let you down in the winter months as cold will drain its power. Check the battery terminals for security as well as

| State of Charge | Battery Voltage | Specific Gravity | |
|---|---|---|---|
| 100% | 12.70 | 1.265 | Okay |
| 80% | 12.50 | 1.233 | Okay |
| 60% | 12.20 | 1.204 | Slow to crank |
| 40% | 11.90 | 1.176 | May not start |
| 30% | 11.75 | 1.162 | Will not turn starter |
| 20% | 11.58 | 1.148 | |
| 10% | 11.31 | 1.134 | Potential damage to battery |
| 0% | 10.50 | 1.120 | |

*A guide to battery condition showing both measurements relating to it.*

corrosion (usually seen as a white fluffy residue). Even some maintenance-free batteries have access to the acid and plates, so look for a removable plate and periodically check the acid level and specific gravity with a hydrometer (cheaply available from most motor factors). If you cannot access the plates, check the voltage from a 'rested battery'.

The 126 needs a high-quality and fairly heavy-duty battery: 66Ah rising to 74Ah for all models bar the 560, which demanded a 92Ah battery. The physical size to fit the tray is 278mm long x 175mm wide x 190mm high.

## FLUIDS AND FILTERS

Although checking levels is very important, it is not the be all and end all. The quality of the fluid, and its ability to do its job, is as important, if not more so. It is very easy to neglect fluids if they are not leaking and to forget that they have a working life.

## COOLANT SYSTEM

### Coolant/Antifreeze

In general, the term 'antifreeze' is misleading – it does stop the liquid that circulates the engine from freezing

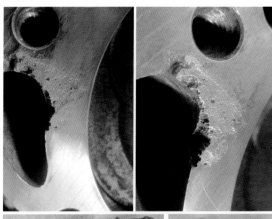

*The damage caused by incorrect coolant to an M103 cylinder head.*

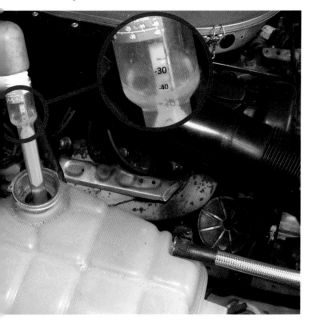

*There are various types of hydrometer on the market but they are all cheap and an invaluable addition to the toolbox. This one shows that the coolant is capable of around -35 degrees.*

in cold temperatures, but it also prevents dissimilar metal corrosion in the engine; prevents build-up of scale; stabilizes the various temperatures around the engine while running; and prevents foaming.

As coolant ages, its ability to do all the above diminishes. More importantly, the longer it is left in a system the more acidic it becomes, with obvious consequences. The coolant in a 126 needs to be changed every two years in order to minimize the damage it can do as its quality dissipates.

If the system needs topping up at any time, only ever use a proper mix of 50/50 with water. There is an important point of balance in percentage of water and coolant; too high a percentage of coolant will actually lower its freezing point and limit its ability to fight off corrosion.

There is much discussion regarding the benefits or otherwise of using distilled or deionized water, as opposed to tap water. Mercedes-Benz 'Specifications for Operating Fluids' (MBD BeVo) does suggest that if you live in a hard-water area you should consider using deionized water, and at the very least think about changing the coolant more often.

Not all coolants are the same and MBD is not trying to make you buy their coolant just to line their pockets. The mix of metals and plastics in the Mercedes engines does require a special coolant mix; extensive use of the incorrect coolant can cause plastic radiator hose outlets such as those on the M103 to crumble away to nothing.

The company that formulates the coolant for most of the MBD range of vehicles also manufactures generic model-compatible coolants under its own name, but those coolants are still not exactly the same formulation as the ones available directly from MBD. Sticking with the MBD-recommended type is probably a good bet.

### Coolant Hoses

The first signs of a potential problem with a coolant hose can usually been seen by eye, so getting into the habit of checking around the hoses every time you open the bonnet could potentially avert a disastrous loss of coolant on the road. Look out for unusual bulges or misshapen edges, white water stains or, in

*This small hose became weak and blew a hole in the top.*

*The small hose at the top of the petrol engine is an expensive part from MBD, as it is made of a tougher material than the usual hose, with 6mm thick walls. Do not be tempted to use 'normal' hose, as it will soon weaken with the heat and blow.*

excessive cases, green or orange jelly forming around the hose edges. Check that worm clamps or Jubilee clamps have not bitten into the rubber.

Pay particular attention to the small hose that sits at the top of the petrol engine, joining the water pump to the radiator top hose and the engine. It is about 80mm long and, although very thick and strong, it will eventually lose some of its tensile strength. If you see it starting to balloon in shape, it is time to change it. It is not easily done without unbolting the housing on top of the water pump, due to the confined space, but lots of plumber's silicone lubricant will assist.

Replace the Jubilee clamps too.

## Thermostat

It seems that whenever there is a problem with the coolant system, whether it is as simple as a vapour lock or a failing head gasket, the first action is the removal of the thermostat. This is never a solution, however. The thermostat is not just there to speed up the engine heating from cold; it also controls coolant flow under all loads and directs the coolant flow by controlling the flow of pressure. Removing the thermostat can actually restrict coolant flow from reaching certain parts of the engine, leaving hot spots.

## ENGINE OIL

Oil is the life blood of an engine, lubricating the moving parts and keeping them cool by lowering the friction between mating surfaces. Changing the oil and filter regularly is probably the single most important thing you can do to aid the longevity of your engine.

There is much talk about the advantages and/or disadvantage of synthetic oils versus the non- or semi-synthetics or standard oils. The more modern fully synthetics are made for the extended servicing periods that are normal on more modern vehicles, but options should be carefully considered when dealing with older vehicles. If you change the oil in the 126 at least once a year, regardless of mileage, or every 6000 miles, there is very limited benefit to using fully synthetic oils, which are generally more costly. It is also said that FS oils do not hold the necessary lead in suspension that older engines need.

Older engines tend to run hotter, have lower oil pressure overall and, as a result, burn more oil and/or increase the chances of losing some of it through gaskets and porous metals.

# Engine Oil Dip Stick

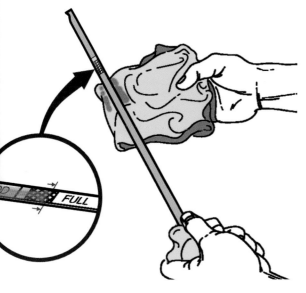

*It is advisable to keep the oil at about three-quarters between the minimum and maximum line.*

With varying temperatures between seasons it is also recommended that you change the oil according to the range change. In France, for example, where my own 126 resides, temperatures can go as low as minus 25 in the winter and as high as 40 in the summer. When it is time to change tyres from winter to summer it is also time to change the oil (see 'Specifications').

Whatever oil you buy for your vehicle, ensure it conforms to the standards of either the ACEA (Association des Constructeurs Européens d'Automobiles) or the API (American Petroleum Institute). Never overfill any MBD engine; if you do overfill by accident, your only option is to drain the excess until the correct level is reached. Do not expect the engine just to burn it off.

Only use high-quality OEM filters. MBD do not cut corners just to make an item cheaper for the market and neither would you want them to, so only use the best for something so important.

## BRAKE FLUID

Of all the fluids in a car, nothing gets forgotten like the brake fluid, perhaps because tinkering with the braking system causes anxiety or perhaps because drivers make no connection between putting their foot on the brake and the fluid that transfers the energy. Braking efficiency degrades so gradually that it is not until something goes wrong – or maybe you drive another vehicle, with good brakes – that you realize that it is not as good as you think. That does not excuse you from the fact that you should have made more regular checks.

MBD recommends that you change the fluid in a 126 every year.

Brake fluid needs to fulfil a number of criteria:

• It must provide consistent operation under soft and extreme conditions alike.
• It must provide optimal corrosion resistance to all components.
• It must provide a consistent feel at the pedal in all temperatures.

The primary reason why brake fluid needs to be changed at least every two years is because it is hygroscopic; this means that even a sealed system naturally absorbs moisture at a rate of about 2 to 3 per cent per year, which permeates the system via vents, micro-pores in rubber seals and flexible brake hoses, especially aftermarket-quality brake hoses that do not have an inner lining.

Six years old Fluid          Fresh Fluid

*Moisture settles in puddles at low points and points of resistance, such as unions and caliper pistons, with obvious results.*

If you were to open the brake fluid reservoir and leave it open for six hours, the quality of the fluid would drop below recognized DOT standards for efficient braking. The boiling point for DOT4 fluid alone would drop from 446 degrees Fahrenheit to 311 degrees Fahrenheit. Moisture dissipating through the system not only lowers the fluid's boiling point but also increases its compressibility, giving a 'soft-pedal' feel.

The DOT also suggests that 50 per cent of all ten-year-old cars have never had a brake-fluid change. A fluid flush and change will cost you around £20 and an hour or so of your time. It is not expensive when you consider that calipers on a 126 can cost anything between £80 and £150 a piece now, depending on the supplier.

## POWER-STEERING FLUID

### Power-Steering Fluid Check

The power-steering fluid (PSF) is another one of those items that gets forgotten, sometimes for years on end. With age, the fluid will darken as it oxidizes and picks up contaminants, will lose its viscosity and become less effective at lubricating and cooling at the internal pressures experienced within the pump and gearbox.

If the fluid has never been flushed or changed to your knowledge, it is time to do it. There is a fair bit of confusion concerning what type of fluid to use and, even though the original written documents provided for the 126 at the time specify that 'only PSF should be used', there is some talk that ATF can be used. According to bevo.mercedes-benz.com, only the following fluids come up to the desired specification quality for use in the power-steering pump:

• MBD 236.3 Lenkgetriebeöl A 000 989 88 03
• Fuchs Titan PSF
• Gonher ATF DIID M 6.3
• Gulf ATF MX
• Liqui Moly Lenkgetriebe-Öl 3100
• Lubral ATF DIID M 6.3
• Petronas ATF Fluid 236.3

*Mercedes PSF should be a translucent cherry red and it should be possible to clearly see the filter at the bottom of the reservoir.*

Note that, just because there are some ATFs listed does not mean that you should use any ATF. With reference to the two specifications, MBD236.3 and MBD-Approved 229.51, MBD advice is that, if the label says MBD 2295.1 instead of MBD-Approved 229.51, it does not have MBD approval.

As the reservoir capacity is only 1.2 litres and you would probably only use a total of 2 litres to completely flush the system, it remains easily obtainable from MBD. There is no reason to skimp purely on price and if MBD suggest that you use their PSF for best results, then it is probably advisable to use it.

There is a filter at the base of the pump which often gets overlooked. Doing a fluid flush at least once every three years is recommended, however, simply emptying the reservoir with a turkey-basting syringe and changing the filter yearly is a good way to keep the PSF fresh.

*At operating temperature, the fluid level should be 18–26mm below the upper edge. Cold, the fluid should be between the minimum and maximum marks.*

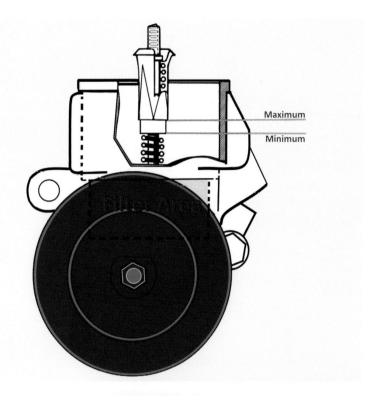

## Power-Steering Fluid Flush and Filter Change

**1)** Before you even attempt to remove the PS pump lid, clear away any loose debris and clean the area around the lid and the unions. As you unscrew the centre bolt fixing you may notice a slight tension from the spring; this usually happens when the clip that holds this spring down is missing. It is a common occurrence as lazy mechanics fail to replace it and just use the plastic level indicator to hold it down.

**2)** Withdraw as much of the fluid as possible with a turkey-baster or syringe (A) until it exposes the top of the filter. Undo the centre bolt and remove the level indicator, being careful not to let the spring fly out. If it still has its clip, remove this carefully with needle-nose pliers. Remove the filter (B) and clean around the bowl, then refit the old filter. (It is also possible to use a disposable filter instead of the reusable version.) Replace the spring, clip, level indicator and fixing nut. Do not top up with fresh fluid yet.

*Use an old turkey-basting syringe to remove fluid.*

**3)** Identify the return rubber hose at the power-steering pump – the one without the pressed fitting and with just a regular Jubilee-style clip. Remove the Jubilee clip and pull off the hose (it may need twisting to get it to loosen). There is not much play in the hose so you will need to attach a second hose to it (A) to enable you to place

*Prepare to flush the old fluid into a can or bottle.*

*Flush until the fluid goes clear.*

the end into a clear plastic bottle away from any moving parts of the engine (C).

4) Loosen the return hosepipe union at the pump and turn it so that the open end faces upwards (B). That way, you will not lose any fluid as you fill the reservoir during the flushing process. Now add fluid to the reservoir, ensuring it does not spill out of the upturned pipe.

5) For the penultimate step you need an assistant. Making sure there is nothing in the way of the pulleys and drive belts, ask them to start the car. As soon as the car starts, the fluid will flow out of the reservoir, through the system and return back through the hose and into the plastic bottle. Be ready to top up the reservoir at the same speed at which it flows out. Do not let the reservoir go dry. As soon as you notice the fluid change colour, you will know it has been successfully flushed with new fluid.

6) Finally, stop the engine and replace the old filter with a new one, or clean the non-disposable one with petrol. Replace the return hose to its original position and tighten the union. Adjust the fluid to its correct level and replace the lid

## REAR-SUSPENSION FLUID (SLS)

The level of the rear-suspension fluid should be checked every time you open the bonnet. It is not unheard of for the rear pump seal to give way, allowing fluid to drain into the engine oil.

Park the vehicle on level ground and open up the bonnet. Locate the level-control system hydraulic reservoir in the engine compartment and remove all traces of dirt from its exterior. Withdraw the dipstick from the top of the reservoir (A) and wipe all the fluid from its end with a clean rag or paper towel. Insert the clean dipstick back into the reservoir as far as it will go, then withdraw it once more. Note

*To replace or at the very least clean the internal filter you will need to disconnect the pipe and undo the main lid.*

the fluid level on the end of the dipstick; it should be between the 'MAX' and 'MIN' marks.

If you notice any sudden loss of fluid, look under the vehicle for any signs of 'dumped fluid', if you see nothing, suspect the rear pump seal and attend to it as soon as possible.

Never overfill the reservoir and keep the filter clean (B).

## AUTOMATIC-TRANSMISSION FLUID

### Potential Problems

The smooth function of the automatic box in the 126 relies heavily on a correct fluid level, at both minimum and maximum. Some say that overfilling can cause catastrophic failure; this may be an over-statement, but all the same great care must be taken. Severe overfilling could cause a build-up of pressure and subsequently blow a relief valve or push fluid through gaskets and seals, but the main problem could be 'foaming' caused by air bubbles building up. The most likely symptom would be sluggish or rough shifting problems and a build-up of heat.

A low fluid level would cause similar symptoms, along with flaring engine revs and clunky up and down shifts. It could also cause excessive wear.

### Checking the Level

In order to check the level of the automatic trans-mission fluid, the transmission must be at operating temperature (fluid temperature of 80 degrees centi-grade). This temperature is reached after driving for approximately 10 miles. Do not attempt to check the fluid level on a cold transmission.

With the transmission at operating temperature, ensure that the vehicle is parked on level ground. With the engine running at idle speed, ensure that the transmission selector lever is in position 'P', and apply the parking brake.

Pull out the dipstick and read the fluid level. The level should be between the 'MIN' and 'MAX' marks (A). If the level is low and topping up is necessary, top it up through the dipstick tube, slowly, using fluid of the specified type (see the 'Service Specifications' section).

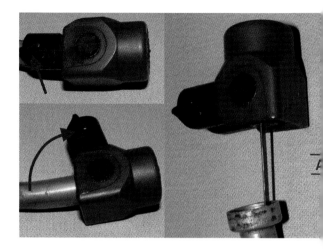

*Release the locking lever, and pull the transmission fluid level dipstick from the dipstick tube. Wipe the dipstick with a lint-free cloth, and then re-insert it.*

It is of the utmost importance when adding fluid to use a funnel with a fine filter. Disposable paint spraying mixing filters work well. The smallest piece of debris can have an adverse effect on gear change.

On completion, re-insert the dipstick tube, and re-check the fluid level. Ensure that the locking lever is engaged when finally refitting the dipstick.

### Auto-Transmission Fluid and Filter Change

When changing the fluid and filter on an automatic gearbox, complete cleanliness is absolutely vital. It cannot be stressed enough. Use latex, rubber or nylon gloves and change them regularly. If you are doing it in your own garage, lay out a sheet of clean plastic on the floor and close any windows and doors, so that nothing can get blown into the valve complex while the pan is removed.

**1)** Unclip and lift but do not remove the dipstick. Get underneath with a collection pan and drain the fluid by removing the plug,

**2)** Once the fluid stops, replace the plug and move to the torque converter drain. You will find a plastic plug in the bell housing (A). To remove it, use an 8mm Allen key to line the tabs front to back; this will also align the keyway so you can pull it out.

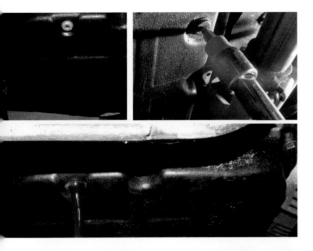

**LEFT: *Ensure the Allen key recess is clean and the Allen key is seated fully. If you strip it by mistake, it will have to be removed with vice grips.***

**3)** While you are under the vehicle you will need someone to turn the crankshaft nut at the front of the engine to turn the torque converter until the drain plug is at the bottom. It needs a 6mm Allen key to remove and drain old oil. It makes a bit of a mess as it exits the slotted housing.

**4)** Replace the plugs as soon as it has drained.

**5)** Lay out the plastic sheet and proceed to remove the six pan bolts. Once they are all removed, pull the pan straight down carefully to expose the

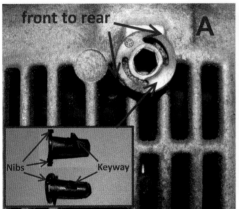

*The torque drain plug is hidden behind a plastic bung. It may be very tight and stuck.*

valve body and filter. It is a messy job and the valve body will drip oil. Do not touch the valve body with anything.

**6)** The interior of the pan will have a residue of fluid remaining, which may have very fine metal filings in it. This is not a problem as long as they are not too plentiful and large (A).

**7)** Refit the pan as soon as possible, seating all the bolts lightly. Most leaks from the fluid-pan gasket are caused by over-tightening, so be very careful. It is very easy to deform the pan seating tabs when over-tightening the four corner bolts. Tighten all the bolts until the gasket starts to bite and then

**LEFT: *The filter is held on with three Philips-head screws (B). Pull down the old one and immediately replace with a new one.***

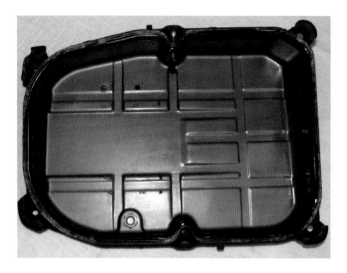

*Thoroughly clean and dry the pan after removing the old gasket. Replace with a new gasket and fit a new sealing washer to the drain plug.*

## Automatic Gearbox Fluid Pan

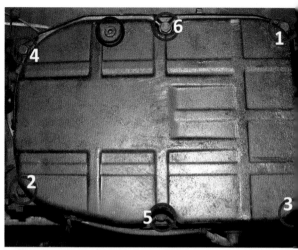

⬤ Torque setting 8Nm    ⬤ Torque setting 14▶

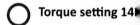
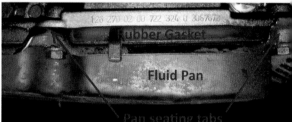

ABOVE: *Do not over-tighten the bolts as the tabs can deform, making it impossible to seal properly.*

work across diagonals making sure the six bolts are tightened evenly (see the illustration).

8) Using perfectly clean rubber hoses, fit a funnel with a fine filter to facilitate pouring of the fluid into the dipstick tube. Pour in approximately 4 litres of the total amount of fluid with the engine stopped.

9) Start the engine and run at idle and in 'Park', gradually adding all but the remaining half-litre of the remainder of the fluid.

10) Once the vehicle is lowered from ramps and back on its wheels, with one foot on the

LEFT: *A homemade filler funnel using tight-fitting hose.*

brake, run through the gears slowly R-N-D-2-1-2-D-N-R.

**11)** Put the car on level ground and check the level again – remembering you will only get an accurate indication of the true level after it has been fully warmed up. Top up as necessary.

If the car has been lain up for an extended period, you are having lazy or flaring gear selection or you do not know whether a fluid change has ever been done, consider doing the job again after 1000 miles. Decent fluid is not cheap but neither is a gearbox rebuild.

## FINAL-DRIVE UNIT OIL CHANGE

The final-drive oil should be changed every twenty-four months or 18,000 miles. The ASR LSD units need different oils, so check with the specifications first.

## FUEL UNIT CHECK AND FILTER CHANGE

The fuel pumps and filter unit for the petrol versions of the 126 are located under the rear right-hand side of the car, just in front of the half shaft.

*Do not just drain the old oil out of the drain plug [B] without checking first whether you can undo the filler plug [A]. They are notoriously difficult to remove if they have been left for years, and you may have to take the car to a garage with a ramp to give you the space to fit a lever bar.*

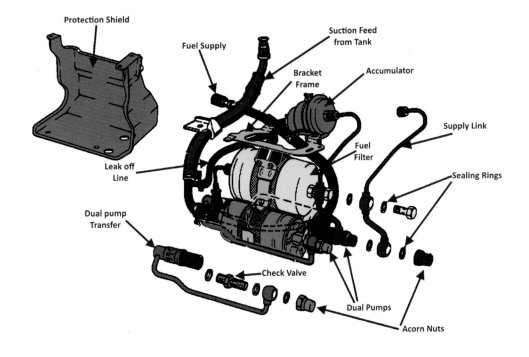

*Fuel pump and filter assembly details.*

## Fuel Filter Unions

*It is a good idea to loosen the fittings on the filter before you try and remove it from its support.*

*As the fuel unit is tucked out of the way, the first you might know of a fuel leak is when it is dumping it on the floor under pressure.*

According to the workshop manual, the fuel filter should be changed every 30,000 miles or three years; if it is left unattended, it can cause misfires and a lack of power. Even though a plastic shroud protects it from the majority of dirt and water, three years is a long time to pay it no heed. Make a habit of checking the fuel unit every year to make sure it is in good order.

First, de-pressurize the fuel system by removing the fuel relay under the bonnet and turn over the engine. Also undo the fuel filler cap to de-pressurize the fuel tank. Once you have removed the road wheel, you will see the fuel distribution unit. You need to remove the plastic protective piece covering the fuel filter, accumulator and pumps, which is held in place by three 10mm hex-head coarse-thread screws. Remove these and place the plastic plate aside for a good clean later on.

The fuel assembly is suspended from the chassis by four rubber hangers or 'doughnuts', as they are sometimes called. Be aware that putting too much twisting force on the filter unions without supporting the cradle could rip them off their mounting if

they have already started to deteriorate leaving the unit hanging by its pipework.

There is a banjo bracket on one side and a fitting on the other, both 17mm. Use two wrenches to remove the lines, one to hold the filter and the other to turn the fitting. With the lines to the filter removed, you may need to loosen the metal bracket that holds the pumps and filter to the hangers, to be able to slide the filter out of its cradle.

If the new filter does not come with a new plastic sleeve (a good reason to buy from MBD), remove the plastic cover on the old filter and reuse it. Install the new filter according to the flow directions (the filter will only fit in one direction, as the fittings are different). Ensure you install the two brass washers between the banjo bolt, and tighten everything up.

With everything in place, turn the ignition on and off a couple of times to re-pressurize the system and check for leaks. Once you are happy all is well, turn off the ignition and reinstall the cover plate.

## FUEL-TANK PRESSURE VALVE

While you are under the rear axle looking at the filter and fuel lines, consider changing the fuel-tank pressure valve. It is not easy to do a visual check, but you may notice that the fuel cap becomes quite difficult to remove. When you do get it open, the tank

*The vacuum can build up very quickly on a journey and will very easily crush the tank inwards if left.*

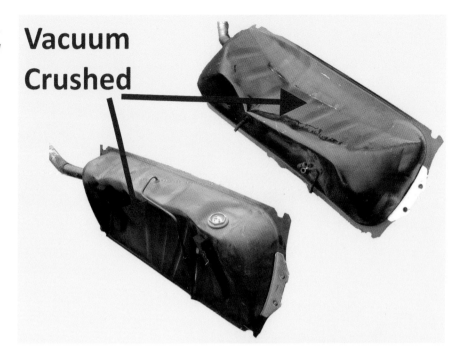

# Vacuum Crushed

vacuum may seem excessive, although there is always a small amount of vacuum hiss. If you hear ticking or creaking noises from the tank, or smell fuel, go to the boot and remove the inner tank cover.

The valve controls the inner pressure, which in normal circumstances improves fuel supply and counteracts the forming of bubbles created by the pump. If an overpressure of 30 to 50MBDar is exceeded in the tank, the valve will open and allow vapour to flow to the charcoal canister under the wing. Alternatively, if a 1 to 16MBDar of vacuum is produced by the tank, the valve will open and admit air in to the tank via the evaporation/charcoal canister under the wing.

*Locate the pressure-relief valve, Part number A 1234700393, just above the left-hand driveshaft.*

## DRIVE BELT

Check the condition of the drive belts before you start to hear a squealing sound. Regular checks can prevent a breakdown and possibly extra damage caused by a belt jumping or disintegrating while at full speed. Get into the habit of visually inspecting the belts every time you open the bonnet. If you see polished rubber, scuffs or a glazed section it could indicate overheating or slipping, which could be a precursor to cracking or shredding under load. Pinch, squeeze and twist the

belts, looking for cracks, fraying, splits or brittle places. On a serpentine belt, also look for missing grooves or places where the belt's layers have separated.

Inspect the pulleys and tensioners, looking for any signs of rubber deposits, uneven shiny spots or rough edges. Ensure all the pulleys line up as they should and wiggle them to check whether they are secure.

Check the belt tension. There should be no more than one-half to one inch (12mm to 25mm) of give across the longest run of the belt.

*Remember, the power-steering belts must be replaced only in matched pairs.*

Anything that seems to be amiss should be taken care of as soon as reasonably possible, as belts can easily shred radiator and gearbox coolant hoses on the path outwards.

## IGNITION

All petrol versions of the 126 are reliant on a good ignition system, from the EZL (ignition module) to the spark plugs.

### EZL IGNITION MODULES

There are various types of ignition module, depending on the age and size of the engine, but as time wears on it seems that some are becoming a little more fragile, especially the eight-pin versions in the later M117 engines. There is not much you can do to preserve them, as they are sealed units. However, there are a number of issues that seem to accelerate their demise: not disconnecting the battery when playing with anything electrical; booster-charging the battery; OVP relay failure; incorrect spark plugs; and heat and damp, to name but a few. The EZL and the terminal plugs must be kept clean from debris and dust.

Unbolt the unit from the body to make sure the white heat-sink paste is still intact; there are more modern options available now in the form of heat-sink sheets, so re-pasting may not be necessary. It

**TIP:** Remove the dirt from the spark-plug recesses using a clean brush, vacuum cleaner or compressed air before removing the plugs, to prevent dirt dropping into the cylinders.

might even be possible to use a small 12V computer fan to keep it cool.

### SPARK PLUGS

The correct functioning of the spark plugs is vital for the proper running and efficiency of the engine. Because of this, it is essential that the plugs are of the appropriate non-resistor type, as detailed in the 'Service Specifications' section.

In this day and age, spark-plug cleaning is rarely necessary if the engine is in good condition. In general, the spark plugs should not need attention between scheduled replacement intervals, however, it is always worth taking a cursory look during a service as this will give you a relatively accurate idea of how well the engine is running and could alert you to any impending problems.

If the marks on the original-equipment spark plug (HT) leads cannot be seen, label the leads to correspond to the cylinder that the lead serves.

# Spark Plug Condition

**Normal:**
Even biscuit brown colour.
Lightly coated core.
Electrode grey in colour.
Ideally suited to engine.
Engine in good order.

**Oil Fouled**
Wet and oily deposits.
Worn bores and/or piston rings.
Worn valve guides.
Occurs sometimes after running in.

**Carbon and Soot Fouled:**
Dry, black, sooty deposits.
Over fuelling.
Over rich mixture.
Faulty ignition system.

**Lean Mixture:**
Signs of overheating.
Glazed appearance.
Patchy white smooth deposits.
Fuel mixture too weak.
Incorrect octane rating.

*Examination of the spark plugs will give a good indication of the condition of the engine as well as combustion.*

Pull the leads from the plugs by gripping the end fitting, not the lead, otherwise the lead connection may be fractured. Unscrew the plugs using a spark-plug spanner, suitable box spanner or a deep socket and extension bar. Keep the socket aligned with the spark plug as best as possible; if it is forcibly moved to one side, the ceramic insulator may be broken off or cracked.

The condition of the spark plugs will tell you how the engine is running:

- If the insulator nose of the spark plug is clean and white, with no deposits, this is indicative of a weak mixture or too hot a plug (a hot plug transfers heat away from the electrode slowly; a cold plug transfers heat away quickly).
- If the tip and insulator nose are covered with hard black-looking deposits, this is indicative that the mixture is too rich.
- Should the plug be black and oily, it is likely that the engine is fairly worn, as well as the mixture being too rich.

- If the insulator nose is covered with light tan to greyish-brown deposits, the mixture is correct and it is likely that the engine is in good condition.

The spark-plug electrode gap is of considerable importance – if it is too large or too small, the size of the spark and its efficiency will be seriously impaired. The gap should be set to between .032 and .035 for optimum performance. To set the gap, measure it with a feeler blade and then bend open, or close, the outer plug electrode until the correct gap is achieved. The centre electrode should never be forced, as this may crack the insulator and cause plug failure.

If using feeler blades, the gap is correct when the appropriately sized blade is a firm sliding fit. Do not attempt to adjust electrodes using a hammer or screwdriver. Special spark-plug electrode-gap-adjusting tools are available very cheaply from most motor accessory shops or from some spark-plug manufacturers.

Over time, the spark-plug holes can get grubby and contaminated, making it difficult to insert spark plugs without cross-threading them, especially in an

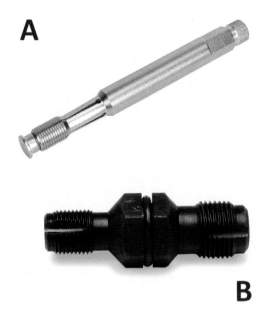

A

B

*Consider using a spark-plug thread cleaner.*

aluminium cylinder head. The reverse-thread chaser (A) is the best option as it clears debris on the way out, whereas the other style of thread chaser (B) cleans the thread going in and, although it has a 'pick-up' slot, you do run a risk of dropping dirt into the bore.

Refit the remaining spark plugs in the same manner. Connect the HT leads in their correct order, and refit any components removed for access.

## IGNITION DISTRIBUTOR

The 126 has been referred to as one of the smoothest cars in the world and much of this praise can be

**TIP:** When refitting a plug, fit a short length of five-sixteenths of an inch internal diameter rubber hose over its end. This will act as a flexible joint to help align the plug with the plug hole. Should the plug begin to cross-thread, you will feel it in the hose as it bites and slips in time to prevent thread damage to the cylinder head. Once it is seated, tighten the plug to the specified torque using the spark-plug socket and a torque wrench.

attributed to the ignition system. The ignition distributor has an extremely important role in keeping the engine balanced between smoothness and efficiency and even the slightest fault can leave the car with frustrating misfires and hesitations.

While the distributor itself should last the life of the car, there are several components that need regular checking, servicing or replacement over time.

The OEM 126 distributor cap has a dual plastic cover; the first cover fits over the orange cap, which provides locating slots for an external shroud that covers the lead ends to tidy everything up. The V8 M116/7 cap has three screws holding it in place. Sometimes, dissimilar-metal corrosion rears its ugly head, between the brass, steel and aluminium, and these can get very stuck. Dab a little anti-seize grease on them before you refit them.

The M103 engine has three turnkey-type screws that pop up as you turn them a quarter turn.

Turn the cap over and check for scorch (arcing) marks on the contact points. Excessive carbon dust inside the cap could also be an indication that the centre carbon electrode has worn. While the cap is off, remove the rotor arm. Check for wear and corresponding arcing marks.

You should notice a keyway in the rotor arm (A) and a corresponding slot on the distributor spindle; do not try and force the rotor arm to fit on any other way than sliding it into the guide key. Under the rotor arm is a plastic sealing plate (B). Keep this safe.

If either the cap or the rotor needs to be replaced, it is always a good idea to replace both at the same time. The M116/7 V8s cap and rotor arm very rarely need replacing within 100,000km but keep a check on them anyway. The M103's, however, seem to need replacing closer to around every 25,000km.

*Thoroughly inspect the cap and rotor arm for any signs of cracks and wear.*

## HT PLUG LEADS

The high-tension circuits are the veins of the engine. Age, heat, oil and fuel vapours are just a few of the issues that will contribute to the deterioration of the HT plug lead wires. The outer insulation sleeve breaks down and sparks stop flowing smoothly, causing rough idle, engine hesitation, hunting, surging or missing.

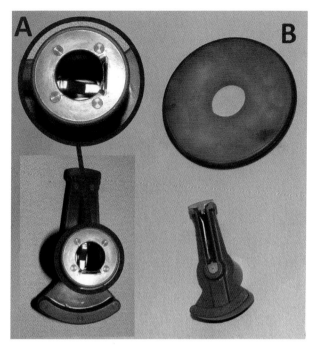

*When refitting the rotor, do not forget the shield and ensure it locates correctly.*

Worse still, the high resistance will stop the flow completely, sending sparks to the nearest ground.

The best way to check HT lead integrity is visually. If all looks well but you are none the less experienc-

*If you do source your leads from an alternative supplier, you need to ensure that they are 'resistor' leads.*

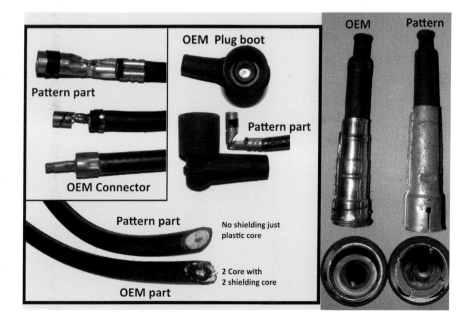

Pattern part

OEM Plug boot

Pattern part

OEM Connector

Pattern part

No shielding just plastic core

2 Core with 2 shielding core

OEM part

OEM     Pattern

ing any of the aforementioned problems, test with a multimeter. New OEM Bosch leads should read around 1.5k to 2.0k ohms from end to end but this can be as high as 7.0k ohms on older leads.

Lead sets are very expensive from MBD directly, but Bosch and BERU sets are available independently and these were both OEM. Again, OEM is by far the best way to go for something so important.

## SUSPENSION, STEERING AND FINAL DRIVE

### STEERING AND BEARINGS

With the car standing on its wheels, have an assistant turn the steering wheel back and forth about an eighth of a turn each way. There should be very little lost movement between the steering wheel and the road wheels. If this is not the case, closely observe the linkage joints and mountings; in addition, check the steering-column universal joint/coupling for wear, and the steering box itself.

Next, raise the front of the vehicle, and support it securely on axle stands. Before removing the road wheels, grasp each one at the 12 o'clock and 6 o'clock positions, and try to rock it back and forth. There

should be no discernible free play, but if any movement is felt, further investigation is necessary to determine the source. Continue rocking the wheel while an assistant depresses the footbrake. If the movement is now eliminated or significantly reduced, it is likely that the hub bearings are at fault. If the free play is still evident with the footbrake depressed, then there is probably some wear in the suspension joints or mountings.

A small amount of play to the front hub bearings is adjustable by removing the bearing cap and tightening the nut, however, the play is better rectified by removing the brake disc, cleaning out the old grease and repacking. If this does not work, a new pair of bearings will be needed (see the 'Brake and Bearing Overhaul' section).

Now grasp the wheel at the 9 o'clock and 3 o'clock positions, and try to rock it as before. Any movement felt now may again be caused by wear in the hub bearings but it could also be attributed to the steering track-rod ball joints. There is a pair on each side and, if they are very worn, it may be possible to spot by eye. If not, it may be necessary to have an assistant move the wheel while you put your hand over each joint to see if you can feel any movement.

Visually inspect all the ball-joint dust covers for splits, chafing or deterioration. Any wear of these

*Apart from checking fluid leaks from the pump, remember to check the steering-box mounting bolts every year.*

components will cause loss of lubricant, together with dirt and water ingress, resulting in rapid deterioration of the ball joints.

Just to double check, ask someone to turn the steering wheel (without getting in the car) in small increments to identify any slack in the joints. Visually check the steering damper for function and leaks. Replace if even the slightest fluid leak is detected.

Check that the steering-box mountings are tightened to the specified torque settings, and look for signs of fluid leakage under pressure from the steering box, which would indicate failed fluid seals within the box. Check all the fluid hoses from steering box to pump for chafing or deterioration, not forgetting to examine the pipe and hose unions for fluid leaks.

## SUSPENSION STRUT/SHOCK ABSORBER

Using a large screwdriver or flat bar, check for wear in the suspension mounting bushes by levering between the relevant suspension component and its attachment point. Some movement is to be expected, as the mountings are made of rubber, but excessive wear should be obvious. Check the condition of any visible rubber bushes, looking for splits, cracks or contamination of the rubber.

Check for any signs of fluid leakage around the suspension strut/shock absorber body, or from the rubber gaiter around the piston rod. Should any fluid be noticed, the suspension strut/shock absorber is defective internally, and will need to be renewed. Suspension struts/shock absorbers should always be renewed in pairs on the same axle.

It is possible to check the efficiency of the suspension strut/ shock absorber by bouncing the vehicle at each corner. Generally speaking, the body should return to its normal position and stop after being depressed. If it rebounds a number of times, the suspension strut/ shock absorber is probably suspect.

The suspension strut/shock absorber upper and lower mountings should also be checked for any signs of wear.

## DRIVESHAFT CHECKS

With the vehicle raised and securely supported on stands, have an assistant slowly rotate the rear road wheel as you inspect the condition of the outer and inner constant velocity (CV) joint for wear or noise. Any appreciable movement indicates wear in the joints, wear in the driveshaft splines, or a loose driveshaft retaining nut.

Check the rubber gaiters by manipulating to open out the folds. Look for signs of cracking, splits or

*There is reasonable access to check the half shafts visually, but you can consider removal if necessary.*

*Remove the 13mm half-shaft retaining nut and washer from the hub centre (B), then remove the six spline bolts holding the half shaft to the diff flange using a No. 12 spline tool (A).*

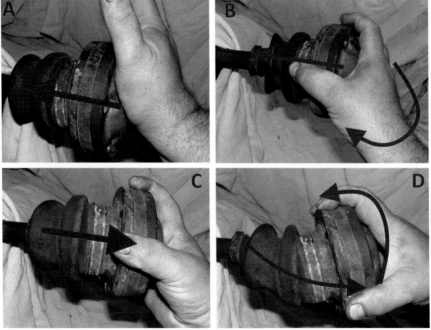

*Hold the shaft in a vice if possible and manipulate the joints in every direction.*

deterioration of the rubber, which may allow the grease to escape, and lead to water and grit ingress into the joint.

There has been some discussion that swapping over each complete half shaft will encourage longevity, as it changes the development of forward wear pattern; this may seem a good idea in theory, but it would probably only be beneficial if done on a regular basis from new, not just once after twenty years.

If you are unsure about the condition of the CV joints or need to renew a rubber gaiter or just the grease, it is not too difficult to remove the half shafts completely.

*The centre support bearing is an amalgamation of a large bearing set in rubber.*

To check the joints in all directions, hold the shaft in a fixed vice. It is necessary to check the joint in both compressed (A) and extended (C) form. The CV joint will obviously not turn on the shaft but, while compressing, rotate the swivel to check for any notchiness (B). Repeat the process while extending the shaft (D) and also about halfway between the two.

There are two flexible propshaft couplings (also referred to as 'doughnuts'); one joins the propshaft to the gearbox and the other joins the other end of the propshaft to the final drive unit. There is also a very important central support bearing where the two propshafts meet.

Check the rubber for any separation from the outer metal ring and check the bearing for any play. If they are worn, they may also make a 'thrumming' vibration noise through the floor when the car is being driven. If they are left for an extended period of time, the vibration can encourage them to break free from their rubber mounting, causing real problems.

## BRAKES

If the brake situation is an extreme one, you will need to carry out a complete overhaul; for more information on this, see the relevant section later in the book. As always, however, the more attention you give these items, the less likely it is that you will have to do a complete overhaul.

The 126 uses a combination of manufacturers, but the systems are all the same. Brake servo units are either Girling or ATE. Calipers are either Bendix or ATE, or a combination of the two. There is very little difference between them and to the untrained eye the only way to identify them – apart from spotting the manufacturer's name on the side, which is usually difficult to see – was the wire pad retaining clips used by Bendix and the sprung plate used by ATE. Confusingly, however, after around 1988 Bendix calipers employed a similar spring plate to the ATE set-up. Sometimes the roll pins that held the Bendix pads in place did not have the interference collar, but had little tiny pin retaining clips also. There was no difference in the actual pad for either the Bendix or the ATE calipers.

New calipers are still available OEM at about £70 each so all is not lost if you prefer to change for new. Alternatively, there are plenty of companies willing to refurbish the old ones for around £40, including a bright coat of paint if your heart so desires.

Note: if an excess of dust is found, do not attempt to blow it out with an air line. Use a proprietary brake cleaner instead.

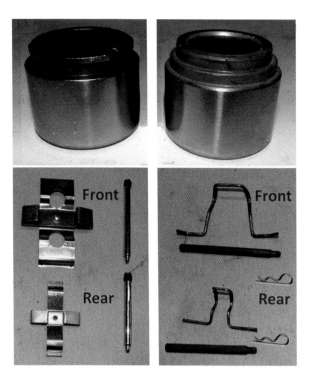

*Internally, the pistons are slightly different, as are the external rubber dust seals.*

*New calipers remain available and should be replaced in pairs.*

## FRONT AND REAR BRAKES

Firmly apply the handbrake/parking brake and put the gearbox into 'Park'. Jack up the front of the car and support it securely on axle stands. Remove the front road wheels.

For a comprehensive check, the brake pads should be removed, the dust seals and the operation of the caliper checked and all the excess dust cleaned away.

Turn the discs to check the condition of their faces and the overall thickness. If any of the pad's friction material is worn down to the minimum specified thickness, all four pads must be renewed as a set.

Visually check the condition of the flexible brake hoses.

## HANDBRAKE/PARKING BRAKE

The use of the handbrake/parking brake is often neglected in a vehicle with an automatic gearbox, with drivers habitually relying on the 'Park' facility instead. To check the shoes properly and to clean out the dust it will be necessary to remove the rear calipers and discs, to expose the brake shoes. However,

the handbrake/parking brake can be adjusted, and this should be done if the pedal or lever can be depressed or pulled more than four notches. (For more information, see the 'Brake Overhaul' section.)

## LUBRICATION

Something as simple as a regular lubrication regime can be the backbone of preventive maintenance. However, car owners have become so accustomed to sealed-for-life items on newer vehicles that many have forgotten how to do it. A considerable amount of failure of an item is down to either no lubrication maintenance or the wrong lubrication. Correct lubrication has the potential to preserve the functionality of a part, perhaps for the life of the vehicle. It is important to use the correct type of grease and also to apply it in the right place; it is not just about plastering the part with any random grease pot or long-nosed aerosol lying around the garage.

There are no quick fixes and it takes time. The sunroof mechanism is a case in point, involving a

*Part of my collection of application tools.*

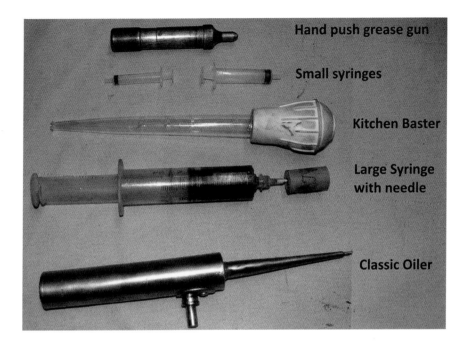

Hand push grease gun

Small syringes

Kitchen Baster

Large Syringe with needle

Classic Oiler

mixture of different types of plastics, nylons and metals in the unit; and the over-use of generic petroleum-based greases is the main reason why parts become fragile. The website bevo.mercedes-benz.com gives information on the correct grease to use for specific items. It is not vital to go to MBD every time you need a pot of grease, but the website will give the correct type as well as alternatives.

## ACCELERATOR LUBRICATION

Problems can arise when the accelerator is neglected, as its joints and knuckles generally sit hidden tucked away under the air filter in the dry heat from the engine. It is absolutely imperative that they are cleaned and lubricated at least once a year and the only way to do this is a long-winded one that involves popping off the knuckles, pivot points, joints, spindles and clips. There are plenty of short cuts you could take but it is not advisable. Do not use spray grease or universal paste grease. Use only ATF or other hydraulic oil; go to bevo.mercedes-benz.com and check 'Sheet 343' for advice.

Every time you carry out a minor service to the engine, make a conscious effort to put a little ATF into a small syringe and freshen up the joints.

Engine M103

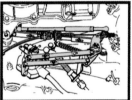

Engine M110

Engine M116 and M117

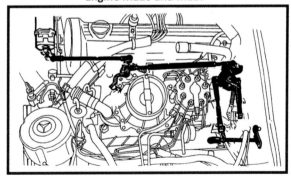

*The accelerator linkage.*

The longitudinal shaft connects the linkage from the bulkhead/firewall to the main linkage and has plastic ball and socket joints that need dismantling, checking and lubricating. The main linkage has push-fit ball and socket and pivot points (B). Ensure the 'regulating rod' (A) moves freely internally via its

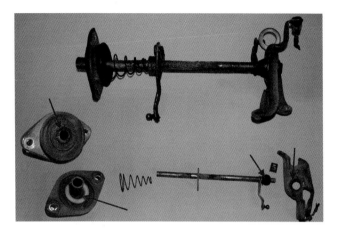

*With a mix of nylon, hard plastic and metal in this area, it is imperative that you lubricate everything regularly.*

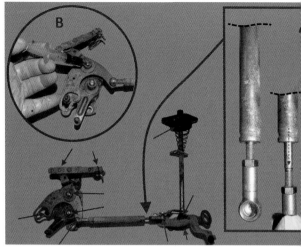

*Check, clean and lubricate all pivot points.*

spring; this damps the action of the accelerator and is essential to smooth running.

## IGNITION DISTRIBUTOR LUBRICATION

If at any point you have to remove the ignition distributor, take the time to lubricate the ignition advance weights, which are located in its base. Look for the little steel access trap in the body and pull this off with a screwdriver. Turn the spindle until you see the two points from which the weights pivot (B). Apply a drop of ATF on each one.

The easier point to lubricate is the rotor spindle (A) which can be attended to any time you remove the cap and rotor. Look for the little felt pad pushed in the centre hole and just dowse it in ATF.

Keep the spindle clear from rust by scrubbing with a scourer or 'wet and dry' paper – do not use wire wool as this may cause tiny bits of wire to fall into the magnetic pick-up.

## BONNET HINGE PIVOT LUBRICATION

The bonnet on the 126 has a complicated system of hinge pivots, which not only allows you to lift the weight with ease but also lifts the bonnet into a vertical position for easy access all around the engine. It is not unknown for these pivots to seize and in extreme conditions to shear off.

*Even the distributor has a couple of lubrication points.*

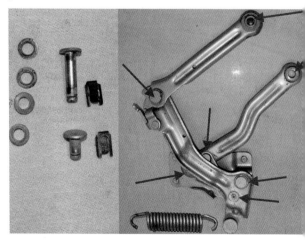

*There are seven pivot points in total, only two of which have removable pins.*

**The first time you carry out a lubrication task on the bonnet hinge pivots, consider removing the roller pins on each side to check for wear to the pin or the nylon collars.**

First, lock the bonnet hinges into their vertical position. It is preferable to remove both pins on each side so you can check the nylon collars for wear and lubricate the pivot point properly, but this should be done only if you have someone to help you to hold the bonnet firmly. Do not attempt it on your own. If you have to carry out the task single-handed, you must remove only one pin at a time. Tap it out with something similar in size – a 10mm bolt should be fine. Remove the spring retaining clip from the inside and tap the pin out towards you, using the bolt to take its place.

Check there is no wear. If it is corroded or dry, clean it up with wire wool. Put a blob of grease on the hole and re-grease the pin so that, as you insert it, it pushes the grease through with it. The pin head has a locating bar that must match up with the corresponding notch on the bonnet (A).

You will be surprised how easy it is to lift the sprung-weight-compensated bonnet when it all moves freely. If you still feel there is some resistance from the hinges, you may need to consider removing the bonnet completely and work on the pivot points individually. Again, do not attempt this on your own. To carry out this task safely, three people are needed – one at each hinge to support the bonnet and one to remove all the pins.

**Push the pins out with something of similar size.**

Protect the front windscreen from any slip-ups with a sheet of cardboard and a dust sheet and set up a table, or at least a couple of trestles, to place the bonnet on. Do not forget to disconnect the screen-wash tubing from the motors.

Once the bonnet has been removed, remove the large spring, but make sure you remember its location – there are a couple of 'spare' notches in the attachment plate.

**If you prefer not to drop the bonnet shut, lower it by hand and push it from the top of the grille frame, to avoid denting the panel; this is especially important for the aluminium bonnet.**

Using a syringe with a long nose or needle, apply drops of ATF and then swing the arm back and forth to work the oil in. If you have a compressor, shroud the area with a cloth and use the air gun to push fluid into the joints while manipulating the arms until they are moving freely again. Place them in the upright position and reattach the spring before refitting the bonnet.

The bonnet should hold itself in the first position and you will be able to open and close it with consummate ease, assisted by the spring.

## BONNET LATCH LUBRICATION

The aluminium 126 bonnet may be lowered by hand and then pushed shut from the top of the grille frame, so there is no risk of denting the panel. To close the steel version, you should be able to drop it from about 30cm and both latches should click cleanly into place.

Even though the two bonnet latches sit behind the bonnet edge they are still exposed to the elements. If they are over-packed with grease they will collect road grit and start to stiffen up. Occasionally, the bonnet latches may jam completely and releasing the bonnet may well cause damage to it.

To clean the latches properly it is much better to remove the headlights and take the latches out to soak. This will also give you access to check and lubricate the pull cable. Otherwise, flushing the latches out with WD40 or alternative grease cleaner and a bottle brush should suffice.

*Access to the latch is via the removal of the headlight side cover; pull the pin and post and slide the shroud upwards to release it.*

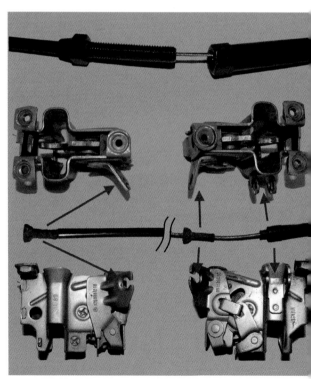

*A full strip-out and clean is a lot less frustrating than trying to open or close a sticking bonnet on your own.*

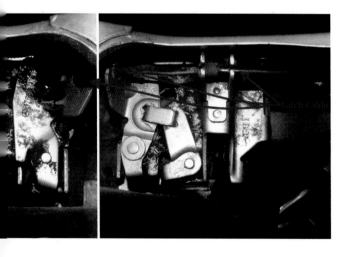

*The bonnet latches easily pick up road grime.*

## DOOR LOCK AND HINGE LUBRICATION

The doors are extremely heavy, solid items and re-greasing them will keep the hinges smooth and free from wear. Due to the position of the hinges, a flush concave nipple has been used so you may need to acquire the correct grease-gun end. It is possible to adapt an old hand-pump grease gun, but you can also buy a pointed nozzle for a standard grease gun that will push in the nipple bearing as it loads.

Pump the gun until the dirty grease squeezing out from between the hinge gaps changes to clean grease.

The latches involve an incredibly complicated mechanism and they are not easy to remove from inside the door – they have to be manipulated at the correct angle before they can be withdrawn past the window runners. You can try to lubricate the correct parts while they are still in place, but this is not the easiest thing to do either. You may prefer to delay carrying out a 'proper job' until you have occasion to remove a door panel.

## DOOR-CHECKS LUBRICATION AND REBUILD

As with most things Mercedes, the door-check levers are not merely the simple pressed-steel, flimsy affairs found in an ordinary vehicle. The frames are made from 3mm thick steel and contain two 15mm hardened ball bearings held under tension by an extremely strong spring. The only way to lubricate them is to remove the unit; no amount of spraying, with or without a straw nozzle, will get the grease into the correct places. Again, it is perhaps another job to add to the list when the door panels are off.

If you start to hear a 'graunching' noise when opening and closing the door, it is time to consider it sooner rather than later. It is not unknown for them to lock up completely and nine times out of ten it will be in the fully open position – and inevitably at the most inappropriate time.

To remove, first remove the door panel (see the 'Interior' section). Remove the spring clip (1) from the bottom of the roller pin (2) and tap the pin upwards, making sure you do not lose the little plastic spacer washer. Undo bolts 3 and 4 from the

*Not many owners realize that there are grease load nipples on all four door hinges.*

*At the very minimum, regularly clean the external door latch.*

inner edge and then undo bolt 5 from the inner flat skin, remembering that the check unit will now drop if you allow it to.

The front units usually have a black plastic sleeve; just slide this off. Using a paint brush and degreaser, brush away all the old grease so you can check the slider channels.

It is not difficult to grease the tracks, but this is only a small part of the job. Unfortunately, the only way to see whether the ball bearings are still up to

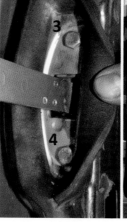

Be aware that, once the door check has been removed, the door will float freely. Allowing it to fall open or pushing it too far could result in damage.

An old door-check frame cut in half, to show what happens to the track as it starts to corrode (A). Coupled with corroded ball bearings (B), it is easy to see why it locks up.

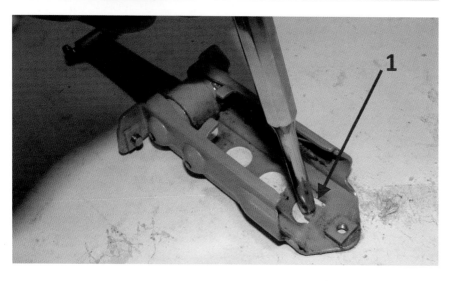

In order to dismantle the arm from the cage you will need to straighten a small tab at the back that prevents the arm falling out. The first thing to do is to knock this flat.

scratch is to dismantle it. Care must be taken as the spring is very strong and may fling the ball bearing into a far corner.

Although complete originals are still available from MBD they are quite expensive at around £50 each; pattern parts are available, but the quality may be suspect. You could try buying a pack of twenty high-quality 15mm ball bearings for around £15 and experiment. If you do so, ensure you clean any corrosion off the cage track using wire wool or 'wet and dry' silicon carbide paper and re-grease the track with good-quality lithium grease. Refit the collars and pack with grease before sliding in the spring. Use one hand to hold the cage firmly and the other to guide the arm and bearings into place; they will be slippery with grease, so exercise care.

Line up the top bearing (A) with one hand and use the other to steady the cage in place, then, using both of your thumbs, push the bearing against the spring (B). It is very strong but doable.

As you feel the bearings give, pull your hand round in an arc (C) while pushing forwards; it should just slide into the first recess.

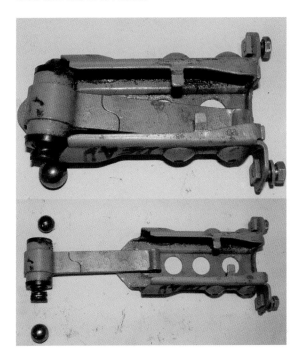

*Gather the parts, clean them thoroughly and check them over.*

*Before you consider knocking the arm out, wrap it in a thick cloth. Using a soft-faced hammer or mallet, tap it sharply to move it to the next recess. Make sure you have a tight grip and tap it again, remembering that this time it will leave the cage with a snap.*

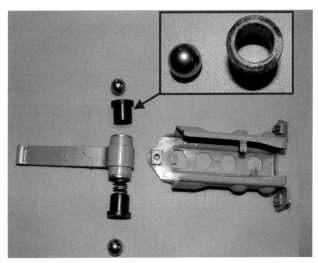

*The ball bearings should be bright and shiny without any flat spots or corrosion and the black plastic sleeves should be a tight fit and not worn oval by the spring.*

You will need to bend up the two cage tabs (A) to lift the arm back over into place (B). Flatten the cage tab that controls arm lift (C) and straighten the end-stop tab back into place (D).

If you have sourced a second-hand or new item, the check-strap bar (E) should be body colour.

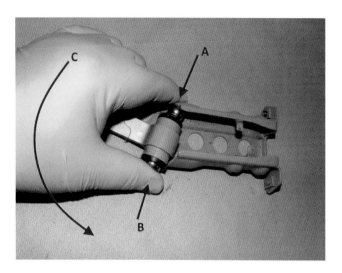

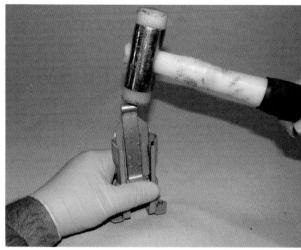

Reinstating the arm in to the cage requires strong fingers and thumbs.

Carefully turn the cage on its end and tap the arm down firmly until it reaches the base recess again.

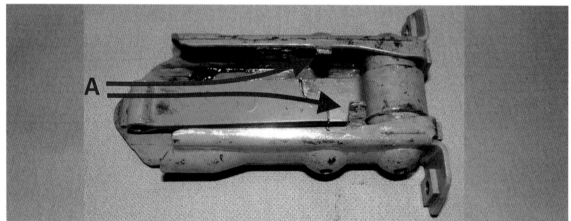

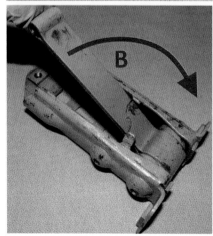

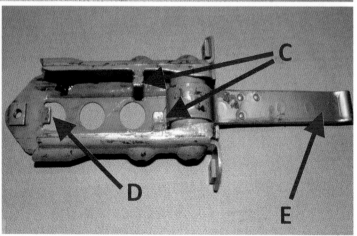

Swing the arm back into place.

Finally, clean and grease the roller pin ready to reinstall.

From fully open, the door should hold firmly then close to half set, holding firmly in that position too. The final stage of the check should catch the door just at the end and assist with latching it shut. The action should be firm, smooth and quiet.

## DOOR-LOCK BARRELS LUBRICATION

Of all the lubrication jobs on any vehicle, the door-lock barrels remain the most frequently forgotten; at least, that is, until they stop working. At that point, the first port of call is usually a can of WD40. WD40 might have 101 general-household uses, but it has no place as a final solution in the garage. It might clean off a sticky residue after tape removal or wash out a bolt thread, but it is no good as a permanent lubricator. 'WD' stands for 'water displacement', and that is what the product does best. It will also degrease to some extent, however, when the carrier has dispersed, the miniscule amount of oil left is not enough to lubricate sufficiently. To top it all, its non-drying coating just attracts more dirt. The crux of the matter is that it is a quick-fix solution that is not appropriate for any lock, least of all on a 126.

Locks should be an essential part of a lubrication service for two reasons. Any lock barrel relies on fine machine tolerances to enable it to work correctly and these tolerances are easily undermined, even in normal use.

Repeated insertion and twisting of the key into the locking mechanism will begin to impact dirt and grit into every free space of the mechanism, however miniscule, and it will not take much for the delicate parts to clog and eventually jam. The finally important consideration is that adding all this to a lock that has lacked lubrication over an extended period will undermine the security of the lock, to the point at which it could be turned with a small screwdriver.

If you have never done it before, you are unsure as to the condition of the barrels or they feel slow or notchy to turn, especially in the winter, it is worth taking the time to remove the handle completely.

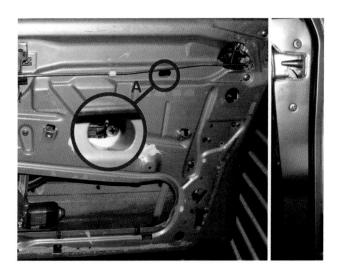

*Removing the handle is a two-minute job while the door panels are off.*

*The rear handles will simply come loose, but the front handles need to be held steady and removed using the key.*

There are two large Philips-head screws holding the handle in place, one (A) behind the door panel and accessed through a small hole in the inner skin, and

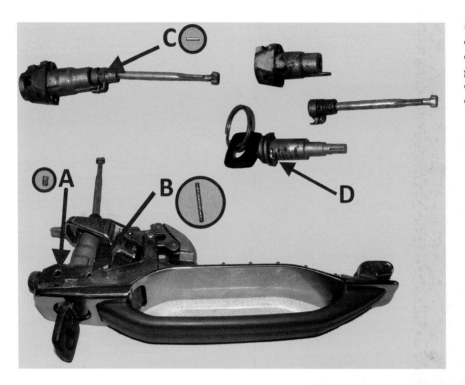

*Use an old dinner tray when dismantling small parts; if anything drops, it should not end up on the floor.*

the other (B) in the door shut behind a black plastic cover cap, which just pulls off.

The front door handle will fall loose but will not fall out unless you insert the door key and turn it a quarter turn as you withdraw it from its position, to release it from its keyway slot.

Although you may be able to flush the barrel through, there is no way of doing a thorough job without removing the barrel from the handle. Although it will take a little time and care, it is not difficult. First, remove the black gasket trim around the handle before you start knocking it about. It is fairly brittle and might snap if you catch it on something. It is best to heat the gasket with a hot air gun or hairdryer; alternatively, dip the complete handle in hot water for a couple of minutes so it becomes supple enough to remove. Return it to the hot water or warm it up to reinstate it too.

There are two roller pins holding the barrel in the handle; one (B) passes all the way through so is easily knocked through; the smaller one (A) is a little fiddly as you have to put in a small screwdriver or bradawl and then turn and lift at the same time. It is quite small, so take care not to lose it. You will be able

*A lock barrel just after removal, clogged up with dry, greasy grit.*

to push the barrel out, without the key in place, and manipulate it into a position to withdraw completely.

Before you remove the tiny roller pin (C) that holds the lock shaft, reinsert the key as this will stop all the little levers and springs going 'ping' if the barrel drops out.

Soak the lock barrel in petrol or white spirit and brush it clean, taking care not to soak the plastic part of the key. Do not remove the key at this point unless

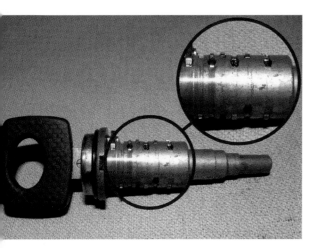

*With the barrel cleaned you will be able to see if there are any raised levers, which indicates wear in the key or the levers themselves.*

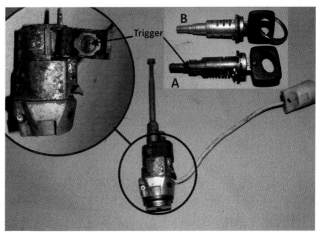

*Later-style trigger barrel used in conjunction with a factory alarm.*

you know exactly what you are doing – the levers are small, but the springs are minute.

If you have a compressor, use a small air-jet nozzle to blow out the holes and crevices. Only when everything is clean and dry, is it time to lubricate. Graphite powder is the best lubricant to use on locks, as it remains dry and will not attract dust, grit or moisture. Aerosol-based graphite is available for ease of use now, with a carrier that flows the graphite into the lock and then evaporates. This is ideal for later applications when you are not dismantling it all.

The later lock barrels have a wire and plug attached, which acts as a trigger (A) for the alarm and pump. With the barrel removed, you can ensure that the insert is thoroughly cleaned.

## SUNROOF MECHANISM LUBRICATION

Many 126 owners seem to be very nervous about doing any work on the sunroof, which ironically is probably one of the reasons it often fails to work correctly or jams up. Although it can be complicated and expensive to put right when it goes wrong, basic maintenance is not difficult.

Only the MBD sunroof paste – Gleitpaste Part # A0019891451 – should be used. It is expensive, as it is supplied only in a 500g tin, so it might be a

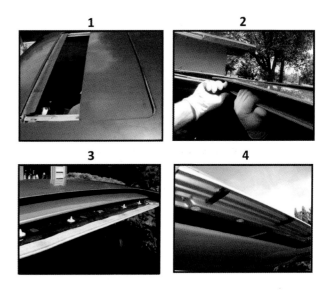

*Once a year at least you should be removing the lid under cover to give you better access to the majority of the mechanism, the main track and the drain holes.*

good idea to get together with fellow owners or club members to do a group buy.

The maintenance procedure is as follows:

1) Open the sunroof about halfway on its slide mechanism.
2) Push a flat screwdriver or trim remover between the cover and the metal of the lid.

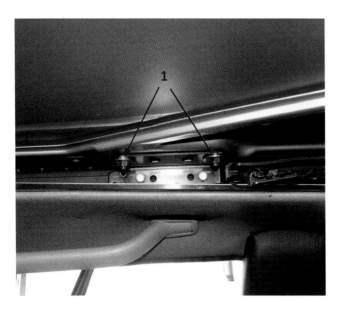

*Removing the lid involves just four bolts and makes accessing the mechanism easier.*

*Late-Generation 1 and Generation 2 vehicles had a tilt mechanism.*

**3)** Once all four of the post fixings have released; pull the cover forward slightly.

**4)** Pull back the sunroof again and pull the cover all the way forward to release.

**5)** Clean out the leaves and debris that accumulate in the back of the cassette and on the lid cover.

**6)** Then, either close the lid, mark the position of the bracket and unbolt it. This is by far the preferred method as you will be able to access a lot more of the mechanism and track.

**7)** Or move the lid back and forth as you access the moving parts and each part of the track.

**8)** For the Generation 2 models that have the lift/tilt facility, bring the lid right forward, and set the tilt/lift to its maximum. This not only allows access to the arms but also allows you to reach the back part of the track, as well as the rear drain holes.

**9)** Use a long flexible rod to access the drain holes; make sure the end is not sharp, as you could very easily push it through the rubber tubes that extend from the cassette.

The sunroof mechanism is not a fragile item, but misuse, bad lubrication and lack of maintenance will finish it. One lift arm will cost nearly £350 from the

*Run something flexible through the front drains to ensure they are free from debris.*

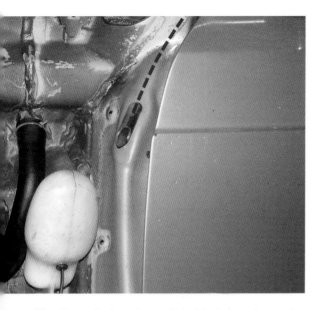

*The front drain tubes exit behind the wing and are accessible by opening the front doors.*

*Access to rear drains is not so easy.*

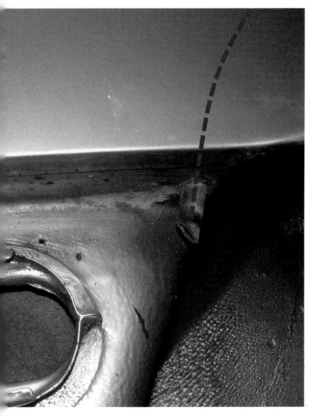

*The rear drain tubes exit just inside the rear bumper but you may have to remove the shield to see it.*

main dealer so it pays dividends to make sure it is well looked after.

## WINDSCREEN-WIPER MECHANISM LUBRICATION

According to MBD, the 'wiper console unit', as it is referred to, is available only on back order. There is no date given and, more importantly, no individual parts are available. This is not good news for such a complicated mechanism and for a unit that cannot be overlooked, as there is a legal requirement for it to work exactly as it should. As with most things MBD, however, problems are avoidable with a little maintenance and time.

(**Note:** both left-hand-drive and right-hand-drive versions of the console are shown. Although there are a few differences, the process is the same.)

As with any wiper mechanism, the most vulnerable areas are the pivot points and the ball joints. The length of the spindles on the 126 can also exacerbate the problem if they are not properly lubricated. The illustration shows the results of issues of moisture penetration due to broken rubber O-rings and no lubrication. There should have been an O-ring on the top of ball joint (B). This is the ball joint that gets bolted to the small thread on the rusty spindle (C).

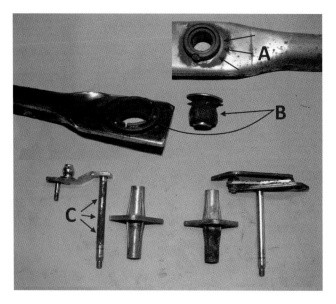

*Although the owner was unaware that there was a problem until he took his car for its MOT, and the wipers were working, the technician decided that the wipers were moving too slowly to pass the test.*

Clearly, there has been a detrimental effect of the rust gripping the spindle and ball joint on the joint (A). The joint should be solidly in place but the wear marks show how much it now moves inside the socket.

At first glance, it is difficult even to see the wipers. It was a great, aesthetically pleasing design by Bruno Sacco for MBD, intended to cut down on wind noise through the exposed blades, as well as keeping the blades tight against the screen. Most manufacturers have taken to adding little wind deflectors on the wiper arms themselves.

### Removing the Blades

There are a number of ways to remove the blades. It is possible to remove them with the bonnet in its first open position but it will mean having to stretch over it or under it to reach them and there is always the possibility that the bonnet might close on you if you knock it. It is much better to latch the bonnet in its vertical position first. You can also make it easier to remove the blades by activating the wipers and switching off the ignition when they reach a third way up the screen.

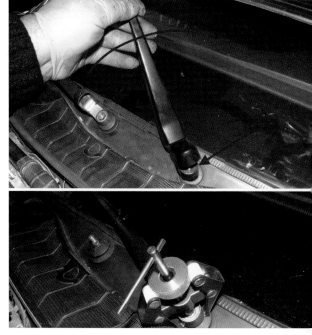

*Removing the wipers is the only way to access the mechanism.*

First, lift the plastic cap that covers the spindle to reveal the fixing nut. The best way to do this is to swing the wiper arm up vertically with one hand while gripping the plastic end cap with the other; the act of swinging the arm up then back down loosens the cap enough for you to pull it up.

Look for the nut in a little recess and remove it using a 13mm socket or ring spanner. Once this is done, spray a little penetrating fluid around the spindle to assist in releasing the grip. To remove the arm from the spindle, pull the arm back up to the vertical position; the arm pivot has a strong spring and will lock into place.

Hold the blade end with one hand, with the other at the spindle; wiggle from side to side and pull upwards at the spindle as you do so. Try not to turn them on the pivot at this point as it is very easy to strip the locating striations from the aluminium wiper arm. You could end up with the wiper going out of control and possibly doing damage to bodywork or the linkage itself. Sealey produces a cheap, neat extractor tool, which means you will never have to suffer a stuck wiper again.

Once the wipers have been removed, you can proceed. The plastic scuttle cover is in two sections, two-thirds and one-third in overall size. Pull off the rubber seal (A) along the bottom edge and remove the metal clips (B). Remove the screen seal carefully by pulling it up the screen (C); they are steel-wound and easily distorted as they age.

A button clip holds the two parts together (D). Remove the smallest section first by twisting it out from behind the hinge. Lift the front section of the tray (A) while pushing down to release the clips at the screen (B).

There are only three 10mm fixings holding the console. The more awkward factor is the plug as it is fitted on the outside of the bulkhead but threaded through it, so it looks reversed (A). Remove the feed plug (A). To remove the plug from the firewall, push the wings in from the back (B) and turn it back through the bulkhead (C).

Fitting it is a reversal of the procedure: thread it through the bulkhead and click the wings in place.

*Check the rubber seals; they are only loose fit but they limit the amount of water and debris entering the scuttle area and on the wiper unit itself.*

*Exercise care when removing the screen seal as it is NLA (no longer available) from MBD, although you can acquire something 'similar' elsewhere.*

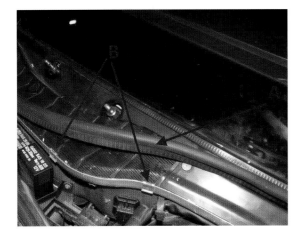

*Remove the bottom seal and clips.*

*Lift the scuttle tray out in two sections.*

*Remove the three fixings to release the console.*

*The console after removal from the vehicle.*

*The plug is awkward to remove.*

## Basic Lubrication

If you prefer not to do any dismantling there are still a few things you can do to make sure the mechanism is well lubricated. All the ball joints have rubber seals that can be cleaned and repacked with grease, and all the plain collar joints can be lubricated with ATF.

The spindles on the other hand are over 4in (10cm) long, inside a tight sleeve that is sealed at both ends by an O-ring, and are a little more difficult to lubricate thoroughly along their entire length. Fit

*The technique may look a little 'Heath Robinson' but it does work in getting ATF down inside the spindle housing and it can also be done with the console remaining in situ.*

a 4in (10cm) tube over the sleeve and tighten the worm clamps thoroughly, then put the airgun nozzle in the opposite end after half-filling the tube with ATF and apply a small amount of air pressure. You should see it working its way out the opposite end of the sleeve.

Consider a more thorough re-grease at some point, especially if you feel the wipers are not operating in a smooth manner.

### Dismantle Lubrication

First, remove the arm connected to the motor – this does not involve removing the motor, or losing any of the positioning, so do not panic. Check the ball and clean and preserve the rubber seal cup.

Removing the arm allows you to push it back and forth, mimicking the motor movement, to check the action. Is there any stiffness in the movement? It should be smooth and there should be no play in any of the joints.

Turning to the spindles, the little spring clip is small and awkward to open but it can be done with a correct positioning of circlip pliers. As it is not the normal-style circlip, with holes in it, it does tend

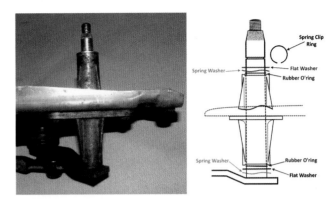

*The spindle locked into the sleeve.*

*Slip a screwdriver or small bar in between and lever carefully; the clip should pop right off.*

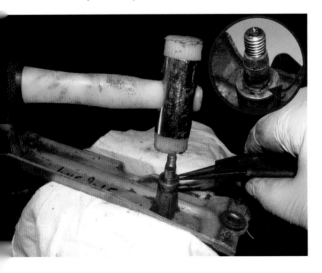

*The easiest way to release the clip is to have circlip pliers in one hand and a soft-face hammer in the other; as you open the clip, hit the top of the spindle sharply. It should be enough to dislodge the clip out of its groove and slide it up the shaft.*

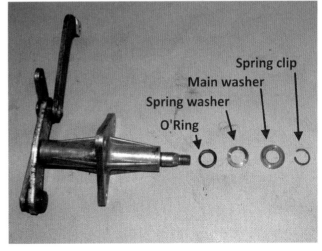

*Keep the spindle fittings in the correct order for ease of replacement.*

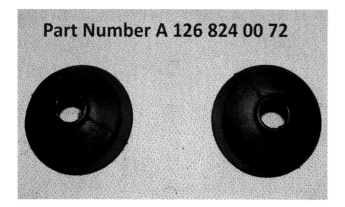

## Part Number A 126 824 00 72

*When refitting the spindles, buy new scuttle to spindle gaskets.*

to slip. Do this to both spindles, then remove the washers and O-rings. You will now be able to slide out both spindles with the linkage attached. Clean with wire wool and ensure they are free from rust; clean the alloy spindle housings thoroughly and apply a blob of grease in either end.

The striations that hold the wiper arms pick up aluminium swarf from the wipers, which stops them from gripping fully, so they need to be cleaned out with a small wire brush. Grease the shafts and reinsert after renewing the O-rings.

Once everything is clean and greased, it is only a matter of yearly lubrication.

### Wiper-Motor Re-Grease

The Bosch motor is a triple-brush, five-wire unit. It is extremely robust, but the composite gear wheel does need to be considered carefully. The use of a composite material relates both to safety and practicality; the motor is of necessity a very strong, high-torque unit and, in the case of an accident in which something jams the wiper arms, the gear will strip, ultimately stopping the wipers. On a practical level the same will happen should the wiper get stuck due to heavy snow or freezing: the gear becomes a shear point to save the motor.

Even though the unit may be working, it is still a good idea to change the grease in the gear unit. This will certainly add a few more years to its life. The grease tends to harden to a treacle-like substance, which has no flow movement and is pretty much

*Remove the main drive arm.*

useless as a lubricant. Following these instructions carefully, you will be able to remove the gear, clean out the hardened pack of grease and replenish with new, without creating any park timing issues. It will give your motor a new lease of life.

First, pop the arm joint that attaches to the motor spindle regulating arm with the spring on it (1) and then mark the position of this arm on to the aluminium console (A-A). Remove the spindle bolt (B) and spring washer and lever up the regulating arm carefully so as not to rotate the motor. Remove the motor mount bolts (C).

You will see on the back side of the gear case that there are three slot-head screws (1, 2, 3, 4). Remove these and keep them safe. Turn the unit over and remove the spindle circlip (A). Using a narrow punch, tap the pin locators (1a and 2a) alternately, a little at a time, to loosen the cover. Once the cover has started to open, turn it back over and pull the lid up by hand, gently wiggling it. Once the lid has been removed, you will see the condition of the composite wheel. You should be able to push the spindle and pull out this gearwheel with ease. Do not lose the little bearing (A).

You can see that the alignment of the contacts on the lid (A-A) line up with the locating pin, this enables you to line up the 'Park' indentation (C) in the gearwheel with the locating pin hole (B-B),

*Remove the casing screws to gain access to the gear wheel.*

*Carefully push the gear wheel out by the spindle. Take care not to lose the little bearing.*

*Clean the gear casing and composite gear thoroughly, ready to repack with new grease.*

*Ensure the park mechanism is positioned correctly by reconnecting the motor and running it through its cycle of on and off.*

*Refit the wiper arms, with the cranked one closest to the bottom of the screen.*

only after brushing in new grease. Refit the spindle circlip and the little ball bearing before refitting the lid.

The easiest way to ensure the park mechanism is positioned correctly is to reconnect the motor before refitting it to the console, and to run it through its cycle of on and off. Refit the motor to the console and refit the motor regulator arm to the marks you made before you dismantled it, then reconnect the linkages.

Once the console is returned to the vehicle, reconnect it and run it through its cycle again with the blades attached. This will position the spindles correctly for the replacement of the wiper arms. You will notice that the wiper arms are a different shape, one from the other. The cranked arm goes on the

bottom and the straight arm goes on the top. (The wipers are marked in red.)

The part numbers for new wiper blades are: Mercedes Part number 126 820 03 45, Driver's Side Wiper, and Mercedes Part number 126 820 04 45, Passenger's Side Wiper.

The issues covered here are not the only points on the 126 needing lubrication, but they are those that have consistently proved to be problematic. Make a pledge that, whatever you do on the car, you will use some form of lubrication. If you remove a bolt, use an anti-seize paste when you replace it; if something moves, swivels or hinges, use appropriate grease or oil. You will be surprised how quickly these small actions will add up to protect the future of your 126.

# CHAPTER THIRTEEN

# INTERIOR MAINTENANCE

## SWITCHES

Often, a perceived problem with an item being activated can be narrowed down to soiled or corroded contact points inside the switch. This guide should give you enough confidence to attempt a proper clean-up of the switch instead of buying an inferior part from an auction site, or using a junkyard item that might be just as bad.

Please do not be tempted to use WD40, unless it is the proper contact cleaner product. The basic product will leave a residue that will just attract more dirt and dust and you will be back to square one in very short order. You can start with a brake or car-burettor cleaner if you have nothing else, but there is nothing better than a proper switch cleaner, which will have been formulated to keep the internals clean over a lengthy period. There are a number on the market, including Deoxit, Servisol Super 10, and CRC contact cleaner, to name but a few.

There are quite a few tiny parts in the switches, so ensure you have something available to catch any pieces that may fall, such as a small white plastic food tray (B). Use whatever you can to clean the internal part of the switch, but if you choose a cotton bud, ensure you do not leave behind cotton-wool residue. Different-sized firm make-up brushes are always handy for cleaning small items as well as for applying grease (A).

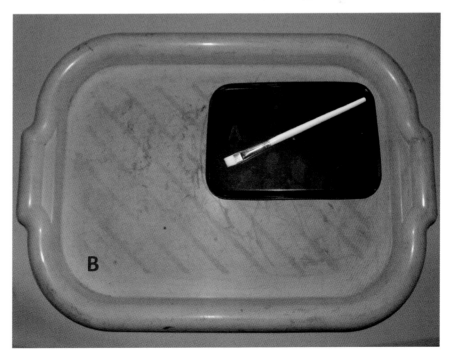

*Using general household items to collect and clean small parts.*

## Dialectic Grease

Dialectic or silicone grease is a non-conductive insulator, so you cannot simply smear terminals and contacts with it, thinking it will assist with conductivity. Low mechanical strength, push-fit connectors benefit from having the grease smeared around the rubber or plastic bodies, but not on the metal part of the connectors before connection.

Although there are two styles of accessory switch in the centre console and doors, they operate in the same way. The only difference is visual and the way they fit into the panel. The buttons to access the interior are slightly different. The switch without shoulders is like a cap and fits over the collar; the switch with the shoulders fits internally.

## REMOVING AND REINSTALLING

To remove the button, slide something thin between the button and collar, levering outwards very slightly to pop out the locating pin (A).

Pull the switch head out and look for the ball bearings sitting on top of the rocker. Carefully remove these

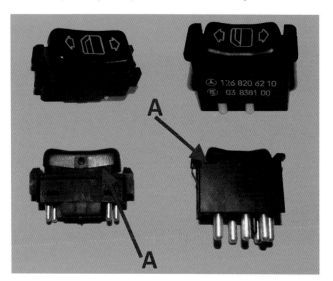

*Find the point where the rocker head attaches to the body.*

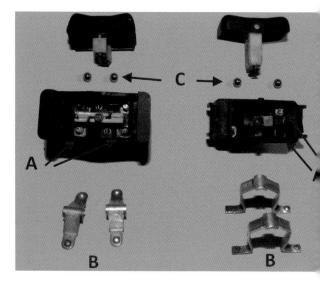

*The component parts of the window switches: (A) contact terminals; (B) rockers; (C) ball bearings.*

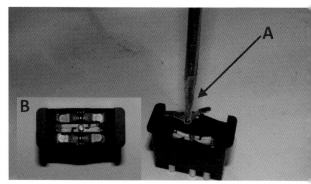

*Refitting the rockers can be fiddly.*

and clean everything up. Do not use wire wool as this may cause small threads of metal to be left inside. Use something like a green kitchen scouring cloth instead.

When you reinstall everything, use a bit of dialectic grease on the back of the rocker, but not on the terminal faces. If your fingers are small enough you may be able to slip the rocker back into place. Alternatively, try using a screwdriver (A) with a bit of double-sided tape to hold the rocker, and lower it in place; it will need a little push as you twist it in place to locate the slots.

Once you are sure the rockers are sitting correctly, put a bit of grease on the ball bearing and drop them into place (B). The springs in the switch will seat them properly.

## SEAT-ADJUST SWITCH OVERHAUL

The seat-adjust switch is not as easy to clean as the single rocker switches but if you do it once you will never forget how. It requires a steady hand and a few held breaths, but you should be able to cure 99 per cent of seat-adjustment problems. The trouble with the switch is that it sits in the door and is not protected by the plastic sheet; it will get damp at some point but the worst issue by far is that it seems to pick up greasy, sooty road grime, which eventually clogs the terminals.

You will have to find the most comfortable way to release the tabs, remembering that, as soon as tension is removed from the lid, the internal items will loosen. The little ball bearing that sits atop the springs will be the first thing to drop off. Once you have removed the screw in the back, lie the switch face up on the tray.

To help you pull up the lid, some pieces of wiper-blade strengthener are excellent as they are strong and thin. A couple of small screwdrivers or even toothpicks will work too – just be careful not to overstretch the tabs as the sides can crack. Put the first two in position 3 and 4 so that when you lever from position 1 and 2 the lid should pull straight up. If you hold the body of the switch very still as you pull up the lid, most parts should stay in place. Just do not twitch.

Have a good look to get a feel for the way it works before you dive in and remove all the bits and pieces. The only way to clean it properly is to empty it into a plastic tub and clean each piece in turn.

The centre actuator will not fall out as it is held in place with two clips; just lever one end up carefully and preserve the clip.

Thoroughly clean the main body and make sure the brass contact tracers are all bright.

The single bearing in position (E) is the headrest actuator, which does not have a brass rocker. It exists only on Generation 2 vehicles.

Using tweezers or a magnetized screwdriver, drop a bearing into each actuator, then add a spring on top of the bearing. Add a blob of grease to the top of the spring, so that the top bearing will hold in place while you reposition the lid. Lightly spray everything with

*Main seat-adjustment switches. The black-bodied one has no memory facility; the grey/blue-bodied one is the memory version, with a switch pad. The tabs, numbered I to 7, hold the lid in place. The only lid-retaining screw (A) is the first item that needs to be removed.*

contact cleaner as most cleaners have a preserving agent.

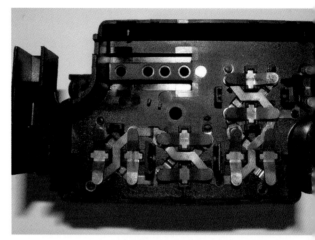

*Accumulated road grime and dust can interfere with the contacts. A good clean can restore movement.*

TOP: *Clean each individual brass rocker and reinsert into the notches; they sit in place, held by tabs.*

ABOVE: *The first actuator to replace is the only one that is fixed into place (A); reinsert the clips to hold it in.*

Slowly lower the lid, adjusting the actuator arms so they slide through the slots smoothly and firmly click into position. Ensure it is fully closed and shake it to make sure nothing is loose. Check that each actuator arm moves smoothly as it should. Do not forget to replace the small screw, and clean the connector poles and plugs on the car with contact cleaner.

RIGHT: *Add the rockers, ensuring they locate into the little tabs.*

BELOW: *The correct set-up before refitting the lid.*

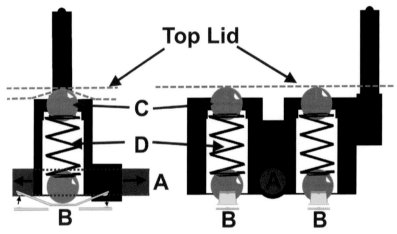

Top Lid

## THE CLUSTER

Before attempting to remove the cluster, make enough space by adjusting the steering wheel so that it is as far away as possible. Disconnect the battery, too, as there are a few electrically sensitive items that can be affected by a short. The clock power connector is a simple spade connector and can easily touch something metallic.

It is possible to buy cluster removal tools online but a handmade item will work just as well. Use something with a decent tensile strength – a cut-up steel coat hanger is too soft, but an old bicycle-wheel spoke or even a broken cheese-wire handle will do the job.

Mark the tool about 40mm from the end – there are little locating nibs on the side of the pod, which will give you an idea where they are (A). Slide the tool in about halfway between the bottom and top corners, turn so that the hook faces inwards, and pull each side a little at a time. There will be some resistance from the retaining spring (B) and then it will release.

Start by removing the main multi-pin plug. This will give you a little more movement of the pod so that you can get your hand around the back to pull the other plugs and connectors. The most awkward connection will be the vacuum gauge tube, which is very tight, although it does just pull off.

There are three separate units. The exterior temperature unit (screw 1 and 2) just slides out.

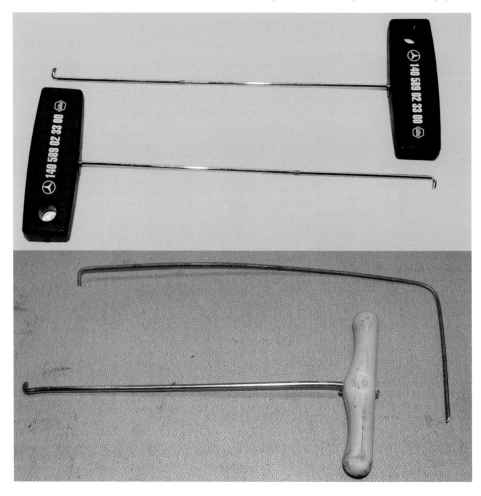

*The available cluster removal tool is cheap but you can also make your own.*

*Pull evenly on each side of the cluster.*

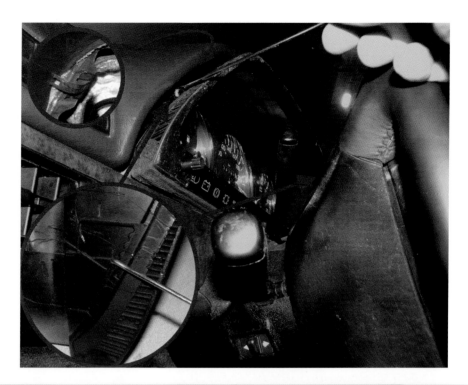

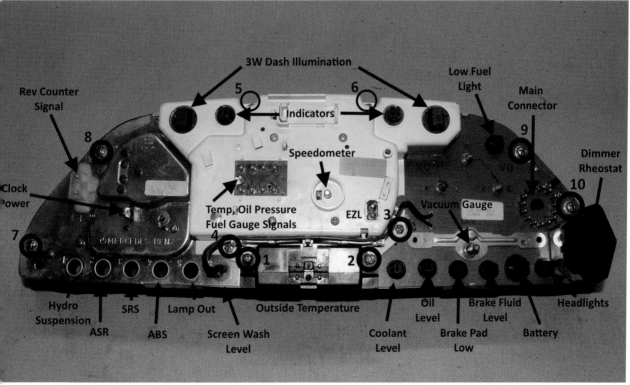

*The rear view of the pod.*

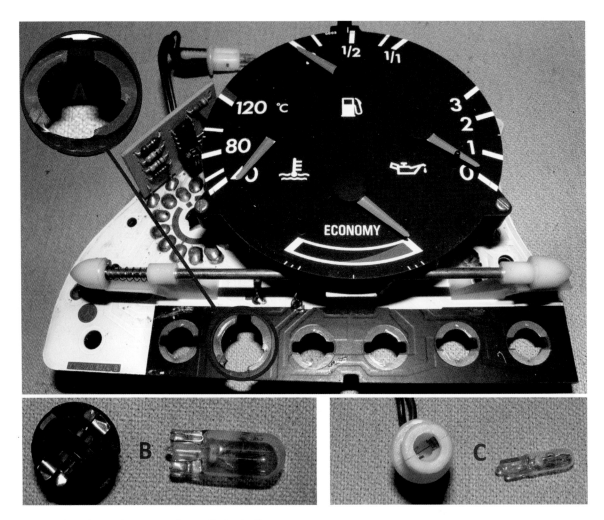

*While the cluster is out, replace all the bulbs.*

The centre unit, the speedometer, comes out first – remove screws 3 to 6, lift it out very carefully and set it aside for later work. Do not rest it on its face as the indicator needles are easily damaged. Remove screws 7 to 10. Try not to touch the matt-finish dial faces.

The interior will be dusty, so take the time to give the pod a good clean, being careful with certain types of detergent as it is all plastic.

## CLUSTER LIGHTING

If you are going to take the time and bear the cost of removing the cluster, it is worth replacing all the bulbs. Do not leave the originals even if they look as though they are working – you will only have to remove the cluster again when the next one goes out.

Any issues with intermittent tell-tale and warning bulbs can usually be put down to the way the bulb holder sits in the circuit board (A) or the way the bulb sits in the holder. Make sure that the bulb contacts are not twisted, broken or missing (A and C); check the contacts on the holders are nice and tight and there is no corrosion. Take a close look into the holder – even the remains of old bulb wire contacts sitting in the base can cause shorts.

One issue that does require extra attention relates to the large 3-watt cluster illumination bulbs. These are commonly replaced, in error, with 5-watt bulbs as they are similar in appearance to the more common side-repeater light bulb fitted to newer cars. However, as they age, the glass blackens inside and they lose their intensity. The issue is that, while the 3-watt bulbs do emit enough heat over time to distort and tarnish the frame, using a 5-watt bulb can really damage the white plastic frame and the prism the directs the light to the front of the cluster. If you prefer to fit incandescent bulbs, ensure they are 3-watt and not 5-watt and consider lining the frame with silver ducting tape (not duck tape) to aid reflecting light. Check that the light prisms in the top of the pod have not distorted with the heat (A) as this is one of the reasons why light will fail to reach the front of the pod.

LED replacements are an excellent alternative in this case. They have a very low operating temperature, very low power consumption and, if the diodes are forward-facing, the bright light is more economically directed.

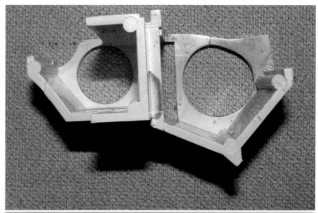

RIGHT: *Main cluster lighting can be easily burnt out with the incorrect bulbs*

BELOW: *Distorted prisms are often a reason behind a lack of light reaching the front.*

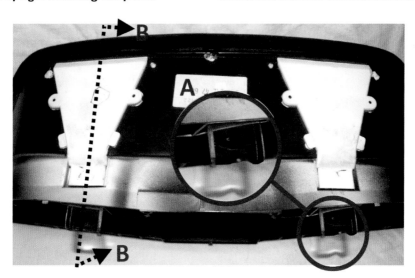

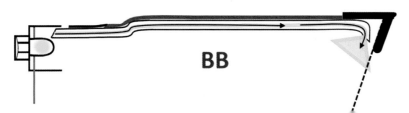

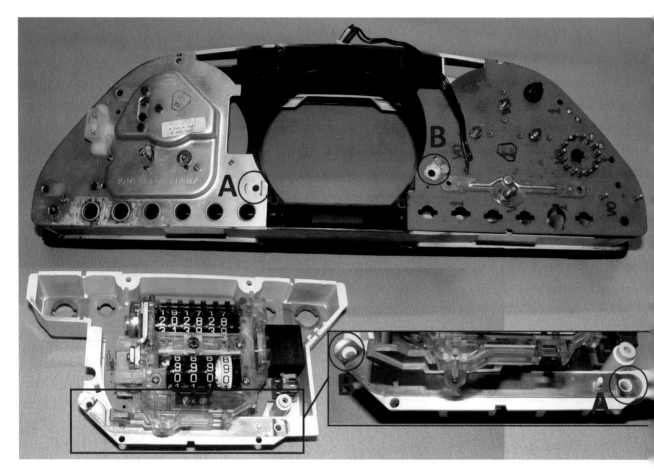

*Clean the main ground strip to ensure good contact.*

## CLUSTER GROUND STRIP

Because the cluster body is plastic, a 'ground' strip is required to evenly distribute an earth across the three separate dial units (A, B). While you have the centre odometer unit removed, check the metal strip that runs along the bottom edge; it is fairly thin and easily creased, so be gentle with it. Roughen up the two contact points where it meets the dial units, and clean with contact cleaner.

It is essential this part works correctly – it has been the cause of many cluster faults and fluctuating instruments – so, if there is any doubt about its integrity, consider creating an alternative using a wire and spade connectors at the fixing points. It is very easy to pick up a ground point from the 'ground nest' behind the cluster.

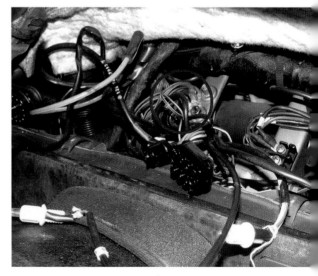

*Take the opportunity to clean up the 'ground nest' behind the pod.*

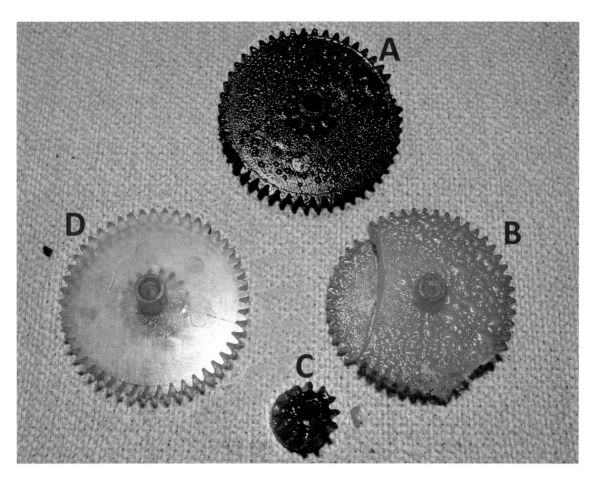

*A crumbling gear is the most likely reason why the speedometer has stopped working.*

## CLUSTER GEARS

The number-one cause of failure of the cluster speedometer and odometer is related to the gears on the side of the unit. The originals are made from very strong polyurethane plastic, which is impossible to destroy by hand, even with pliers. Deterioration of the gears seems to be more prevalent in hot countries, but UK-based cars suffer the same problems, so excessive heat cannot be the only factor.

It is very easy to spot a problem by looking at the yellow gear. In good condition it has a clear yellow, see-through appearance (D) but as it deteriorates it becomes opaque and appears to be covered in sweat beads (B). By the time it looks like this it will have turned from a strong, almost indestructible material into a crumbly biscuit. As it breaks apart, the risk of

more damage is increased as the tiny crumbs find their way around the internals.

Do not be too nervous about replacing gears. The unit seems to be extremely complex, but you will only have to remove a fraction of it, so, as long as you exercise care, the risk of damage is very small. New gears are available from MBD or you can buy remanufactured items in plastic from various online sites, including garagistic.com, for very little money.

If you have not already done so, remove the centre unit by first removing the exterior temperature unit and then the four screws that hold it in place. Lift out the unit, taking care not to damage the face or the needle. The gears are loose on a loose spindle, so watch out for them falling out at this stage and be ready with a container to keep them in. The small

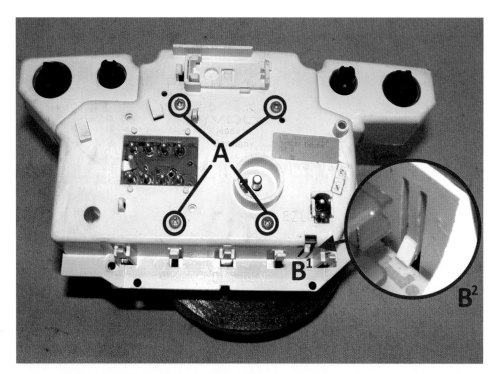

A stripped-down odometer set. Remove the four small screws on the back of the unit (A); the control board will not drop out until the tab (B) is released. The view from the inside (B2) should help with this job.

Put the rubber buffers aside for replacement.

*The shield protecting the gears is secured by two very small screws, sometime Philips-head and sometime slot-head (A). To remove it, you will need to gently pull the face down a little to give you space between the gears and the black relay.*

**1**

**2**

ABOVE: *Make a note of the gear positions. The inner gears (A and B) are hard plastic and do not need to be replaced. The flexible gears (C and D) need to be removed.*

LEFT: *The flexible gears have been removed and the spindles (A) and brass collet (B), which holds the drive gear, reinserted.*

drive gear comes off less easily as it is usually glued on to the brass collar, which is crimped in place.

Once the gears have been removed, ensure everything is as clean as you can get it, using an air compressor to blow out any debris remaining from the crumbling gears. The mechanism is a very low-torque unit and even the slightest bit of debris left behind can halt the gears.

*Replace the hard plastic gears (D and E) and the main flexible primary drive gear (H).*

*Fit the clear yellow flexible gear (F) and then the flexible black gear (G).*

Carefully refit the gear cover with the tiny screws. Do not forget to refit the rubber buffer rings to the circuit board.

## CLUSTER DIMMER RHEOSTAT

There were two types of rheostat used to dim the cluster lights to the desired brightness. A simple

*Unfortunately, there is next to nothing you can do to the IC version if it goes wrong, apart from replace it. The electronically minded might be able to replace the odd resistor.*

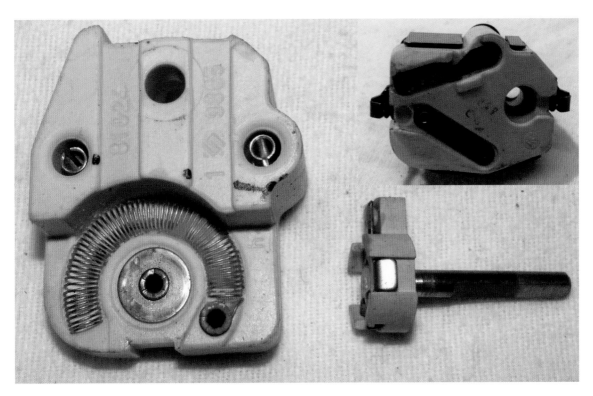

*The ceramic version is a different matter from the IC version. If the cluster lights are intermittent or the dimmer is not working, it is very easily dismantled and cleaned.*

ceramic and resistance spring type was used until autumn 1989 and after that an electronic version.

## IGNITION STEERING LOCK: REMOVAL AND REPLACEMENT

The ignition lock is reasonably reliable, but it can jam up, which will cause all sorts of problems if it does so. If the key becomes stiff, notchy to turn or difficult to remove without wiggling, act immediately. If you leave it, it will undoubtedly fail and when it does you will not be able to remove the key, unlock the steering or even start the car. However, that will be the least of your problems. Replacing the barrel when everything is still working is a maximum one-hour job and will cost around £40 in parts. If it has jammed up on you and you cannot turn the key, you will not be able to remove the barrel. Not only will you need a complete new steering lock unit but your only option will be to cut the old one out, and the outlay is likely to be closer to £400.

A new barrel with your original key profile is not difficult to buy from the main dealer, as long as you show them your VIN and proof of ownership.

There are two types of barrel for the 126: the first type, the most common, was used from 1979 until 1988; after the 'park lock' was introduced, making it necessary to place the driver's foot on the brake with the ignition on before being able to select 'Drive', the barrel changed. Each barrel has to be removed in a different manner but it is necessary in both cases to be able to turn the key to position number two first, to line up the locating hole/s. Both barrels have a hardened security collar.

First, disconnect the battery; you do want the ignition to come on or the engine to start in error.

Second, carefully remove the escutcheon surrounding the lock. It is tricky to remove without breaking the pins (A), as they are held with metal spring clips but they are still available and very inexpensive to buy.

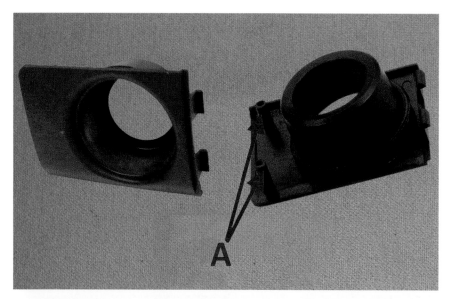

*Removing the escutcheon plate around the ignition lock will probably break the securing pins.*

**The early-style barrel requires only one spoke to remove it, but the shroud does need to be unscrewed.**

*The post-1988 barrel requires two spokes to remove it and the shroud pulls straight off.*

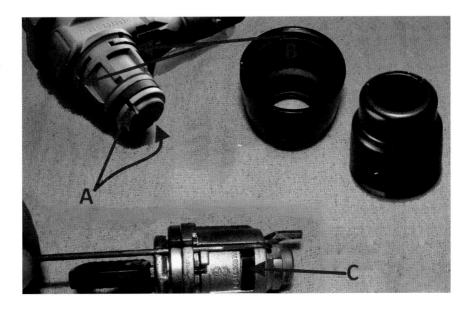

Before attempting to remove the early barrel from the steering lock unit, prepare yourself a single wire, fairly strong and about 10cm long. A cycle spoke with a 45-degree angle sliced from one end and the other end bent over at a 90-degree angle is ideal.

Insert the key and turn the ignition to position two, then insert the wire spoke and wiggle it a little to make sure it seats fully and pulls in the retaining pin (A). You will know you have been successful when you are able to turn the black collar to unscrew it. There was a special tool available, but a piece of suitably sized rubber coolant hose does the job of giving you extra grip.

As it reaches the 'heel' of the key, give the wire spoke another wiggle to ensure the secondary nib

(B) releases the barrel too. The collar needs to be unscrewed as you ease the barrel out (C).

The post-1988 barrel needs two wire spokes (A), the uppermost spoke will release the barrel lock (C) and the locating keyway (B), which holds the security collar, while the lower spoke just releases the second collar keyway (B).

## DOOR PANEL REMOVAL

A number of preventive maintenance jobs necessitate the removal of the interior door panels, so it is useful to be familiar with the correct method of doing this. Do not be frightened of removing the

*Inside the door panel. If you do not have a set already, acquire a set of trim-removal tools. They will come in handy for all manner of jobs, including on the door panels.*

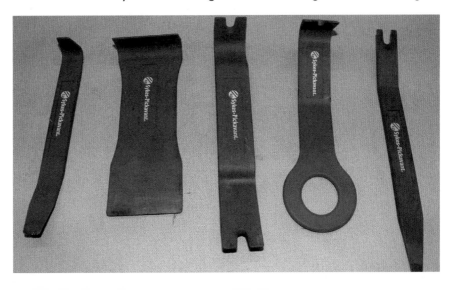

*The front-door panel tab fixing locations.*

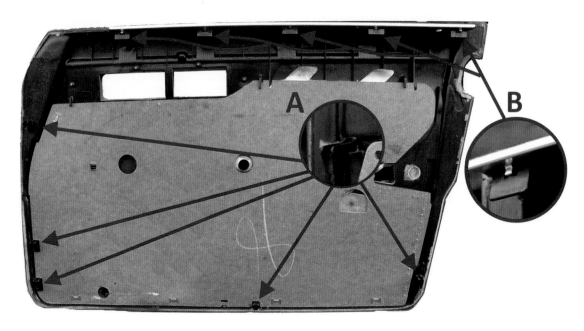

*The front-door panel fixing hooks.*

panel; once you have completed it once or twice, it will become only a ten-minute job and it is well worth the effort.

The plastic tabs on the panels are strong in normal use but are very easily broken if you simply tug at the panel, assuming it is on push-fit clips. Most 126 door panels now have at least one broken tab, it seems. The weakest tabs are the ones along the top line (B), where they fit into a rubber seal with a slot in it. If you do not know what you are doing, you might see the gap and be tempted to grab the top roll and pull. You can generally see where this has happened in the past, and it has been broken, even on a fitted panel – as you slam the door, the top roll of the panel appears loose. Unfortunately, once it is broken, there is not much that can be done that will hold it as well as the original tabs, so make sure you exercise great care.

*The rear-door panel tab fixing locations.*

*The rear-door panel fixing hooks.*

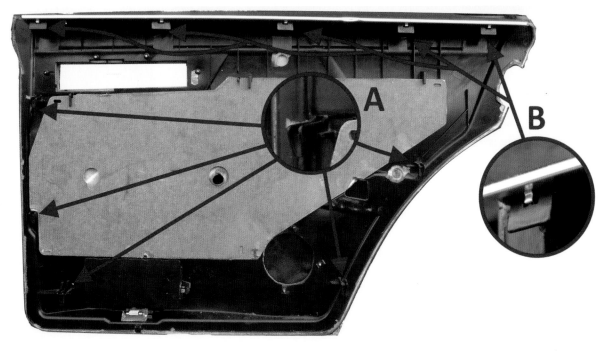

It is not entirely necessary to remove the triangular trim piece that hides the mirror fixings, but it does give a better view of the panel. The moulded frame inserts are held on with only one screw; once it has been removed, pull the trim piece out and up to unlatch it (A). The rear piece has two very small Philips-head screws (B).

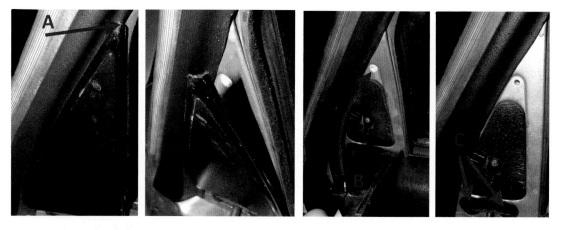

*Ease the plastic trim from the top point by pulling back. There is only one friction-fit post holding it in place, apart from the locating tabs along the bottom edge.*

## Front                    Rear

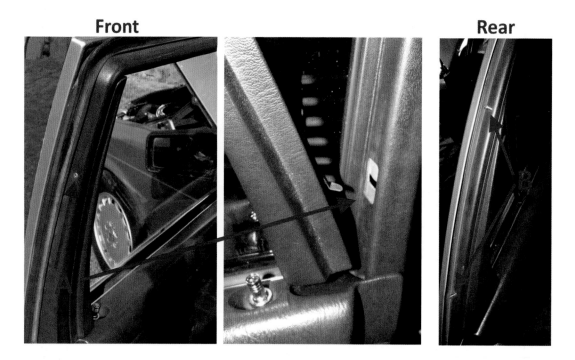

*It is necessary to remove the frame insert trim to enable you to lift the door panel off its hooks.*

*Carefully remove the electric seat-adjust switches and keep them safe.*

*The door handles have a plastic cover piece lodged behind the handle.*

*Remove the seat-button backing plate by levering from the inside edge, not the outer.*

Slip a flat-edge trim removal tool behind the plastic interior handle backing piece and lever it out carefully. Behind, you will find a small Philips-head screw that holds the trim escutcheon in place.

Where the front panels have electric seat-adjust buttons, you will need to use a trim tool to lever these buttons off; keep them safe as they are easily lost, especially the little headrest button found on the Generation 2 cars.

All other doors have similar plates around window buttons, depending on options available, so the same applies. Lever from the straight inner edge as this is where the latching tabs (B) and locating tabs (C) are located. Tabs marked (A) are holding tabs. The plate is only removable completely when the armrest has been removed.

RIGHT: *Remove the window-control switch.*

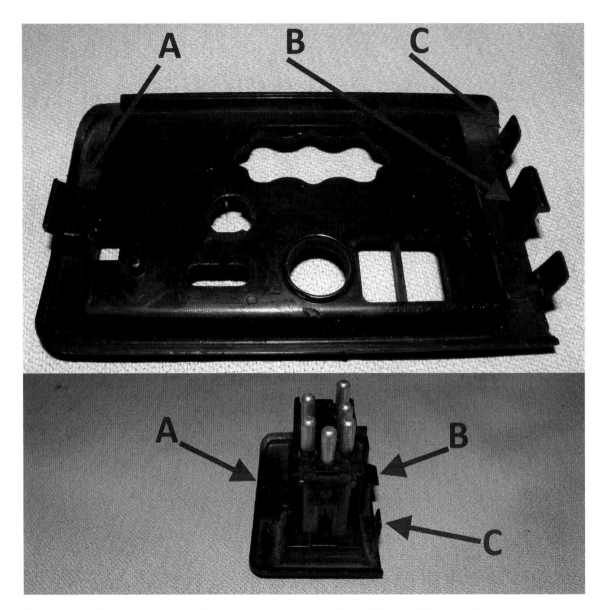

*There are various covers depending on option, however they all lever off in a similar way.*

Safeguard the foam square (A) as this stops noise and draughts from finding its way into the cabin.

It is not entirely essential to remove the interior handle to be able to lift the panel enough to remove it, although it does help, especially if you do not have the help of a third hand to ease the edge of the panel outwards as you lift. If you have the electric seat-adjusting switch box it is a good idea to remove the screws (1) to give the parts movement.

It is necessary to remove the puddle light (A) and thread the wires back through a hole to free the wires from the front panel. The rear puddle light terminal is visible, but there may be additional wires if the model has the ashtray with integral lighter (B).

If the inner protection sheet is no longer intact, make another from a sheet of medium-duty plastic. It will protect the panels from damp as well as the

*Once the handle escutcheon plate is loose, pull the handle outwards to be able to move it enough to reach the large Philips-head screw (B) that holds the top of the armrest.*

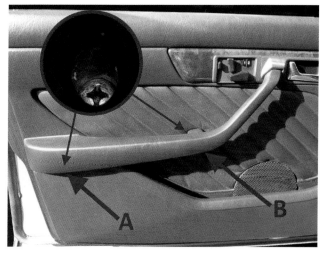

*Remove the two large Philips-head screws from under the armrest – they are at a tight angle – then set aside the armrest.*

*Remove the chrome trim around the door lock.*

*It is easier to remove the panel after having removed the screws in the handle and the seat switches, but it is not essential.*

interior of the vehicle from fumes, draught and noise. Use double-sided adhesive tape to hold it in place.

As always, refitting is the reversal of removal, but there are a few pointers that may help you. Hold the top roll against the glass and slowly lower it while locating the top tabs and the door-lock pins; once you feel the top tabs bite, change your hand position to the sides where the hook-locating tabs are,

ensuring the interior handle and, if applicable, the seat switch block do not get trapped behind. Last, run your fingers around the edge to ensure the panel is sitting square and true.

You do not want to be removing these panels too often, so make the most of the opportunity and do everything that needs doing while they are off.

Check the window regulators, locks and latches, wiring, door checks, metal integrity, drain holes, and anti-drum pads, as they can drop off and get stuck under the window and do not forget to revitalize the cavity wax covering.

*With everything removed, place your hands at the bottom of the door panel and lift straight up sharply.*

*As the panel frees itself, grab the edge of the top roll at the lock edge and pull the panel up so the top tabs leave the rubber strip and the lock button exits the hole before you pull the panel forwards.*

*Remember to disconnect the wires to the puddle lights.*

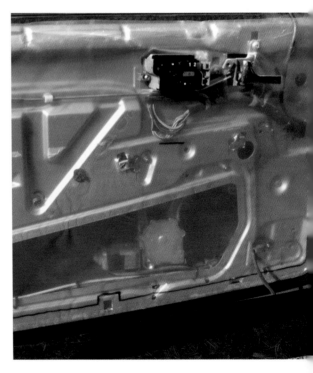

*If the plastic weather sheet is missing or in a bad condition, replace it.*

# CHAPTER FOURTEEN

# EXTERIOR MAINTENANCE

## PLASTIC SIDE CLADDING REMOVAL

The external door trim is there for a number of reasons and can suffer damage in performing its role, which will then make the 126 appear very untidy. As long as the trim is not damaged beyond repair there are many things you can do to bring it back to a good condition. If it needs repainting, check the 'Paint Data' section for the correct original colour combination.

Although it is not difficult to do once you know how, the first time you remove the panel can be daunting. You can actually do some serious damage if you just start tugging and forcing blindly. The first piece of advice is to try to remove the cladding only on a warm day. If the weather is not complying, warm each panel prior to removal with a heat gun, a hair-dryer or even a kettle of hot water. This will minimize the risk of you breaking the clips or, worse still, cracking any of the ribs that hold the white clips.

Pull out from the bottom edge (1); if you cannot get your fingers under the bottom edge, use a wide-angled trim remover and then slide the panel downwards to release the hook catches (2). There is only one hook on the rear wing but there are three on the front wing.

The door panels require a bit more thought. Grip the panels along the bottom edge and pull outwards evenly, as you did with the wing and arch pieces. As

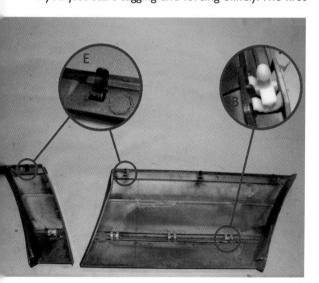

*The interior of the A- and C-post cladding after removal, giving an idea of where to apply force.*

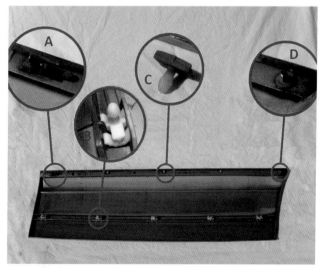

*The interior of the door cladding.*

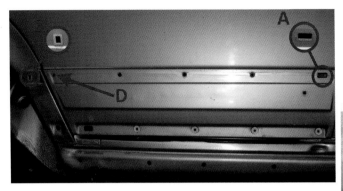

ABOVE: *The door skin behind the panel.*

RIGHT: *The front-wing and rear-wheel-arch pieces are by far the easiest to remove.*

## Rear arch

## Front wing

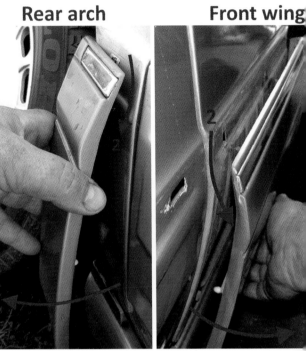

Follow the rubber door seal until you see a dimple around the same level as the top of the cladding. Pull out the rubber to reveal a hole, behind which is an 8mm plastic nut holding the panel. In the rear door, the nut is close to the hole (A).

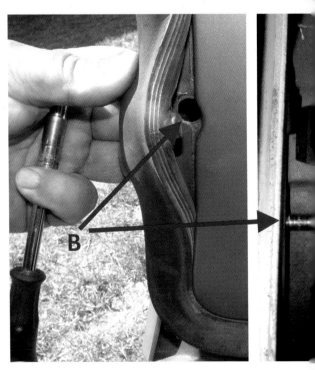

In the front door, the nut is set back about 50mm (2in) and will need a small extension bar to reach it (B).

you get close to the 'S'-shaped clip, support the far end of the panel so it does not twist it.

Take this opportunity to clean behind the panel, and replace the post fixings and the small gaskets

around all the 'S'-clip holes. The 'S' clips can go rusty and attract rust around the holes too.

Again, remove and clean and check the sill and jacking points for any corrosion.

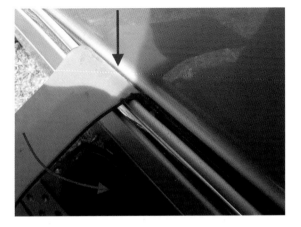

*If you just tug at the top you are likely to crease the stainless-steel trim and, due to its shape, it is not very easy to take the crease out. Use a wide trim-removal tool or a wide plastic spatula to slip down the back of the top edge and gently lever the panel forwards.*

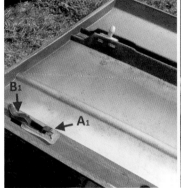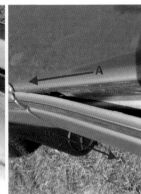

*Once all the post clips are free and the only thing holding the panel is the 'S' clip, you need to push forward (A) and then angle the panel outwards to release (A1). Then, as you pull the panel backwards (B), it will release (B1).*

*The sill cover on the Generation 2 cars is fixed along the floor edge with 8mm hex-head screws (B) and push post clips along the top edge (A). The fixings (C) are different from those on the main panels and a little more fragile, so ease the cover outwards with care.*

## FRONT WING REMOVAL

Removing the wing sounds like a bit of an overkill but it is simple to do and will take no more than an hour to do, so it is a viable option if you need more space to work or want to check and clean the wheel arches.

It is not necessary to remove the inner plastic lining first as it is not fixed to the wing shell. Take the time to check and clean the whole area – catching something now is very satisfactory. Check where the wing bolts to the sill area and the scuttle-drain tubes. Once it is all clean and dry, spray vulnerable areas with cavity wax.

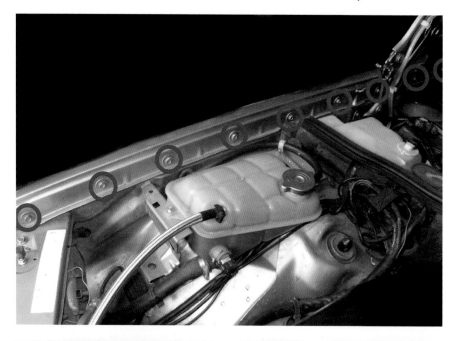

*Each wing has eight top bolts with loose thread plates.*

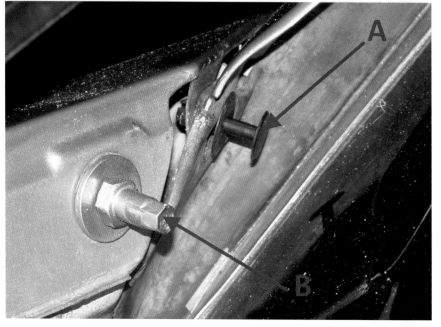

*One large bonnet locating pin at the top edge (B) and a plastic post clip secure the screen trip to the wing (A).*

*There are three hex threads inside the door shut (A) and two bottom wing hex threads (B).*

*There are two bolts behind the indicator and one bolt holding the valance under the headlight (C).*

*Front brake set-up.*

## BRAKE AND BEARING MAINTENANCE

The brakes on a 126 are a simple twin-piston-per-caliper system using Bendix/Girling or ATE/Teves items, and are remarkably simple to work on. If you replace any item, ensure you use only the correct manufacturer's part for ultimate reliability.

### PADS, DISCS AND CALIPERS

Roller pins (A) hold the pads in place. Sometimes on a Bendix caliper these have spring clips holding them in place, but most of the time they are interference fit with a sprung collar. The pad wear sensors (B), on the front brakes only, just pull out of the socket. A retaining and anti-vibration plate (C) holds the pads tight.

Both front and rear calipers are held on to the frame via two 19mm bolts; if you have to remove the calipers, ensure the car is firmly supported as you will need to exert a fair amount of pressure with a longer bar to be able to 'crack' the bolt. Doing this does run the risk of destabilizing the vehicle.

Never let the caliper just hang on its flexible connecting hose; be prepared to hang it up somewhere.

Ensure you use a thread-lock paste when you reinstall the caliper bolts. Spraying releasing fluid through the wheel bolt holes and leaving for twenty-four hours may help. The single non-vented discs are easily deformed if hit with a hammer, so you should consider this only if you are going to replace the disc. Shocks from a rubber or soft-face mallet while turning it should dislodge it eventually if you do not have a puller.

### FRONT WHEEL BEARING

When you get to the stage of having to remove the front hub assembly, for whatever reason, never just replace it without carrying out a proper clean-up and checking the condition of the bearing.

Start by just cleaning off all the surplus grease with clean, lint- free cloths to check the condition of the bearing taper rollers; if there were no signs of excessive play or rumbling noises before you took the wheel off, and the roller surface is a smooth,

*Removing the rear disc is usually simply a matter of removing the caliper and undoing the small Allen key fixing bolt, however the disc often sticks to the hub flange.*

*The front discs come off with the hub by removing the bearing nut and pulling the disc forwards, taking care not to drop the first bearing on the floor.*

To remove the disc from the hub you will need to turn it over and remove the Allen key bolts from the rear.

Fill the bearing cap to the edge bead with approximately 15g of grease. The other 45g is used to squeeze into the tapers, under the seal and around the stub axle.

*While everything is apart, clean the reluctor ABS sensor ring with a wire brush attached to a drill.*

*Clean up behind the disc and clean and check the stub axle to ensure it is not scored, worn or burnt (A).*

even grey colour, they should be in good condition. However, if you see any kind of blemish or discolouration to the races they will need replacing sooner rather than later.

If all is well and all you need to do is to repack with grease, measure out a total of 60g of 'high-temperature, anti-friction bearing grease' as per Specification Sheet 265 for each wheel. The 126 is reliant on the correct amount of grease; if it is over-packed, it has nowhere to squeeze out and will just overheat.

Refit the disc with the bearing hub attached, push in the outer taper bearing with the large thrust washer and loosely fit the hub nut until it bites. Turn the hub as vigorously as possible to distribute the grease internally. Tighten the hub nut while turning the disc until it starts to grip, making it difficult to turn further, then back the nut up by a third of a turn. Smack the wheel spindle with a plastic hammer.

Tighten the hex socket screw to lock the hub nut into place and re-check the play. Refit the radio suppression contact and lastly the bearing cap.

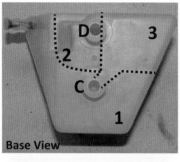
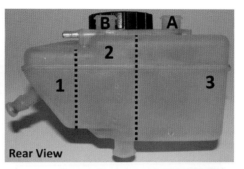
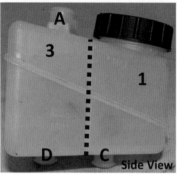

*Brake reservoir partitions.*

## BRAKE-FLUID RESERVOIR

The brake-fluid reservoir has a reputation for being difficult to fill and carrying out fluid changes is also tricky. It is not uncommon to see expletive-sprinkled forum posts online, describing how the rear calipers have refused to bleed.

A first point of note is that the exit tubes in the bottom of the reservoir are vice versa, that is, the frontmost tube (C) supplies the rear brakes and the rear tube (D) supplies the front. It is not much of an issue but it may help to know.

The fluid reservoir has a very clever combination of safety chambers:

- Chamber 1 is the main fluid compartment and controls the front brakes.
- Chamber 3 controls fluid to the rear brakes but, due to the baffle system, will not allow any fluid from chamber 1 and 2 to escape should there be a catastrophic failure of the rear brakes.
- Chamber 2 is simply there to act as a fast drain chamber to allow for minimal fluid loss but a fast response from the front sensor (B).

The siphoning effect of pulling fluid from chamber 1 into 2 before exiting the reservoir at (D) slows the flow considerably should there be a catastrophic fluid failure on the front brakes.

Because of these safety features, it is necessary when filling the reservoir on a 126 from empty – after cleaning, for example – to monitor the rear left corner chamber (3), as it fills only after the main and secondary chambers have been filled. The way to do this is to pour the fluid until it fills the main reservoir (1) and then siphons into the secondary (2). It will seem as though you are going to overfill the reservoir but if you continue to pour slowly you will see compartment 3 start to fill.

Once compartment 3 is full, you can draw off the excess with a syringe or something similar, after you have completed bleeding the brakes. Pay careful attention when bleeding the brakes manually. If you are not careful, the rear chamber might be emptied without you noticing it.

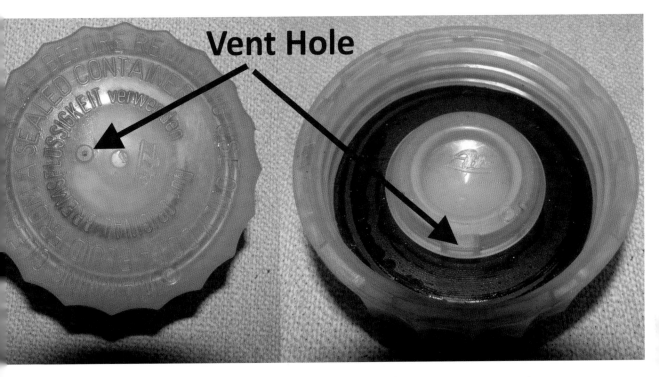

## Vent Hole

*Ensure the lid is clean at all times and that the vent hole is free from contamination.*

## HANDBRAKE/PARKING BRAKE MAINTENANCE

The handbrake/parking brake is a slightly complicated issue. European and US cars have a foot-controlled pedal while the UK and right-hand-drive market 126s have a hand-applied brake. Apart from that part of the mechanism, everything else works in the same way.

Tucked away behind the rear disc, the parking brake rarely gets any attention, let alone mainte- nance, at least until a safety test reveals an issue with it. Recently, there have been a number of failures in which the parking brake has been applied and has then locked into place. Although it is not a great catastrophe it can be very inconvenient and may even involve getting the vehicle lifted on to a truck.

The small brake shoes sit in a confined space behind the disc and hub and are subject to a great deal of moisture, heat and brake dust, even in normal use. Couple this with the number of times the brake may have been left applied in error over twenty years or so, and at the very least it must be time to take a look if you have never done it before.

### ADJUSTING WITHOUT REMOVAL

If the parking brake seems to be slow to release, stiff or not efficient enough to hold the vehicle, the shoes can be adjusted without the hassle of removal.

Jack up both wheels via the bottom of the diff and remove the road wheels. Get on your knees and turn the disc while shining a torch into one of the wheel- nut holes, so that you can see the adjuster wheel as it comes around.

Putting a screwdriver tip high and levering from low to high will loosen the shoes. Putting it low and levering from high to low will tighten the shoes.

### DISMANTLING FOR REMOVAL AND REPLACEMENT

As long as your disc is free to turn and the shoes have not locked up, removing the disc is a simple

*Adjust until the disc becomes difficult to turn and then back off the adjuster a little at a time.*

Tighten Shoes

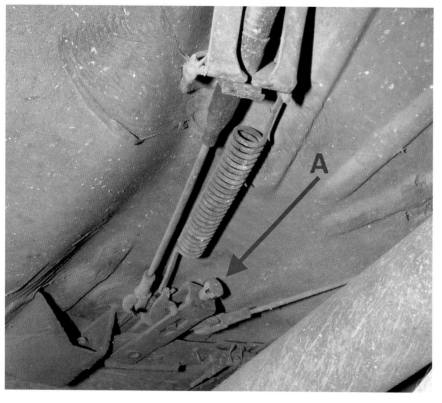

*If you feel the pedal or hand pull still has excessive travel, the cable can be adjusted under the floor with a single 13mm socket or spanner.*

process. However, if they have locked up and cable adjustment fails to release them, your only option will probably be to put a cut in the disc rotor with a metal cutting disc.

Remove the caliper and hang it out of the way and then remove the disc-locating screw, as described earlier. Once the disc has been removed, you will see the shoes are held secure against the back via a locating spring (A). The best way to remove it is using the correct tool; they are very cheap and easily available on auction sites, but you may also be able to adapt a screwdriver to fit (C).

Insert the tool, push and turn until the spring is released (D).

Unhook the opposite end. You will not be able to remove it until the shoes have been removed. Open the shoes and slip over the hub centre in one piece with the adjuster attached.

*The spring-removal tool is the best way to remove the retaining spring, but a screwdriver with a slot ground in it will suffice.*

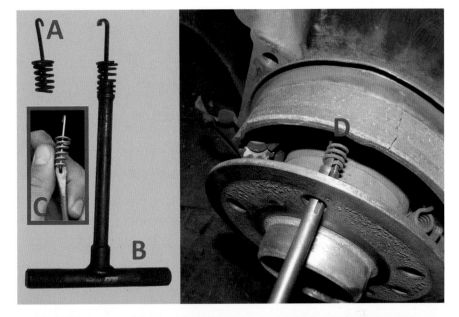

*Using a flat screwdriver, slide it under the spring hook (A) and lever against the hub (B) to lift it out of its locating slot.*

*To remove the holding spring (A) you need to tip it over at the top and turn it slightly to back it out from behind the cable connector shoe.*

Now, clean everything as well as you can. Dismantle the adjuster, clean it and lubricate it (A). Assemble the shoes with adjuster (B) and spring (C) and slip the complete unit back over the hub centre, taking care not to let the adjuster slip out. Reinsert the double spring (D) into the lower shoe slot and lever it back into the top slot using the screwdriver.

Once the shoes are seated correctly, refit the two shoe holdback springs. Refit the rear disc, tapping the shoes to ensure that they seat correctly and then adjust the shoes following the earlier instructions.

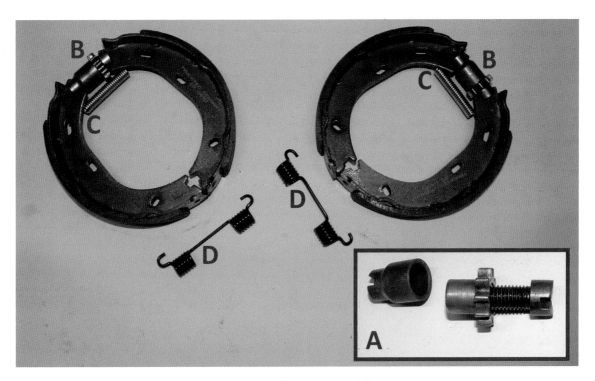

*Fit the adjuster to the shoes (B) with the top spring on the inside (C).*

*Reinstall the holding springs and refit the disc using a brush stroke of anti-seize grease on the hub flange (A).*

# CHAPTER FIFTEEN

# PUTTING IT AWAY

There are a number of reasons why you will, at some point in the future, have to lay up a 126 for an extended period of time. It could be due to work needing to be done or lack of finances, or because you want to protect it over the winter from road salt and water. Whatever the reasons, a few careful considerations can save you a ton of trouble in later months and years.

## FUEL

The primary consideration before any extended lay-up must be fuel. This is especially in more recent times with the introduction of bio-ethanol-laced fuels, but even 'normal', non-ethanol fuels will start to degrade from the moment they have been transferred to a vehicle tank. All fuels will become more or less useless in around six months.

When E10 or ethanol is brought into the mix there are more problems to consider than just 'dead' fuel. Ethanol itself is not particularly acidic but it is hydrophilic, which means it will attract moisture from the air. This will encourage a type of bacterial growth called Acetobactor, which in turn excretes acetic acid (similar to vinegar). This is extremely corrosive and will eat through most materials in quite short order.

Regardless of which fuel you use or even if you are just considering a winter-time lay-up, you should think about using a fuel stabilizer. It is easily obtainable from most motor factors and will give you more peace of mind. Ensure that you drive the vehicle a little after putting in the stabilizer, so that it blends throughout the system.

You might also want to consider 'brimming' the tank. A full tank will help to minimize condensation developing during temperature changes and slow the degrading process considerably.

## COVERING

To cover or not to cover, that is indeed a big question. If you are storing your 126 inside, a light, breathable cover will keep it dust-free and may protect it to some degree from falling items.

If your only option is to store it externally, then there are more serious considerations. The material of the cover must be breathable but waterproof. It must also have a very good securing system – you do not want it to disappear in the wind or, worse, have it flapping around for six months during which it may scratch or rub the paintwork.

Consider the options and go for the best you can afford, preferably a reputable brand. Do not use simple blankets or dust sheets as they will get damp and could cause problems to the paintwork.

## TYRES

The 126 is a heavy vehicle and, if it is left in the same position over an extended period, the tyres will flatspot, which could lead at the very least to severe vibrations in steering and cruising.

If you want to leave the car sitting on its tyres so that is easily accessible if needed, you could consider adding around 10 to 15 PSI more air to each tyre. If you are unsure how long your 126 will be off the road, consider putting it up on axle stands, although not so high that the suspension is hanging on its stops. Judging the point where the stands are taking up about half of the suspension travel will keep the weight off the tyres, as well as avoiding too much stress on the joints.

If the car is left outside, care should also be taken to protect the tyres from sunlight/UV, as the tyre walls can dry and crack in a very short time.

## BRAKES

Ensure the handbrake/parking brake is released, to stop it from seizing in place.

Remove the lid of the brake-fluid reservoir, cover the opening in plastic and refit the lid; this will stop the fluid absorbing moisture through the vent hole.

If you know that the vehicle will be off the road for a year or so, consider removing the brake pads.

## ENGINE

If you decide to run the engine regularly, do not just start it and leave it idling. Running it at a fast idle speed for around half an hour will get it up to a reasonable temperature as well as clearing any moisture from the engine and exhaust.

If you are leaving the engine non-running over the lay-up period, consider putting a couple of drops of oil through the spark-plug holes.

## BATTERY

Automotive batteries are referred to as 'starter' batteries, which means that they have enough high-energy power to turn over an engine but very little deep charge. This in itself makes them susceptible to discharge and subsequent damage very quickly when left unused.

There are many 'intelligent' battery-saver items on the market now to maintain the charge of a vehicle battery, but there are a number of measures you should take to conserve the integrity while it is dormant. Disconnect the battery, check fluid levels if it is possible and then fully charge it overnight to ensure it is at its maximum.

If you are storing a battery off the vehicle, find somewhere with a stable cool temperature and humidity level. Make sure it remains accessible, so that it can be charged periodically if it is not connected to a maintenance charger.

Always bear in mind that an automotive battery will produce hydrogen gas while charging, which is highly explosive. Most batteries have a vent pipe, so the storage place must be adequately vented and nowhere near anything that may create a stray spark,

such as a central-heating boiler, plug sockets or light switches, bench grinders or any other power tool that may spark from a motor. Care should also be exercised when dealing with the connection or disconnection of cables.

## INTERIOR

Give the interior a good clean, then crack the windows open a couple of millimetres. If the car is to be left in a secure garage, latch the doors on the first click, not fully shut, to allow a little air flow.

Clean and spray the door seals in a rubber preserving fluid, to help prevent them from sticking to the metal.

Feed the leather and leave it to soak in.

If the car is left in an accessible garage, on good days open up the building's doors and windows to let the sun and air stream in.

If you decide to use a de-humidifier, remember to empty the water tank regularly.

## SECURITY

A garage door is rarely anything more substantial than a light steel sheet with a flimsy lock, so pay particular attention to security wherever you keep your treasured possession. If you have a secondary door, consider actually fixing the main door with screws on the inside.

Exterior lighting or CCTV cameras will deter the opportunist thief, but windows and doors must be adequately secured for the more determined. If it is not possible to connect to an integrated alarm system, consider a simple audible system that will blast 100Db of noise at an intruder should they gain access.

Do not just discontinue your insurance and do not rely on your domestic contents to cover you should the worst happen. Make a call to your insurance company and inform them that you are laying up a car for a period of time but still require cover; you may even save some money.

Finally, do not just leave the keys in the car. Put them somewhere safe.

# APPENDICES

## Appendix I: Dimensions and Capacities

### FLUID CAPACITIES

**Engine Oil (Including Oil Filter)**
V8 M116/117 engines: 8.0 litres
Straight-six engines: 6.0 litres
Five- and six-cylinder diesel engines: 8.6 litres
Quantity difference between upper and lower marking on dipstick: 2.0 litres

**Cooling System**
Eight-cylinder models: 12.5 litres
Six-cylinder models: 10.0 litres
Five- and six-cylinder diesel models: 12.0 litres

**Transmission**
Manual transmission (approximate), five-speed unit: 1.5 litres
Automatic transmission (approximate): from dry 8.6 litres; at fluid change 7.7 litres

**Final drive unit**
All models (approximate): 1.3 litres

**Power-assisted steering**
All models (approximate): 1.2 litres

**Fuel tank**
All models (approximate): 90 litres (with 12.5 litres reserve)

**Brake System**
All models (approximate): 0.53 litres

**Windscreen-washer and headlight-wash system**
All models (approximate): 5.0 litres

**Hydraulic Suspension**
All models (approximate): 2.0 litres

### DIMENSIONS

**Front Wheel Bearings**
All models: 60g each

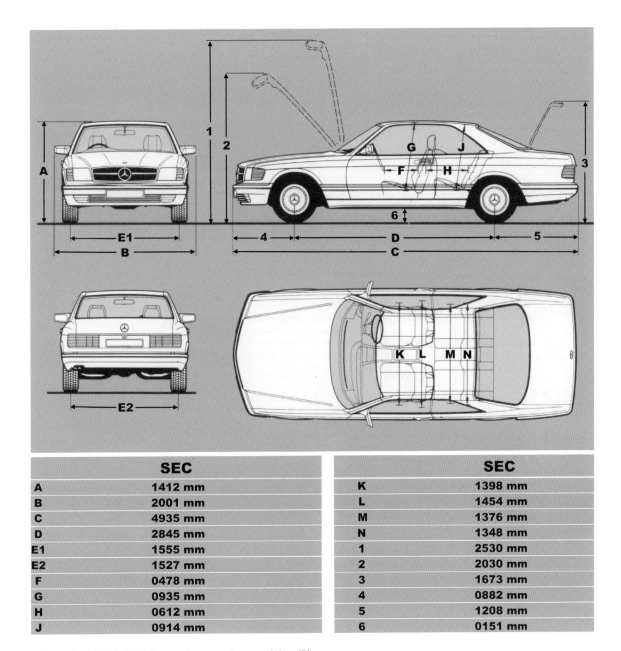

| | SEC | | | SEC |
|---|---|---|---|---|
| A | 1412 mm | K | | 1398 mm |
| B | 2001 mm | L | | 1454 mm |
| C | 4935 mm | M | | 1376 mm |
| D | 2845 mm | N | | 1348 mm |
| E1 | 1555 mm | 1 | | 2530 mm |
| E2 | 1527 mm | 2 | | 2030 mm |
| F | 0478 mm | 3 | | 1673 mm |
| G | 0935 mm | 4 | | 0882 mm |
| H | 0612 mm | 5 | | 1208 mm |
| J | 0914 mm | 6 | | 0151 mm |

*Mercedes W126 SEC dimensions and capacities (1).*

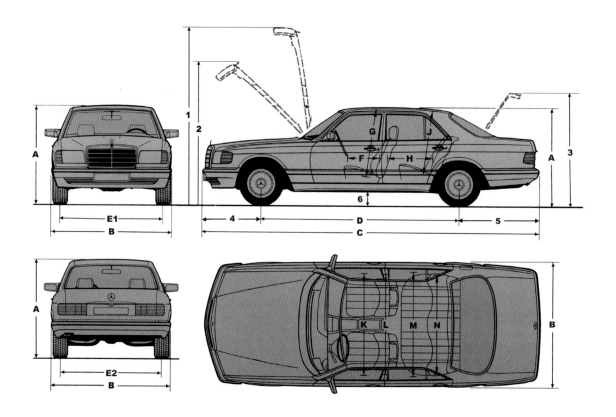

| | SE | SEL | | | SE | SEL |
|---|---|---|---|---|---|---|
| A | 1437 mm | 1446 mm | K | | 1432 mm | 1432 mm |
| B | 1820 mm | 1820 mm | L | | 1428 mm | 1428 mm |
| C | 5020 mm | 5160 mm | M | | 1468 mm | 1468 mm |
| D | 2935 mm | 3070 mm | N | | 1416 mm | 1416 mm |
| E1 | 1555 mm | 1555 mm | 1 | | 2541 mm | 2539 mm |
| E2 | 1527 mm | 1527 mm | 2 | | 2025 mm | 2023 mm |
| F | 477 mm | 474 mm | 3 | | 1652 mm | 1650 mm |
| G | 979 mm | 948 mm | 4 | | 882 mm | 955 mm |
| H | 704 mm | 844 mm | 5 | | 1203 mm | 1208 mm |
| J | 943 mm | 944 mm | 6 | | 160 mm | 145 mm |

*Mercedes W126 saloon dimensions and capacities (2).*

# Appendix II: Service Parts Specifications

Part numbers are for guidance only. Check any upgrades or changes via your VIN.

## ENGINE

### Oil filter part numbers
### Engine numbers M110, M116, M117
Bosch, Part number: 72104
MBD, Part number: A00 118 46 525
MANN, Part number: H929X
KNECHT, Part number: OX32D

### Engine number M103
Bosch, Part number: 72165
MBD, Part number: A102 184 05 01
MANN, Part number: W719/13

### Engine number OM617
Bosch, Part number: 72126
MBD, Part number: A601 184 01 25

### Engine number OM603
Bosch, Part number: 1 457 434 123
MBD, Part number: A11533002
MANN, Part number: WK817/3X

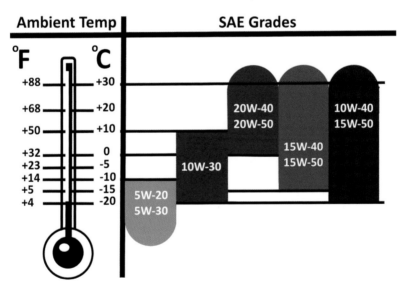

*Recommended oil grades.*

## COOLING SYSTEM

### Antifreeze mixture:
Antifreeze/corrosion agent, 5.75 litres, Protection down to -37 degrees C (-34 degrees F)
Antifreeze/corrosion agent, 6.75 litres, Protection down to -45 degrees C (-49 degrees F)

ONLY MBD antifreeze is recommended, Part number: A000 989 08 2510
ONLY use MBD Citric Flush for system flushing, Part number: A000 989 10 2511

**Note:** Refer to antifreeze manufacturer for latest recommendations.

## AUTOMATIC TRANSMISSION

**Fluid:**
   ATF Dexron 11D and above, MBD236.6

**Filter:**
   MBD, Part number: 1262770295
   Mann, Part number: H 1914/2
   Mahle, Part number: HX 48
   Filter and gasket kit, Part Number: 126 270 02 98

| 280 S | 1980 to 1982 | 722.301 |
|---|---|---|
| 280 SE/SEL | 1980 to 1982 | 722.300 |
| 260 SE | 1985 to 1990 | 722.412 |
| 300 SE/SEL | 1986 to 1991 | 722.351/319 |
| 380 SE/SEL | 1981 to 1982 | 722.304 |
| 380 SE/SEL/SEC | 1982 to 1985 | 722.310 |
| 500 SE/SEL | 1980 to 1984 | 722.302 |
| 500 SEC | 1980 to 1985 | 722.311 |
| 500 SE/SEL | 1984 to 1986 | 722.311 |
| 500 SE/SEL/SEC | 1986 to 1991 | 722.356 |
| 420 SE/SEL/SEC | 1986 to 1990 | 722.355/324 |
| 420 SE/SEL/SEC | 1990 to 1992 | 722.355 |
| 560 SE/SEL/SEC | 1986 to 1989 | 722.323 |
| 560 SE/SEL/SEC | 1989 to 1992 | 722.350 |

*Mercedes W126 transmission codes.*

## FUEL SYSTEM

**Air filter element:**
**Engine numbers M110, M116, M117**
MBD, Part number: A001 094 78 04
Mahle, Part number: LX276
**Engine number M103**
Mahle, Part number: LX114
MBD Part number: A003 094 5404

**Engine number OM617**
MBD, Part number: A603 090 01 40
MANN, Part number: 0020940404

**Engine number OM603**
MBD, Part number: A603 094 02 04
FRAM, Part number: CA6388

**Fuel filter:**
Mahle, Part number: KL38
Mercedes, Part number: A002 477 17 01
Bosch, Part number: 71047

**Engine number OM603**
MBD, Part number: A1457434123
Mahle, Part number: 6010901452

**Engine number OM617**
BOSCH, Part number: A1457434153
MANN, Part number: 0010920401

## IGNITION SYSTEM

**Spark Plugs:**
**Engine number M116, M117 Non-Resistor Only**
NGK BP6ES, Beru 14-7DU, Bosch W7DC, Champion N9YC
Electrode gap (all models): 0.8mm/ 0.34in

**Engine number M103, M110 Non-Resistor Only**
Bosch H8DC0, NGK BP5EFS, Beru 14K-8DU
Electrode gap (all models): 0.8 mm/ 0.34"

## POWER STEERING

**Power-steering fluid Mercedes recommended only**
Mann filter, Part number: H85
Mahle filter, Part number: HX44
Bosch filter, Part number: 1457429416

## BRAKES

Brake fluid DOT 4 and above
Brake-pad friction material minimum thickness: 2.6mm
Rear-brake disc thickness: Max 10.0mm, Min 8.4mm
Front-brake disc thickness: Max 28.0mm, Min 25.4mm

## DRIVE BELTS

**Engine numbers M116, M117**
Fan, water pump, power steering: 2 x 9.5 x 1100, MBD Part number: A0059978492
Alternator: 1 x 9.5 x 1005, MBD Part number: A0059975392
Air conditioning: 1 x 12.5 x 960, Continental Part number AVX13X960
342 M116/117 Belt routing with AC Image

**Engine number M103 Ribbed Belt**
Without AC compressor 6 ribs 21.36 x 2175, MBD Part number: A0089976992
With AC compressor 6 ribs 21.36 x 2257, MBD Part number: A0089977092
343 M103 Belt routing with AC Image

**Engine number M110**
Alternator 9.5 x 980, Continental Part number: AVX10X980
AC Compressor 12.5 x 1285, Continental Part number: AVX13X1285
Power steering 12.5 x 818, Continental Part number: AVX13X818
344 M110 Belt routing with AC Image

## Engine number OM617

Alternator 10 x 1000 (single), MBD Part number: A0049978592

Alternator 10 x 1035 (double), MBD Part number: A0049973992

AC Compressor 12.5 x 925, MBD Part number: A0049979392

Power steering 12.5 x 1145, MBD Part number: A0049979992

**Length of belts for Engine OM617**
**A) Power steering 13 x 1145 mm**
**B) AC Compressor 13 x 925 mm**
**C) Alternator 10 x 1000 (single)**
**C) Alternator 10 x 1035 (double)**

**1) Crankshaft**
**2) Coolant pump**
**3) Alternator**
**4) AC Compressor**
**5) Power steering pump**

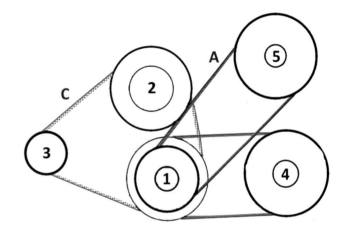

*Pulley layout for OM617 engines with AC compressor.*

## Engine number OM603

Serpentine .96x 21.36 x 2145mm, MBD Part number: A0089973892

Serpentine .97x 21.36 x 2120mm, MBD Part number: A0089973492

**Length of belt for:**
**Engine OM603.96X... 2145 mm**
**Engine OM603.97X... 2120 mm**

**1) Idler pulley**
**2) Crankshaft**
**3) AC Compressor**
**4) Alternator**
**5) Power steering pump**
**6) Coolant pump**
**7) Guide pulley (.97X)**

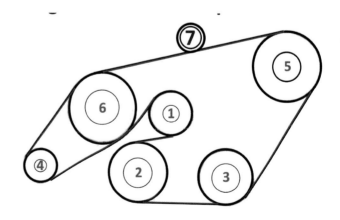

*Pulley layout for OM603 engines with AC compressor.*

*Pulley layout for M116/7 engines with AC compressor.*

Length of belts for engine M116/7:
A) Alternator  9.5 X 1005 mm
B) Power steering pump  2no 9.5 X 1100 mm
C) Air Pump (USA)  10 X 1200 mm
D) AC compressor  12.5 X 960 mm

1) Crankshaft pulley
2) Coolant pump
3) Alternator
4) AC compressor
5) Tensioner roller
6) Power steering pump
7) Air pump (USA)

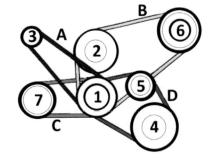

Length of belt for engine:
M103... 2255 mm

*Pulley layout for M103 engines with AC compressor.*

1) Tensioner pulley
2) Cranckshaft
3) AC Compressor
4) Cooling fan
5) Alternator
6) Deflector pulley
7) Power steering pump
8) Coolant pump

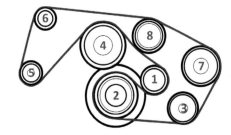

Length of belts for engine M110:
A) Power steering 12.5 X 818 mm
B) AC Compressor 12.5 X 1285 mm
C) Alternator 9.5 X 980 mm

*Pulley layout for M110 engines with AC compressor.*

1) Crankshaft pulley
2) Coolant pump
3) Alternator
4) AC Compressor
5) Tensioner pulley
6) Power steering pump

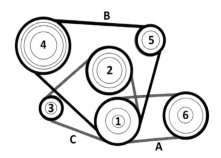

## FIRING ORDER

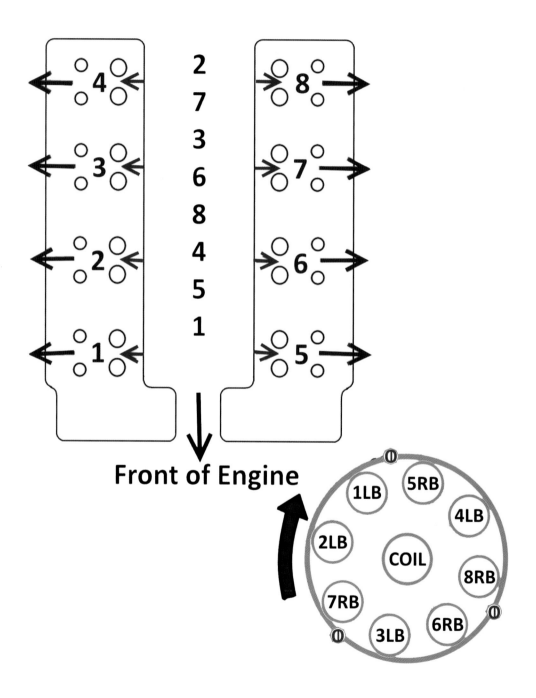

2
7
3
6
8
4
5
1

**Front of Engine**

*Firing order of M116/117 V8 engines.*

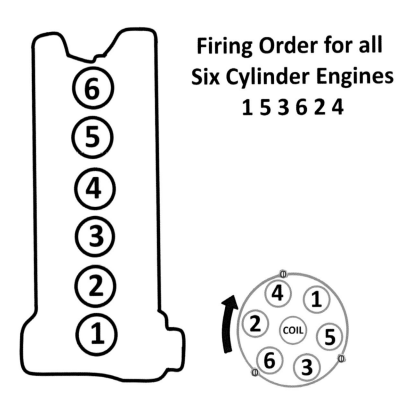

## Firing Order for all
## Six Cylinder Engines
## 1 5 3 6 2 4

## Front of Engine

*Firing order for all six-cylinder engines.*

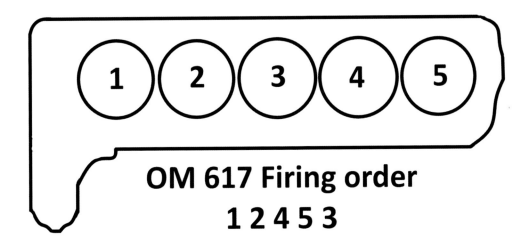

## OM 617 Firing order
## 1 2 4 5 3

*Firing order for OM617 six-cylinder engines.*

| 126 Lighting | MB Part Number | Osram Bulb # | Power |
|---|---|---|---|
| **FRONT LIGHTS** | | | |
| High/Low beam headlamp | N 000000 000374 | H4 | 60/55w |
| Front Fog | N 072601 012290 | H3 | 55W |
| Front Indicator | N 072601 012190 | 7506 | 21W |
| Side light | N 072601 012900 | 03893 | 4W |
| Indicator repeaters | N 072601 012250 | 2825 | 5W |
| **REAR LIGHTS** | | | |
| Rear Indicator | N 072601 012190 | 7506 | 21W |
| Rear Fog | N 072601 012190 | 7506 | 21W |
| Brake light | N 072601 012190 | 7506 | 21W |
| Number plate light | N 072601 012130 | 6418 | 5W |
| Tail light | N 072601 012702 | 5008 | 10W |
| **INTERIOR LIGHTS** | | | |
| Boot light | N 072601 012120 | 6411 | 10W |
| Rear roof rail Dome light | N 072601 012120 | 6411 | 10W |
| Front roof rail Dome light | N 072601 012120 | 6411 | 10W |
| Glove box | N 072601 012130 | 6418 | 5W |
| Belt warning light | N 072601 012130 | 6418 | 5W |
| Step/Puddle light | N 072601 012130 | 6418 | 5W |
| Front reading light | N 922008 012000 | 64111 | 5W Halogen |
| Rear reading light | N 922008 012000 | 64111 | 5W Halogen |
| **CONTROL LIGHTS** | | | |
| Instrument Cluster (Tell tale lights) | N 072601 012230 | 2721 | 1.2W |
| Fibre optic bulb | N 072601 012230 | 2721 | 1.2W |
| Main cluster illumination lamp | N 072601 012240 | 2821 | 3W |
| Charge control lamp | N 072601 012240 | 2821 | 3W |
| Gear Selector | N 072601 012230 | 2721 | 1.2W |
| Ash Tray | N 072601 012110 | 3898 | 2W |
| Headlight switch | A 000 825 0094 | 2712 | 0.5W Frosted |

*Mercedes 126 bulb list.*

# INDEX